Putting the Tea in Britain

Putting the Tea in Britain

The Scots Who Made Our National Drink

Les Wilson

BIRLINN

First published in 2021 by
Birlinn Limited
West Newington House
10 Newington Road
Edinburgh
EH9 1QS

www.birlinn.co.uk

ISBN 978 1 78027 657 1

British Library Cataloguing in Publication Data. A catalogue record
for this book can be obtained from the British Library.

Typeset by Initial Typesetting Services, Edinburgh
Printed and bound in Great Britain by Clays Ltd, Elcograf S.p.A.

In memory of
Carl Reavey (1956–2018)
and for
Ivy Jean Hunter (born 22 August 2019)

'For me starting the day without a pot of tea would be a day forever out of kilter.'

Bill Drummond, *$20,000*

'Tea is the best substance in the world. I love tea. It makes me feel jolly – tea is the substance.'

Billy Connolly

Contents

List of Illustrations

Introduction

Two centuries ago, all the tea drunk in Britain came from China. Tea bushes, and the techniques of preparing their leaves, were the Celestial Empire's jealously guarded secret. Any Chinese who betrayed them to the Western barbarians faced severe punishment, even death. This book tells how Scots broke that monopoly, made tea Britain's – and the world's – favourite drink and transformed the histories of China, India, Sri Lanka and much of Africa.

In 1664 the East India Company imported a single chest of tea into Britain from China. But Britain quickly developed a thirst. By 1800, the Company was buying more than 25,000,000 pounds of China tea a year. The self-sufficient Chinese didn't want industrial British manufactured goods in exchange – they just wanted silver, and the United Kingdom's reserves were dwindling. In this ignominious age, Britain paid for the tea with Indian opium – smuggling opium into China, causing misery for millions, infuriating the Chinese government and igniting two opium wars. A more rational way for Britain to balance its tea-trade deficit was to find somewhere in its vast empire where it could grow its own tea and then acquire the plants and the know-how to make them flourish. Enter a remarkable group of Scotsmen. Essentially, they 'stole'

China's tea, successfully replanted it in India and then discovered an indigenous tea in Assam. These two different *jats* (types or 'castes') of tea were successfully raised in Darjeeling, Assam, South India, Ceylon and Africa – breaking China's tea monopoly forever.

The seed from which this book grew was planted in Darjeeling, in the foothills of the Himalayas. I have had a long love affair with India, and on a visit to this beguiling region I discovered, to my astonishment, that the first person to grow tea in Darjeeling was a Scottish doctor, Archibald Campbell. Campbell was the son of a gentleman but, as the third son, and being neither the 'heir' nor the 'spare', had to make his own way in the world. He graduated in medicine at Edinburgh University and joined the East India Company, which eventually sent him to establish a sanatorium and hill station that would provide white *sahibs* with temporary relief from the sweltering heat of Calcutta. A keen amateur botanist, Campbell planted China tea bushes in the garden of his Darjeeling estate. Campbell's tea thrived, and within a decade other Brits had followed his example and tea gardens sprouted up all over Darjeeling's hillsides.

Archibald Campbell is a neglected figure. He came from Islay, the Inner Hebridean island that has been my home for many years – yet I had never heard of him. He founded Darjeeling – but it was only on my second visit to the town that I discovered who he was and what he had done. Intrigued, I began to read and enquire. Very quickly, I discovered that an extraordinary proportion of the men who caused tea to become the favourite drink of half the world were Scots.

Here is a very brief list:

+ Islay's Archibald Campbell.
+ Robert Fortune, a Borders 'lad o' pairts', who – disguised as a Chinese man – risked arrest, robbery, piracy and murder to bring tea plants to the British Empire.

+ William Melrose, the son of an Edinburgh grocer and a pioneer trader in a tiny European enclave in hostile Canton.

+ Edinburgh's Bruce brothers – Robert and Charles – who discovered that wild tea grew in Assam, thereby becoming the fathers of another great tea region.

+ Robert Kyd, the Angus-born soldier who founded Calcutta's botanic garden, where tea was first nurtured in British India, and the subsequent dynasty of Scottish botanists who succeeded him as the garden's superintendents.

+ James Taylor of Kincardineshire, who first grew tea commercially in Ceylon and brought the economy of the island back from the brink of disaster.

+ Thomas Lipton, who brought affordable tea to the masses and made it our national drink.

+ Edinburgh gardener Jonathan Duncan, who planted two tea bushes from the city's botanic gardens at the Church of Scotland mission at Blantyre, Malawi; and Henry Brown of Banff, who founded Africa's vast tea industry with a handful of seeds scrounged from that mission garden.

These men's stories read like something from Robert Louis Stevenson or Joseph Conrad, but there is a genteel lady to soften this macho crew. The entrepreneurial and artistic Catherine Cranston's fashionable Glasgow tea rooms gave full scope to the imagination of Scotland's most famous architect, Charles Rennie Mackintosh, and his artist wife, Margaret Macdonald, and provided gathering places for unaccompanied ladies at a time when women were clamouring for the right to vote.

And there are the assorted entrepreneurial Scottish mill-owners, grocers, adventurers, soldiers, scientists, planters and chancers who risked their capital, reputations, health and lives for tea What characters! What stories! Tea is interwoven with centuries of Scottish, British and world history. My serendipitous discovery of Archibald Campbell of Islay and Darjeeling sprouted wings.

With such a litany of Scottish names prominent among those who put the tea in Britain (and a good many other places), I quickly came to face the questions: Why Scotland? What was it about the Scots that made them such pioneers? It is clear that the tea men were part of what Professor Tom Devine has called 'the relentless penetration of Empire by Scottish educators, doctors, plantation overseers, army officers, government officials, merchants and clerics'.[1] Essentially, Scotland's tea men were economic migrants, escaping poverty – or at least a lack of opportunity – at home.

With about 9 per cent of Britain's population, Scots at one point held 25 per cent of the British jobs in India and were clearly the right people, in the right place, at the right time. Their relatively small country had recently united with a neighbour that was busy building a global empire. That empire badly needed likely lads – white English-speakers, if not necessarily Englishmen – to run it. Scots, hungry for betterment, were able to take advantage of that. Their education, an inheritance of the Reformation and the Scottish Enlightenment, had equipped a far greater proportion of Scots than of England's people to fulfil a wide range of imperial roles.

While they brought much needed skills to England's imperial enterprise, they often came with a very non-English attitude to it. The historian Michael Fry argues that 'A small poor country could never think of domination, but at best persuade larger and richer ones to treat it on equal terms. So they sought to make themselves useful, to thrive through adventure and enterprise, and so to approach other societies not with a desire of conquering, ruling and changing, but of understanding them.'[2] The role of two Scots, Allan Octavian Hume and George Yule, in the creation of the Indian National

Congress – which eventually led India to independence – certainly supports Fry's view. However, there is no shying away from the fact that the business of tea production was a ruthless and exploitative one, and that Scots too were capable of the cruelty and racism that besmirched the British Empire.

Scottish administrators, scholars, soldiers, merchants and engineers all played their roles in the growth of empire, but the profession with the biggest impact on the tea industry was medicine. Time after time while researching this book, I found that a medical degree from Edinburgh or Glasgow University, followed by a spell as assistant surgeon on an East India Company merchantman, was almost a prerequisite for anyone to make their mark on the development of tea. The list of Scots medics I encountered reads both like a professional directory and a gazetteer of Scotland – Campbell of Islay, Falconer of Forres, Roxburgh of Symington, Buchanan-Hamilton of Callander, Jameson of Leith, Govan of Cupar, Hooker of Glasgow and Helensburgh, and Wallich of Denmark (but with an Aberdeen University medical degree).

Scottish medicine had developed alongside a strong tradition of plantsmanship. From the seventeenth century, Scotland had been recognised for gardening – a skill necessary to overcome a harsh environment, or starve. But as Scotland became the world's leading nation in medicine, physic gardens were cultivated to grow and study plants for their healing powers. In 1670 such a garden was established near Holyrood Palace in Edinburgh by Andrew Balfour and Robert Sibbald, and within a decade more than 2,000 plants flourished there. Not long after, Edinburgh alone would boast three physic gardens.

The gardens, which serviced the medical profession's interest in plants and the environment, were integral to the development of Scots as leaders in the creation of botanical gardens at home and abroad. Scots were

the key figures at the Kew Gardens and the Chelsea
Physic Garden in London, and founded and maintained botanical gardens across the diverse lands of
the British Empire.[3]

Of course, English doctors understood botany too, but Oxford
and Cambridge didn't train students in surgery. English sawbones learned their trade by becoming apprenticed to surgeons.
Scottish universities allowed students to take classes in both
medicine and surgery and granted degrees to these 'hybrid
healers'. In an age of relentless war, exploration and expansion, broadly trained Scottish medics, who could amputate a
limb or extract a bullet, as well as treat tropical diseases, were
invaluable to Britain's army, navy and East India Company.
The medical services of these engines of empire became 'largely
staffed' by Scots, particularly Edinburgh graduates.[4] A massive public relations victory for the East India Company was
won in 1815 by Scots surgeon William Hamilton, when he
cured the painfully swollen groin of Farrukhsiyar, the Mughal
emperor, allowing his delayed royal marriage to go ahead. So
relieved was the emperor that he rewarded the Company with
land and privileges in Bengal that were the starting point for its
eventual domination of India.

For many Scots, the passage to India was with the East
India Company, and many Company men played important
roles in the development of tea. Then came the independent
traders – entrepreneurial Scots who went east to make money.
A Calcutta Business Directory of the 1840s might be mis-
taken for a Scottish one: Jardine Matheson; Jardine, Skinner
& Co.; Begg, Dunlop & Co.; Andrew Yule & Co.; MacNeill
& Co.; and James Finlay – all Scottish companies with a tradition of recruiting fresh blood (often with blood ties) from
the homeland. Meanwhile, back in Scotland, Gorbals boy
Thomas Lipton founded a retailing empire with a keen pricing

policy that made sure that even the poor could enjoy tea. Tea then entered Scottish politics as the Suffragette, Socialist and Temperance movements embraced it as 'the cup that cheers but does not inebriate'. Tea rooms sprang up throughout the country and the Glasgow of the 1890s was described as 'a veritable Tokyo of tea rooms'.

The tea that Scots travelled the world in pursuit of has now taken root in their native land. In the 1960s the tea expert Denys Forrest visited the Loolecondera estate, where a Scot, James Taylor, pioneered Ceylon's tea industry. Looking across the broad glens blanketed with tea bushes and up at the craggy tops of the mountains, he commented: 'It is, one feels, what tea growing in the Cairngorms would be if such a thing were possible.' How prescient! Today there are a fair number of tea growers in Scotland, some of whom feature in this book. My journey into the wide world of tea, which began in Darjeeling, finally ended in Angus.

My first memory of tea is from about the age of four, when I noticed that my father took his tea with sugar – presumably revelling in post-war plenty – while my figure-conscious mother didn't. I took her side and have been a confirmed 'no sugar, just a wee splash of milk' man ever since. I've drunk a lot of it. All the television documentaries I have made and books I've written have been fuelled by tea, and on my travels I have drunk it in many ways: delicate Darjeeling in that very town, mint tea in Turkey, aromatic spiced tea in Jordon, sweet and milky chai from Indian street stalls, with lemon and sugar in the Ukraine, British Army stewed 'brew' with lots of milk and sugar, Sri Lankan teas sipped on the estates where they were grown, the slightly astringent fresh green teas of Japan . . .

I first encountered the process of growing and producing tea in Japan. Introduced from China a millennium ago, tea is now at the heart of Japan's custom and culture, and its people ascribe medical and even mystical powers to it. The Okamoto family, who live close to the city of Shizuoka, had been tea planters for seven generations when I visited them. In 1948 they had been photographed, along with eleven other farming families from around the world, for an American magazine. Half a century later, I worked on a BBC2 documentary that traced these same people to discover what had happened to them in the intervening years. It was an extraordinary privilege, and the Okamotos were a warm and hospitable family with whom we enjoyed much sake as well as tea.

Ichie, the patriarch, had grown old and tired of the chills and rheumatics brought about by living in a beautiful, traditional home with its paper walls. On a warm night the 300-year-old house looked like a paper lantern, but when it got cold the heavy wooden shutters had to be slid shut. Ichie's choice was between being chilly in natural light, or warm in the dark. When we first contacted him with a request to film him and his family, he had just decided to replace the paper walls with double-glazing, sweeping away the tradition of generations. His wife, Etsuko, was sorrowful about this, but he felt his health depended on it. However, Ichie postponed the double-glazing so that we might film his home and family in the style they had lived for a century or more, and we spent several days with them in the final days of that fine and historic house.

Just outside were the manicured tea bushes, grown on the sixty acres of land that the family had been granted at the end of the Edo period, 120 years previously. Ichie and Etsuko had three daughters and they, their husbands and children helped with tending, weeding and plucking the bushes to make a high-quality tea, just as the family had always done. When the American photographer Horace Bristol had been there half a century before (when Ichie was a small boy) the farm was remote, looking down on distant Shizuoka from the hillside. Today, the suburbs of the city end where the Okamotos' tea garden begins; the old house is overlooked by a three-storey block of flats. No doubt property developers look on the garden with envy. What price a cup of tea?

The beauty of the traditional house, the warmth of our hosts and the loveliness of their tea garden entranced me. However, I have a confession to make. I don't much care for Japanese green tea, or green tea at all. In this, I happen to be in good company. The sage of Ecclefechan (and Chelsea), Thomas Carlyle, living in penury when he first went to London in 1831, would splash out on black tea at home if there was the slightest danger that anybody he was about to visit might serve him the green stuff.[5] More recently, the satirical website the Daily Mash told of a box of green teabags that had been around an office for longer than any current member of staff. Like a yoga mat, it had been bought in the vain hope of making a 'healthy change'.[6] However, my visit to the Okamotos' tea garden has stayed with me, was the first of many visits to plantations and sparked my interest in tea as more than just a thirst quencher.

The 1867 edition of the Edinburgh-published *Chambers's Encyclopedia* warned:

> It is impossible to protest too strongly against the habit occasionally adopted by students of keeping off their natural sleep by the frequent use of strong tea. The persistent adoption of such a habit is certain to lead to the utter destruction of both bodily and mental vigour.

This is advice that I have chosen to ignore. I have no doubt that tea improves my concentration, memory and stamina. For me, coffee is the quick-start fuel of the poor wage-drone who needs six-cylinder propulsion to get her or him through the hugger-mugger of corporate life. Tea, however, is a gentler stimulant – refreshing, relaxing and likely to induce contemplation rather than hyperactive and rash action. Students may 'cram' on wee-small-hours coffee, but it is tea – mugs of it, strong and dark with the tiniest splash of milk – that gets me through the working day. I'm an at least eight-mugs-a-day man – although on this book my consumption rose dramatically as I reflectively sampled single-estate teas, green and white teas, teas from China, Assam, Darjeeling, Sri Lanka, Malawi, Kenya and Scotland. Sipping tea while staring into space – and they call it work? But work it has been, fascinating, delightful and rewarding, just like tea itself. This introduction was completed while drinking a pot of the splendidly named Bannockburn estate tea from Darjeeling. All it took to make was a teaspoonful or two of desiccated leaves and a kettle on the boil – but, like all tea, it comes with a history as rich and dramatic as Scotland's own.*

Les Wilson

Port Charlotte, Isle of Islay

30 January 2020

---

* So that readers can plunge straight into Scotland's adventures in tea, I have relegated the technical matters of what tea is and how it is made into an appendix, *Notes for the Botanically Curious*, which appears at the end of the book.

CHAPTER 1

To Drink a Dish of Tea, Sir?

It is said that when the bride-to-be of King Charles II stepped off the ship that brought her to Britain in 1662, she called for a reviving cup of tea. She was horrified to find that none was available, as the exotic Chinese infusion was little known in wine-drinking, ale-swilling England. The disappointed bride was Catherine of Braganza, a Portuguese princess whose matchmaking father longed for an alliance with England. At this time the Portuguese dominated trade with the East and were the first Europeans to seriously take to *Camellia sinensis* (the Chinese camellia).

Fortunately for Catherine, amidst her lavish dowry were two cases of tea for her own use. The Stuart court, never slow to flatter, was quick to follow the queen's taste. Poet and politician Edmund Waller – a practiced sycophant who wrote verses in praise of both Oliver Cromwell and Charles II – penned a birthday poem for the queen in which Portugal and its empire in the East is thanked for furnishing Britain with both a queen and tea.

> The best of Queens, the best of herbs we owe
> To that bold nation which the way did show
> To the fair region where the sun doth rise
> Whose rich productions we so justly prize.

The Royal Stuart seal of approval encouraged the Scottish aristocracy to embrace tea and it was first served to them amid the grandeur of Edinburgh's Holyrood Palace. In 1680 Charles II appointed his younger brother, James, Duke of York, as Lord High Commissioner of Scotland. James and his wife, Italian Princess Mary of Modena, were tea drinkers and, for the three years of their residence at Holyrood, their guests and courtiers followed the fashion they set. In her classic book *The Scots Kitchen*, F. Marian McNeill tells us that tea 'was denounced by both medical men and clergy, and its acceptance was slow, but by 1750 its conquest of the womenfolk was complete, and wine was reserved for gentlemen'.

James, Duke of York, became king on the death of his older brother, but he was deposed in the Glorious Revolution and replaced by William of Orange. King James II of England and VII of Scotland had reigned for just three years, but the taste for tea he introduced the Scots to has never left us. King William's Dutch background may even have reinforced the tea habit. The Dutch were confirmed tea drinkers long before the British, and Holland's traders in China even named a tea in tribute to the House of Orange – orange pekoe – which, unlike Earl Grey, contains not a whiff of citrus.

Tea was, in the beginning, a luxury item. The first known seller of it in Scotland was George Smith, a goldsmith who, in 1705, sold green tea at sixteen shillings a pound and Bohea (black) tea at thirty shillings from his premises at the Edinburgh Luckenbooths.[1]

Apart from the ladies who attended the gracious Mary of Modena at Holyrood, and those fortunate enough to be able to pop into an Edinburgh goldsmith's for an ounce of their favourite leaf, who were Scotland's tea drinkers?

My old edition of *Rough Guide to Scotland* says: 'Scotland's staple drink, like England's, is tea, drunk strong and with milk.' How did the desiccated leaves of a jungle tree become

Scotland's favourite drink? Before exploring how Scots contributed to the acquisition and exploitation of tea, let's look at Scotland's history of drinking it.

The history of our nation is full of tantalising references to the newly fashionable drink. Tea was not always welcomed. William Mackintosh of Borlum was 'old school': not only did he so disapprove of the usurping House of Hanover that he commanded units of the Jacobite army in the 1715 Rebellion, but he also strongly disapproved that his morning dram had been replaced by tea. In 1729 he lamented:

> When I come to a friend's house of a morning, I used to be asked if I had had my morning draught yet. I am now asked if I have had my tea. And in lieu the big quaich with strong ale and toast, and after a dram of good wholesome Scots spirits, there is now the tea-kettle put to the fire, the tea-table and silver and china equipage brought in, and marmalade and cream.[2]

Such a table and equipage are seen overturned and flying in an amusing drawing from Penicuik House, now in the National Museum of Scotland. It depicts blows and harsh words being exchanged over the rights and wrongs of the Jacobite cause.

When the English traveller Edmund Burt roamed throughout the Highlands in the late 1720s, he ate in numerous hostels and private houses. His *Letters from the North of Scotland* infuriated Scots, with its constant references to the dirt, poverty and superstition that he found, but it also records him drinking 'wine', 'very good wine' and 'good claret' – although they never mention him being offered a *cupa tì*. Burt was in Scotland to oversee and collect the rents from unsold Jacobite estates that had been forfeited after the 1715 Rebellion, and he worked closely with General Wade, the Hanoverian Army's commander-in-chief in Scotland and famous builder of roads.

Although Burt never seems to have heard the hospitable Gaelic invitation, *Bheil dìth teatha ort?* ('Are you in need of tea?'), we know that it was being enjoyed by some Highlanders, because Burt writes of 'wines, brandy, tea, silks etc.' that were being smuggled into ports on the Moray Firth. Perhaps Highland tea-drinking was restricted to the Jacobite aristocracy who looked to Europe for the restoration of the House of Stuart, as well as luxuries untaxed by King George II's government in London. These families would have been unlikely to offer such hospitality to a friend of the Redcoats like Edmund Burt. As readers will discover in the following chapter, there was a direct connection between Jacobitism and tea smuggling.

Because Scots doctors had a firm grounding in the medicinal powers of plants, the effect of tea on the human constitution was of great interest to them. Thomas Short, from Moffat in the Scottish Borders, moved south to set up his practice in Sheffield, where he conducted exhaustive scientific experiments on tea. *A Dissertation upon Tea, Explaining its Nature and Properties by Many New experiments . . . to Which is Added the Natural History of Tea and a Detection of the Several Frauds Used in Preparing it* was published in 1730. Discovering that tea 'promoted the circulation of the blood', Short concluded that 'the person who frequently drinks it is not terrified by frightful dreams' and that 'Green tea is an antidote against chronic fear or grief'. Thomas Short clearly believed that a nice cup of tea was both relaxing and fortifying – a view still widely held nearly three centuries later – and that it relieved 'Disorders of the Head', like migraine, by 'increasing the blood flow to the brain.'*

---

* A view certainly shared by that most famous of doctors, Doctor Who. On being regenerated as the Tenth Doctor, David Tennant proclaimed: 'Tea! That's all I needed! Good cup of tea! Super-heated infusion of free-radicals and tannin, just the thing for healing the synapses.' Russell T. Davies, *The Christmas Invasion*, 2005.

Short's experiments also indicated that tea affected the sexes differently:

> Tea, if moderately drunk, and of a due strength, is generally more serviceable to the fair sex than to men. Because Nature, having framed them with a more lax and delicate Fiber, they are more liable to a *Plethora*, or Fullness of Juices; and also because they are more exempted from exercise and hard labour.

While the jury may still be out on whether tea affects men differently from women, Short's observation makes it clear that the women who were drinking tea around 1730 were indeed from the class 'exempted from exercise and hard labour' – unlike the common mass of women labouring long and hard in agriculture, industry, in service and in the home. However, Short did believe that tea was beneficial to society as a whole, even those who could not afford to drink it, noting, 'what a great revenue the duty upon the little crumbled leaf returns to the Crown of England whereby the general taxes are so much lessened to the Poor'.

Tea, in this era, was certainly still a luxury item, even a decadent one. In 1744 the clan chiefs of Skye – Sir Alexander MacDonald of MacDonald, John Mackinnon of Mackinnon, Norman MacLeod of MacLeod and Malcolm MacLeod of Raasay – gathered in Portree and agreed to 'discontinue and discountenance' the luxuries of brandy, tobacco and tea.[3] It was not, however, a decadence that tempted the common folk of the Hebrides. Lodged in my memory (but sadly not recorded in any notebook) is a story I heard about a Gaelic seaman returning home from a long voyage to the East with a 'poke' of tea as a gift for his mother. The *cailleach* had never encountered this sophisticated product before, so her son carefully instructed her to pour boiling water over it and then left the house to visit friends. When he returned, his mother served him the boiled leaves on a plate, having poured the liquid away. I have no idea where I heard this story, but folklorist Margaret Bennett has heard the tale told in Nova Scotia about a seaman returning home there. While it may well be apocryphal, the story neatly illustrates how completely alien this fashionable drink of the upper classes was to the common folk. However, if these accounts are true, these confused Scottish and Nova Scotian mothers weren't entirely off the mark. In 1823 the Scottish explorer Robert Bruce found the Singpho hill tribes of the upper Assam region boiling and eating tea leaves as a vegetable. These Indian tribesmen were ahead of the game. Until the late nineteenth century the vast majority of Indians didn't drink tea; it is largely due to Scotland's pioneering tea men that India is now one of the heaviest tea-drinking countries in the world.

Teatime certainly came late in the Hebrides. One traveller noted in 1875 that a field at Dalbeg, on the north-west coast of Lewis, was known as 'the tea field'. This was because when chests of tea were washed ashore from a shipwreck the local people hadn't known what the contents were and used the leaves to manure a field. He added that 'tea has not been at all used in the west more than twenty years' and even then was only drunk occasionally when the family was well-off.[4] Hebrideans have certainly made up for it since; in all my stravaigs among the islands I've almost never visited a home where a *strùpag* wasn't pressed on me.

There were those who believed that tea was an indulgence too far for the common folk. Duncan Forbes of Culloden, Scotland's top legal officer and a man who did much to suppress the 1745 Jacobite Rebellion, fulminated against the 'excessive use of tea' in the belief that such a luxurious import threatened the economy of the country. Nobody who earned less than £50 a year, he argued, should be allowed to buy tea.[5] Forbes had accompanied General Wade's forces sent to Glasgow to suppress the Shawfield Riot against the imposition, in 1725, of the Malt Tax. The tax, a clear breach of the Treaty of Union, increased the price of beer – and it can only have stimulated the demand for tea. Forbes, however, generously and personally supported the Exchequer in the drive to collect liquor tax. On the day of his mother's funeral, he plied his fellow mourners with so much drink that when they got to the churchyard they found they had forgotten her coffin.[6]

Whole communities of common folk resolved not to succumb to the 'tea menace' that was corrupting their 'betters'. The sturdy tenants of William Fullerton, of Fullerton in Ayrshire, pledged:

> We being all farmers by profession, think it needless to restrain ourselves formally from indulging in that foreign and consumptive luxury called *tea*; for when we consider the slender constitutions of many of higher rank, among whom it is used, we conclude that it would be but improper diet to qualify us for the more robust and manly parts of our business: therefore we shall only give our testimony against it and leave the enjoyment of it altogether to those who can afford to be weak, indolent and useless.[7]

The Reverend Thomas Somerville, the minister of Jedburgh (whom Robert Burns described as 'a gentleman, but sadly addicted to punning'), recalled how, during his childhood in the 1750s and 1760s, the middle classes were beginning to ape the custom of their tea-drinking superiors. 'Most families, both in the higher and in the middle ranks, used tea at breakfast; but among the latter it was only recently introduced, or beginning to be introduced in the afternoon, and then exclusively on the occasion of receiving company.'[8]

We know that James Boswell was well acquainted with tea before he went to London in 1762, because in his *London Journal* he compared a grim London social event to 'one of the worst Edinburgh tea-drinking afternoons'. His journal is infused with references to drinking tea and he kept a supply of it under lock and key in his rooms. 'I am so fond of tea that I could write a whole dissertation on its virtues,' he wrote. Sadly, no such dissertation exists, but his writings do show that invitations to drink tea (or not) offered the priapic Boswell the opportunity of sexual conquest, as the following exchange between him and actress Mrs Lewis (referred to in his journal as 'Louisa'), reveals.

> Boswell: 'When may I wait upon you?'
>
> Louisa: 'What? To drink a dish of tea, Sir?'
>
> Boswell: 'No, no, not to drink a dish of tea. What time may I wait upon you?'
>
> Louisa: 'Whenever you please, Sir.'

Boswell kissed Louisa and took his leave, 'highly pleased with the thoughts of the affair being settled'. Unfortunately, Boswell contracted gonorrhoea from Louisa and the drinking of tea, as part of a very simple diet, was prescribed for his cure. Boswell's friend, the Scottish judge and philosopher Lord Kames, would doubtless have approved of this tea cure, having been told by physicians that sugar and tea were 'no inconsiderable antiseptics'.[9] Boswell's guru, Dr Samuel Johnson, admitted to being a 'hardened and shameless tea drinker'; he must have been relieved that during his jaunt round the Hebrides with Boswell in 1773 tea was firmly established at the breakfast tables of their well-to-do hosts. Tea, along with butter, honey, conserves and marmalade, had Johnson declaim that wherever an epicure wished he could sup 'he would breakfast in Scotland'.[10]

You needed to be a generous host to invite Dr Johnson for breakfast. While staying at Dunvegan Castle on the Isle of Skye, Johnson's consumption of at least sixteen cups of tea at one sitting prompted Lady MacLeod to ask him if drinking from a small basin would cause him less trouble. 'I wonder Madam,' he replied, 'why all the ladies ask me such impertinent questions. It is to save yourselves trouble, Madam, and not me.' Lady MacLeod was stunned into silence. Johnson's rudeness to his hostess went unreported by the sycophantic Boswell in his *Journal of a Tour to the Hebrides*.

An even more ill-tempered tea party was held in the same year as Johnson's visit to Dunvegan – the Boston Tea Party in Massachusetts. In a little-known aftershock of that powerful protest, Scottish merchant Anthony Stewart lost his ship, 2,000 pounds of tea and almost his life when he paid the hated British tea tax after his vessel the *Peggy Stewart* docked with its cargo of the leaf at Annapolis, in Maryland. An angry mob gathered outside Stewart's house and erected a scaffold. The terrified merchant was given an ultimatum – swing from the gibbet, or board his ship and set it and her cargo on fire. The *Peggy Stewart* burned and her owner fled rebellious America to eventually found a settlement in Nova Scotia called New Edinburgh. America was soon lost to the British Empire – and to widespread tea drinking. 'A great republic was born that was soon to become the wealthiest consumer-nation in the world, but with a prenatal disinclination for tea,' commented William Ukers.

Tea was slower to reach the lower orders in Scotland than it was in London. Lamenting that the encouragement of 'idleness and beggary' disinclined the poor to find work, Lord Kames reported in 1778 that paupers in London who lived by parish-charity were in the habit 'of drinking tea twice a day'. But of the Scottish labouring classes, he says, 'Water is their only drink; and yet they live comfortably, without ever thinking of pitying themselves.'

It was at a respectable tea party in Edinburgh in December 1787 that Robert Burns, then the darling of the capital's smart set, met Agnes Maclehose, 'Nancy' to her friends, a lively and pretty Glasgow lady who was estranged from her obnoxious husband. Burns was smitten. They exchanged passionate letters and, while it is possible that their relationship was more textual than sexual, Burns was moved to write 'Ae Fond Kiss', his greatest song of love and loss, after Nancy announced her wish for reconciliation with her husband.

> I'll ne'er blame my partial fancy;
> Naething could resist my Nancy;
> For to see her was to love her,
> Love but her, and love for ever.

The author John Griffiths argues that taking afternoon tea was encouraged from 1794 onwards by the adoption of gas lighting, invented by the Scots engineer William Murdoch, who worked for the company that James Watt founded near Birmingham. Murdoch's gaslit cities extended the working day, increasing the gap between dinner at midday and supper in the evening. It was a gap too far for many middle-class women, who filled it with tea, bread and butter, and cake.[11]

Writing of her life in 1808, the diarist Elizabeth Grant of Rothiemurchus recalls being treated to 'a tea breakfast' after sea-bathing – implying that even for an upper-class family tea wasn't an everyday drink. It was, however, a valuable substitute for stronger stuff. When invasion by Napoleon was thought to be imminent, Elizabeth's father became lieutenant-colonel of the Rothiemurchus Volunteers. His officers, all Strathspey gentlemen, clearly took the threat seriously. Elizabeth recalled, 'It was in this year, 1809, my mother remarked that she saw some of them for the first time in the drawing-room to tea and sober.'

Slowly, tea began to percolate down to Scottish commoners, although, for them, it remained a luxury. Buchan loon James Milne recalled that in 1836 the rent on his father's farm was so high that his parents limited themselves to one cup of tea a day, taken in the morning and sweetened with treacle because it was cheaper than sugar. In 1843 the Royal Commission on the Scottish Poor Law visited Elizabeth McGregor at Newtyle in Angus and found her to be a capable and respectable woman in her eighties, living on six shillings a month from the Kirk Session. 'She never drinks tea except upon Sabbath,' the Commission recorded. It also found that in fewer than a fifth of parishes the labouring classes ate meat and still fewer ever drank tea, although in the south-east tea or coffee with break-fast was a common luxury for the hind (farm labourer) and his family. In the 1880s a New Pitsligo resident recalled that only a few families had tea with their breakfast brose or porridge, but that in most homes it was a Sunday morning luxury, 'the day o' the lang lie an' the tay breakfast'.[12]

Between 1730 and 1805, tea consumption throughout the UK rose more than five-fold to one pound eleven ounces per head. Historian Tom Devine has argued that it wasn't just increasing wages that fuelled this thirst, but the rise of the factory and urbanisation.[13] Country folk migrated to the towns where the new jobs and opportunities were. By 1840 six out of ten inhabitants of Glasgow's Tron district were incomers: the teeming slums had multiplied like the bacteria in the fetid drinking water. In the cholera outbreak of 1832, 3,000 people died in Glasgow alone.[14] Tea would have been more readily available than the fresh milk that country peo-ple were used to, and boiling water for tea sterilised it and made it safe for drinking. The phenolics in tea, which give it its 'tannic' taste, also may have some effect against *bacteria*, so for people living in insanitary industrial towns, tea was the healthy option.

Sir Gilbert Blane, the Ayrshire doctor responsible for preventing scurvy by persuading the Admiralty to introduce lemons and limes into the diet of sailors, was quick to recognise that tea was beneficial: 'Tea is an article universally grateful to the British population and has to a certain degree supplanted intoxicating liquors in all ranks, to the great advantage of society ... the modern use of tea has probably contributed to the longevity of the inhabitants of this country.'

Thomas Trotter, a son of Melrose who also made his reputation as a progressive Royal Navy doctor, noted in 1807 that 'The consumption of the Chinese plant is enormous throughout the united kingdoms: it is a beverage well suited to the taste of an indolent and voluptuous age. To the glutton it gives a grateful diluant after a voracious dinner; and from being drunk warm it gives a soothing stimulus to the stomach of the drunkard.' Trotter recognised that tea was being widely used as a stimulant. 'To sip frequently of green tea, produced wakefulness and gaiety of spirits; hence some literary men who protract their studies to a late hour, use strong tea, like the late Dr Johnson, to keep them awake.' Doctor Trotter was fond of tea himself, although he sometimes refused it, as he believed it aggravated his short-sightedness. He thought it harmless to the strong and athletic, but believed it particularly harmful to women, people with dyspepsia and gout, and 'those who are weak natured'. Like the continual ping-pong in today's newspapers about the benefits – or otherwise – of red wine, Thomas Trotter decided that tea was both good and bad for you.

> Fine tea, where the narcotic quality seems to be concentrated, when taken in an infusion by persons not accustomed to it, excites nausea and vomiting, tremors, cold sweats, vertigo, dimness of sight and confusion of thought. In its more diluted state, sweetened with

sugar, and softened by the judicious mixture of bland cream, it is grateful to the stomach, gives a soothing sensation as if it lulled pain, exhilarates the spirits, produces wakefulness, relieves fatigue; and from being taken down warm, promotes perspiration, and acts powerfully by the kidneys.[15]

In country areas, tea was sold at cottage and farm doors by packmen, including my own ancestors David, John and Charles Jardine, who in the mid-nineteenth-century censuses are listed as 'tea dealers' or 'tea agents' based at Powfoot in Dumfriesshire. Between 1857 and 1903 the price of tea fell by 64 per cent. Working people drank it when they could. Red Clydesider David Kirkwood recalls that in the mid-1880s, after a day's work as an apprentice in a Glasgow ironworks, he came home to supper of porridge and buttermilk 'and sometimes bread and butter and a cup of tea.'[16]

Tea was coming to be a top-selling commodity for Scottish shopkeepers. In 1864 Greenock-born grocer Matthew Algie, who had first sold his customers tea that had been delivered to the Clyde by Clyde-built tea clippers, established a tea-blending and wholesaling business that served businesses around Glasgow. The company rapidly expanded after the Second World War, becoming a leading UK tea and coffee concern but remaining in Scottish hands until taken over by a German company in 2016, although the Matthew Algie brand has been retained. Scottish grocers blending tea to suit their local water, and the tastes and pockets of their customers, had a profound effect on Scotland's other great national drink. The skills required to blend tea led Kilmarnock grocer Johnnie Walker to start blending whiskies to create a smoother, more palatable dram, and Chivas and Ballantine whiskies have their roots in tea-blending grocer shops in Aberdeen and Edinburgh.

In 1888 tea refreshed the crowds who flocked to the International Exhibition of Science, Art and Industry at Kelvingrove Park in Glasgow. At the Bishop's Palace Temperance Café – where waitresses were dressed as Mary, Queen of Scots[17] – Joseph Lyons gained the experience that allowed him to found the Lyons' Corner House chain.[18] Tea was all the rage in Glasgow. Thirteen years earlier, the enterprising Glasgow tea merchant Stuart Cranston had set up tables and chairs in his new shop, at the corner of Argyll and Queen Streets, where customers could sample his teas for tuppence a cup. Others were quick to follow, not least his sister Catherine (Kate) Cranston, who three years later opened the Crown Luncheon Rooms in Argyle Street. Unlike her brother, Kate served proper lunches and afternoon teas at a time when the city suburbs had sprawled out too far for men to nip home for lunch. Women, too, were welcome in Miss Cranston's comfortable premises and could meet there unaccompanied by men. At this time many Glaswegians rejected Clydeside's hard-drinking culture and their city had become a stronghold of the temperance movement. The new tea rooms became respectable, alcohol-free gathering places for all classes of men, women and children. Stuart Cranston now followed his sister's lead and turned his 'sample room' into a fully fledged tea room. Soon the Cranston siblings embarked on an escalating rivalry, each opening new premises and styling them, confusingly, 'Cranston's' and 'Miss Cranston's'. Miss Cranston – as she was known, even after her successful marriage – came to own four grand tea rooms, and from 1888 she had them designed in the emerging Arts and Crafts style that had captivated the imagination of many of Glasgow's creatives.

While Kate Cranston was determined that her tea rooms would be tasteful and artistic, she had the courage to give her architects and designers the freedom to follow their own visions. Such enlightened patronage launched the career of

George Walton, who went on to become a leading Scottish designer and architect. Walton had been working as a bank clerk until Miss Cranston hired him to redecorate her Argyle Street Tea Room and on the strength of that commission was able to set up his own design company. Kate's tea rooms were Walton's galleries, where prospective clients could view his work for the price of a cup of tea.

Miss Cranston's passion for the bold, new style led to her commissioning Charles Rennie Mackintosh to transform a narrow four-storey tenement building in Sauchiehall Street – then the city's most fashionable street – into her finest outlet, the Willow Tea Rooms. 'Sauchiehall' comes from the Scots words 'saugh' (willow) and 'haugh' (meadow), and Mackintosh ran with the folklore-rich willow theme. He collaborated with his wife, Margaret Macdonald, who contributed one of her finest works to the project, a gesso panel inspired by the line, 'O ye, all ye that walk in Willow-wood' from the poem by Dante Gabriel Rossetti. The extraordinary and beautiful rooms opened in 1903; one critic said that a diner in the Willow Tea Rooms could 'dream that he is in fairy land'. *Para Handy* author Neil Munro, writing in his *Evening News* column of the adventures of his 'punter' hero Erchie, noted Mackintosh's signature high-backed chairs: 'The chairs is no' like ony other chairs I ever clapped eyes on.'* Mackintosh also designed Kate

---

* I once interviewed Spike Milligan for a TV programme about his book *Monty: My Part in His Victory*. With time to spare, I took him to see Mackintosh's Glasgow School of Art. One of the staff was a Spike fan and we ended up in the director's office, looking at Mackintosh's drawing for one of his extraordinary high-backed chairs. Spike (whose grandfather was a Glaswegian) launched into an impromptu routine in which Mackintosh showed the drawing to a flabbergasted Glasgow joiner. 'Aw naw, Mr Mackintosh,' ran the punch line, 'this is naw a chair, this is a f****n' stepladder!'

Cranston's temporary White Cockade Tea Room for the 1911 Glasgow International Exhibition. The menu, designed by his wife Margaret, shows that Kate wasn't offering her brother's tea but that of Andrew Melrose, the enterprising tea company of George Street, Edinburgh.

The eccentrically dressed, single-minded and artistically inclined Kate Cranston became a Glasgow treasure. *Who's Who in Glasgow in 1909* listed her as one of the city's leading 461 public figures, of whom only seven were women and of these only one a businesswoman. Kate Cranston's recent biographer summed up her achievement: 'Miss Cranston, her own creation, personified the panache of Glasgow in its heyday: hence the affection in which she was held by the inhabitants of that great city.'[19] Two world wars, an intervening depression and changing social habits ended the great era of tea rooms, but today the Willow Tea Rooms have been fully restored by the Willow Tea Rooms Trust and are once again open for business, run as a social enterprise that provides training and opportunities for young people.

By 1901 the offerings of Glasgow's 'Tokyo' style tea rooms were being copied in the homes of all classes. Tea had lent its name to an entire meal – high tea. Initially a simple meal in which bread, cheese and, in good times, meat was washed down by copious quantities of hot sweet tea, it was the antidote to a long, hard shift down the mine or in the ironworks, mill or factory. Later, perjink little sandwiches, savouries and cakes were added, at least for the better off. At its best, high tea could be a momentous affair, as Lewis Grassic Gibbon's account of the Aberdeen version of it reveals.

> Tea is drunk with the meal and the order of it is this: First, one eats a plateful of sausages and eggs and mashed potatoes; then a second plateful to keep down the first. Eating, one assists the second plateful

to its final home by mouthfuls of oatcake spread with butter. Then you eat oatcake with cheese. Then there are scones. Then cookies. Then it really is time to begin on tea – tea and bread and butter and crumpets and toasted rolls and cakes. Then some Dundee cake. Then – about half-past seven – someone shakes you out of the coma into which you have fallen and asks you persuasively if you wouldn't like another cup of tea and just *one* more egg and sausage.[20]

Two decades later, the pioneering English travel writer H.V. Morton found the tradition unchanged. After an encounter with a tea table in Kelso that 'looked like the prize stall in the bakers' competition' he concluded: 'No southerner can conceive the reckless generosity of Scottish teas.'[21]

An unnamed Fraserburgh woman, interviewed in an Aberdeen care home in the 1980s, remembered that when she was a girl, around about 1910, the fishing boats would sail into 'the Broch' late and her mother would gut and pack herring through the night, fuelled by tea.

When the bairns were beddit I made a pot of tea for the three women in her crew and maybe a loaf and jam. There was no Thermos flask so I just put the tea in a flagon and packed the basket and with that over my arm I went down to the shore. It would be pitch dark, the only light came from those bubbly lamps, and down to the herring yards where I would wait until they had drunk all the tea and had their piece then I took the flagon back home.[22]

In mills and factories, where people increasingly operated complex and dangerous machinery, bosses and unions came to recognise what Buddhist sects, like Zen, had known for a millennium: tea refreshes, energises and aids concentration. Even before mandatory tea breaks in the workplace became law, Scotland's shipyards pioneered them – unofficially brewing up around the fires of the riveters. At the Ardrossan shipyard in the 1920s a foreman discovered an apprentice boiling a forbidden billycan.

'Whose tea is that?' the gaffer demanded.

'Lipton's,' replied the boy.

For millions, the tea break became a recognised part of the working day, relieving drudgery, hydrating those who worked by hand and mentally stimulating those who worked by brain.

And when Scots sought better lives in the colonies of Australia and New Zealand, they took their tea-drinking habits with them, habits that persist in these nations today. Tea also became part of the essential 'kit' of the British Army. During both world wars the British government took over the importation of tea, controlled prices and issued extra rations to servicemen, firemen and steelworkers. Drunk with condensed milk, tea was a luxury for hungry and exhausted men in the First World War trenches, even if the brew was a far cry from that served in Kate Cranston's Willow Tea Rooms. 'March some distance, and then have a meal, the tea seems excellent,' wrote a Cameronian officer in the summer of 1914. 'It has been made in a canteen which is dirty with past meals, a scum of grease on the top, and there is no milk, but we find it finer than any tea we have ever drunk.'[23]

Ian Hay, a writer who served in the Argyll & Sutherland Highlanders, tells in his heavily autobiographical novel, *The First Hundred Thousand*, of life in the trenches as high-explosive shells rained down:

> We sit close, and make tea. Only the look-out men, crouching behind their periscopes and loopholes, keep their posts. The wind is the wrong way for

gas, and in any case we all have respirators. Private McLeary, the humorist of A Company, puts his on, and pretends to drink tea through it.

Tea can make almost anything bearable. In Scotland, we had become so addicted to it that even the most revolting brew, drunk in appalling circumstances, would do. As consumers, we have come a long way since the courtly Mary of Modena sipped tea in Holyrood Palace and the uber-rich bought it from a goldsmith.

Now we turn to how Scots began acquiring their tea.

CHAPTER 2

Without Milk, Sugar – or Tax!

In the sixteenth century, Dutch and Portuguese traders made fortunes in the East, while London merchants looked on in envy. But in 1600 Queen Elizabeth of England issued a charter that gave England's Honourable East India Company her authority to trade with the Orient. Following Elizabeth's death and the Union of the Crowns three years later, Scots believed – now that there was a Scottish king on the throne of a United Kingdom – that they could cash in on the trade. On 31 January 1618, Sir James Cunningham, a Scottish peer and privy councillor, was given leave to found a Scottish East India Company – to the fury of English interests, who launched a campaign to strangle this Scottish upstart.[1] King James, first of England and sixth of Scotland, clearly knew which of his united kingdoms was the more important and revoked the Scottish company's patent on 1 April that same year.

In 1695 the Scots again tried to break the monopoly of the East India Company by launching their own business to trade with Africa and the Indies – and were once more stymied by English interests. The Company of Scotland then turned its attention to the New World, where its attempt to found a trading colony at Darien foundered when the English government refused to assist the disease and Spanish-tormented

Scots on their fever-ridden isthmus. The disaster at Darien played its part in bringing about the eventual Treaty of Union between Scotland and England. In return for Scots losing their independence and parliament, they were offered the commercial privileges of England's empire, a move deeply resented by English merchants.

The 1707 Union may have been a patrician deal done for the benefit of the Scots aristocracy, but the nation's literate classes of minor landowners, professionals and tradesmen surely had the chance to infiltrate England's imperial adventure and make it a truly British Empire. Or did they? A customs bill, passed by the very first meeting of the new British parliament, extended the monopoly of the East India Company over Scotland.[2] Scots could now take part in the Asian trade, but only as employees of the English company.

When Scottish merchants tried in vain to compete against the East India Company, they were taking on what would become the most powerful commercial organisation in the world. 'Commercial organisation' hardly describes the Company, for as well as dominating the world's trade in spices, saltpetre, cotton, silk, indigo, tea and opium, the Company came to wield enormous political and military power and rule over tens of millions of people. It became an empire within an empire, the world's first multinational. It was also a ruthless crusher of indigenous powers, obsessively money-motivated and grotesquely racist. From around 1720, Scots took to it like ducks to water.

The East India Company established its first major 'factories' (or trading posts, for these outposts only traded; they manufactured nothing) on the west coast of India, buying luxury textiles for sale in London, or exchanging them for spices in the Far East. Factories soon became forts, and troops followed traders. Exploiting the feebleness of the dying and chaotic Mughal Empire, 'John Company', as it was commonly known, would eventually come to both rule and loot India. Ironically, 'loot' is a Hindustani word that also fell victim to British acquisitiveness. In 1772 a Dutch former employee of the Company, William Bolts, turned whistle-blower and wrote a book denouncing the Company for having become a despotic oligarchy of merchants who had usurped the status of sovereigns. Precious stones, metals and fine fabrics poured from India into Britain. What was not pouring was Indian tea. The British failed to recognise that a variety of tea, consumed by hill tribes both as a food and as an infusion, was indigenous to India. To eighteenth-century Brits, tea meant China tea.

Britain's obsession with tea created a serious trade deficit. China was not impressed with manufactured goods such as the mill-spun cotton that Britain was hawking around the world. It wanted its tea paid for in silver, and Britain was loath to part with its reserves of the precious metal. The solution was to pay for tea with something that the Chinese people craved, even though their government abhorred it – opium. Enter the Honourable East India Company. In 1758 the British government gave it a monopoly over the production of Indian opium. Some of the drug was processed into Western medicines, but obscene fortunes were made from the misery of Chinese opium addicts – all for 'a nice cup of tea'.

The centre for opium poppy cultivation was Bengal, in north-east India, where nearly a million people were employed in growing and processing the drug. It was back-breaking, labour-intensive work, with each individual poppy bulb having to be nicked by (a non-white) hand, to allow heady-smelling sap to ooze out and coagulate into a sticky gum. The gum was then scraped off and stored in earthenware pots before being taken to the opium factory for processing. Native farmers were 'persuaded' – often by being given loans that they could never afford to pay back – to grow opium rather than useful crops that they could actually eat. The whole sorry process is vividly told through the eyes of Deeti, an Indian peasant woman in Amitav Ghosh's novel, *Sea of Poppies*. Ghosh, an historian and anthropologist by training, partly based his description of the opium factory in his novel on the memoir of J.S.W. MacArthur, an enthusiastic Scottish superintendent of the Ghazipur opium factory, who wrote:

> The factory occupies a large extent of ground and contains several magnificent buildings. The factory collects the production of the whole north western provinces and Oudh and from there the cakes are sent to the Presidency of Bengal to be sold to merchants mostly bound for China.

The Ghazipur opium factory was built by the East India Company in 1820 and is today the biggest opium factory in the world, producing drugs for the pharmaceutical industry. Under British rule, the management of the factory was entirely European, although the physical work was done by coolies, with the most 'tedious and sedentary' work being done by women. Perhaps the tedium was relieved by what MacArthur calls the factory's 'powerful opiatic smell that, acting on the nerves of people not endowed with too strong a constitution, produces what is ordinarily called drowsiness, and in extreme cases brings about complete soporific results'. While the coolies might have been dozy, the security at the factory certainly wasn't. The opium was weighed, checked and meticulously recorded at every stage, and MacArthur states that the East India Company had taken steps to defend the factory from attack.

> There are three guns belonging to the factory – they were probably sent here during the mutiny of 1857, as the factory was then fortified to prevent surprise

from the enemy. Now the guns are only fired every Sunday morning to give notice for the Divine Service to the Christian Residents at the station . . .

Published in Calcutta in 1865, MacArthur's *Notes on an Opium Factory* is meticulous in its detail, glowing in its praise and, consequently, rather dull – although it did attract Rudyard Kipling to visit Ghazipur and write an essay about the production of 'the precious cakes that are to replenish the coffers of the Indian Government'.[3]

Replenishing the coffers came at a cost of Indian as well as Chinese lives. The availability of opium in Bengal had a devastating effect on the peasants who grew it and blotted out the wretchedness of their impoverished lives by getting high on their own supply. In 1839 Scotsman Charles Bruce, of whom we will shortly hear more, wrote about:

> That dreadful plague, which had depopulated this beautiful country, turned it into a land of wild beasts, with which it is overrun, and has degenerated the Assamese, from a fair race of people, to the most abject, servile, crafty, and demoralized race in India. This vile drug had kept, and does now keep, down the population; the women have fewer children compared with other countries, and the children seldom live to become old men, but in general die in manhood, very few old men being seen in this unfortunate country, in comparison with others.

John Company was well established in China's port of Canton (today the city of Guangzhou) but was forbidden by the Chinese government to trade in opium there. Instead, it sold the opium from Ghazipur and other factories at auction to traders in Calcutta, who would then smuggle it into China. By about 1825, almost all the Company's tea exports from China were paid for with Indian opium. A profit from the opium sold to China ... and a profit from the tea exported from China ... these were heady days for John Company. Year on year, China's opium consumption rose. By 1838 about 2,500 tons of opium was entering China every year.[4] The Chinese government made beheading the penalty for opium smuggling, but the profits were too addictive for the traders to break the habit.

Foremost among the drug traffickers was the Scottish-owned company Jardine Matheson. William Jardine was eighteen when he left Scotland in 1802 as a surgeon's mate on the East Indiaman *Brunswick*. He'd been raised on a smallholding at Lochmaben and, as his father had died when he was nine, had been supported at Edinburgh University by his elder brother. Fifteen years later, Jardine left the East India Company to become a 'free merchant' in Bombay. Meanwhile, James Matheson, a Highlander from Lairg in Sutherland, was learning the business of trade in Calcutta. The two formed a partnership, launching Jardine Matheson in Canton in 1832. Matheson was twelve years younger than Jardine, but widely read and an enthusiast for fellow Scot Adam Smith's *The Wealth of Nations* and the doctrine of free trade.

The two Scots made a good, if unscrupulous, team. Simon Schama describes them as 'pounding the bible in indignation against heathen Chinese justice, footbinding and kowtowing,' while engaged in 'narco-imperialism'.[5] Michael Fry calls them 'utter rascals, who distinguished themselves by a ruthlessness bordering on infamy'.[6] Historians Schama and Fry follow in distinguished footsteps. Benjamin Disraeli satirised Jardine in his 1845 novel *Sybil* as 'a dreadful man! A Scotchman richer than Croesus, one McDruggy fresh from Canton, with a million of opium in each pocket, denouncing corruption and bellowing free trade.' Jardine, however, thought that 'Opium is the safest and most gentlemanlike speculation I am aware of'.

By the mid-1830s Jardine Matheson dominated the illegal China opium trade. Chinese laws against the drug were, in the words of James Matheson, 'so much waste paper'.

Travelling disguised as a Chinaman to parts of China where Westerners were forbidden, Scottish plant-collector Robert Fortune had ample opportunity to assess the Chinese authorities' attitude to opium.

> It may be quite true that its introduction and use are prohibited by the Chinese government, but that prohibition is merely an empty sound, which, in fact, means nothing. The whole, or at least the greater part of the mandarins use it, and it is not at all unlikely that his Celestial Majesty himself makes one of the number of its devotees. The truth is, the Chinese government, whatever it may say, has no wish to put a stop to its introduction.[7]

Jardine Matheson's fast clippers delivered the opium to anchorages right under the noses of the Chinese authorities. Smaller river vessels, operated by Chinese dealers, would then carry the drug into the cities of the interior. The dealers paid Jardine Matheson for the opium with bags of silver, which in turn were used to buy tea for export to the UK. With fortunes to be made, attempts at piracy were not uncommon. In one incident, the becalmed schooner *Hellas* fought off eight pirate junks for four hours until a breeze spirited her to safety. Occasionally a ship disappeared, leaving the question – weather or piracy?

Although James Matheson's nephew Donald eventually resigned from the company because of his concerns about the physical and social effects of opium, few traders had any qualms about the trade.[8] Opium was, after all, when diluted in alcohol, a common painkiller in Europe. But in China addiction became an epidemic. Well-informed commentators have made widely different estimates of between two and ten million Chinese being hooked.[9]

Robert Fortune encountered one such addict: 'The effects which the immoderate use of opium had produced upon this man were of the most melancholy kind. His figure was thin and emaciated, his cheeks had a pale and haggard hue, and his skin had that peculiar glassy polish by which an opium-smoker is invariably known. His days were evidently numbered . . .'

In 1839 the Chinese authorities seized 20,000 chests, worth £2,000,000, from British merchants in Canton. The UK maintained that the Chinese had no jurisdiction over British subjects or their property, even in China, and demanded compensation. The Chinese refused, fired on British warships and banned trade with Britain. In retaliation the Royal Navy bombarded Canton and Chusan, and soldiers occupied Hong Kong.

The actions of the warship *Nemeses* show how Western technology triumphed over Eastern tradition. The first iron vessel to be mounted with guns, *Nemeses* was built by Scottish shipbuilder William Laird at his Birkenhead shipyard. Laird's son, John, had adapted the metal-bending techniques of his father's boiler-making business to build iron hulls. Driven by two sixty-horsepower engines and armed with two swivel-mounted thirty-two-pound cannon, five six-pounders and Congreve rockets, the *Nemeses* was the most formidable warship in the world. 'The Devil Ship', as the Chinese named her, pulverised the wooden war junks of the Emperor's navy, along with his shore batteries and fortresses. Hilaire Belloc's lines (albeit about a different weapon wielded in a different war) sum up the uneven conflict:

Whatever happens, we have got
The Maxim gun, and they have not.

Britain's military/industrial complex brought the ancient Chinese Empire to its knees. In August 1842 China was forced to sign the Treaty of Nanking, which ceded Hong Kong to Britain and opened the ports of Canton, Amoy, Foochow (now Fuzhou), Ningpo (now Ningbo) and Shanghai – the treaty ports – to foreign, and particularly British, merchants. As Arthur Herman says in his book *How the Scots Invented the Modern World*, 'Great Britain was now the dominant political power in the region – thanks to John Laird and the Scottish drug lords.' The treaty ports forced open in the First Opium War loom large in the story of Scotland and tea. With China defeated and humiliated, the East India Company continued to grow opium for Jardine Matheson and others to supply to China – all for the sake of a cuppa.

Although it had used middlemen to sell its Bengal opium in China, the East India Company was well-established in Canton and traded legally there. Its agents on the ground, who bought tea from the Chinese Hong merchants, juggled their detailed instructions from London with the cost and quality of tea available. The Company's 'colony' in Canton consisted of about a dozen such agents and seven or eight writers, or clerks, who were looked after by butlers, stewards and servants. The Chinese government restricted Europeans to the tiny footprint of their factories, but in compensation for the lonely and isolated lives they led, John Company's men lived, and feasted, well. With a monopoly on the tea sold in Britain, their employer could afford to be generous. This lordly lifestyle, along with high-quality trade goods and a flawless credit rating, lent kudos to the Company, and some commentators even ascribe a quasi-diplomatic status to its employees in China.[10] The Company men may have enjoyed great privilege, but even staunch critics of the Company agreed that they had 'taken great pains to ensure the goodness of the tea'. Scottish merchants, and their counterparts in Ireland and the English provinces, deeply resented John Company's half-century monopoly over the tea legally imported into Britain. If Scots wanted tea, it had to come from the Company's public auctions in London – and most Scottish merchants were too small to buy directly at these sales; they had to buy through London dealers and pay their premium. By the 1780s, a handful of Edinburgh and Glasgow merchants had grown big enough to deal directly with John Company. Edinburgh's Robert Sheppard bought five tons of tea from the Company in 1798. The accounts of Sheppard's protégé, Andrew Melrose, show how ambitious Scots were keen to cut out the middlemen. In 1816 Melrose spent £16,000 buying tea from a London dealer and only £9,000 directly from the Company. Two years later he bought just £9,000 from the dealer and £11,000 directly from the Company. In years to come he would rely less and less on London dealers.[11]

But whether they bought their tea directly from the Company, or from London dealers, one thing was certain – they were going to pay a hefty tax on it that more than doubled the price of tea. Thirsty, thrifty Scots looked longingly towards Continental Europe, where they had ancient trading links – much older than their political union with England – and where the duty on tea was negligible.

Heavily taxing tea was a very British wheeze. Even as Catherine of Braganza first sipped the infusion with the ladies of the court, her royal husband slapped tax on it. The duty on tea would eventually reach 119 per cent. This swingeing levy, and Scotland's long and convoluted coastline, presented a golden opportunity – for smugglers. China tea was traditionally drunk without milk or sugar, and soon it was being widely drunk in Scotland without tax. As the London government's tariff on tea rose, so did the audacity of the smugglers. Sometimes large foreign ships unloaded crates of tea in remote ports, but more often the Scots smugglers set out in small boats to rendezvous with well-manned and armed ships lurking off the coast, collect tea from them, land it in remote bays and sell it in parcels to grateful locals. Even respectable grocers mixed their tax-paid tea with the smuggled leaves to increase their profit. For many Scots, duty-free tea made the drink affordable for the first time.

Sir Walter Scott caught the mood of widespread acceptance of smuggling in his novel *Guy Mannering*, in which he has Margaret Bertram complain to her brother, the Laird of Ellangowan, about exciseman Frank Kennedy's pursuit of Dutch tea smuggler Dirk Hatteraick:

> 'I wish' replied the lady, 'Frank Kennedy would let Dirk Hatteraick alane. What needs he make himself mair busy than otherfolk? Cannot he sing his sang, and take his drink, and draw his salary, like Collector Snail, honest man, that never fashes onybody? And I wonder at you, Laird, for meddling and making – Did we ever want to send for tea or brandy frae the Borough-town, when Dirk Hatteraick used to come quietly into the bay?'

Margaret Bertram would doubtless have been happy for Auld Mahoun (the devil) to have danced away with an exciseman like Frank Kennedy – as he did in the poem by Robert Burns, who had a brief career as an exciseman himself.

> The De'il cam fiddling thro' the town,
> And danc'd awa' wi' the Exciseman;

And ilka wife cry'd, 'Auld Mahoun,
I wish you luck o' the prize, man.'

In 1783, 150,000 pounds of tea and a large volume of spirits were landed by just one ship in three voyages to Scotland. On shore, a sophisticated network dealt with the storage, insurance, sales and distribution. One dealer in smuggled tea, Aitcheson of Edinburgh, even established a string of retail outlets in the north of England and Yorkshire.[12] By 1785 about 250 ships were engaged in smuggling tax-free tea to Britain, with Gothenburg, Sweden, a major supplier to Scotland. The Scottish entrepreneurs were a serious threat to London, and John Company's, legal monopoly.

The godfathers of the Gothenburg smuggling trade were very often exiled Scots Jacobites who had settled in the Swedish city after Culloden. Their well-honed survival instincts, contacts and knowledge of the Scottish coast, combined with an aversion to paying Hanoverian taxes, made them formidable smugglers. Canny Scottish merchants and the nation's growing consumer culture ensured that there was a ready market for 'Gothenburg tea'. In fact, it seems that only a tenth of tea imported into Sweden was for local consumption – the rest being bound for Britain.[13]

The most tangible evidence of Scottish tea smuggling stands in the Berwickshire fishing port of Eyemouth. Gunsgreen House, which overlooks the harbour, was designed as a mansion house for John Nisbet. With its grand frontage, massive vaulted cellar and fine interiors, it befitted a successful merchant. But Nisbet was a smuggler. In fact, he was almost certainly the most successful and notorious smuggler of his day. The part of the house that John Adam, one of the great Scottish architectural dynasty, almost certainly didn't design was the 'tea chute', a hidden chamber fashioned out of Canton tea chests that could hold 500 pounds of tea – rather a lot for the unmarried Nisbet to have had for his own consumption. There are several other secret storerooms in the house and it is clear that Nisbet ran a major operation. Legal records suggest that Nisbet's entire business was smuggling and that he didn't even pretend to be a legitimate merchant. More than half the tea drunk in Scotland during the mid-eighteenth century is likely to have been smuggled, with Mafia-style *omertà* protecting dealers like Nisbet. Rudyard Kipling's *A Smuggler's Song* has always, to my mind, conjured up the English West Country, but the advice it contained certainly applied to Eyemouth.

If you meet King George's men, dressed in blue and red,
You be careful what you say, and mindful what is said.

Evidence for the Gothenburg–Eyemouth smuggling axis can be found in the 1761 records of Eyemouth's Masonic lodge, which notes the visit of George Carnegie, one of Gothenburg's Jacobite merchants.[14] As Carnegie hailed from Angus, it is likely that his main reason for visiting Eyemouth was business, not pleasure, and that the nature of his business was perfectly acceptable to his brother Freemasons. Often, smuggling was disguised by Sweden's legal trade with Scotland. In the 1780s, John Lyon, captain of the *Elizabeth*, legally carried timber and iron from Gothenburg to Eyemouth, but was also a notorious tea smuggler of whom it was said: 'Getting hold of his vessel will be difficult as he is a most Compleat artfull Fellow for the Business. No capture will destroy smuggling on that Coast as much as securing that vessel.'[15]

Even when the authorities did succeed in seizing contraband, heavily armed bands of smugglers sometimes stole it back. One July night in 1780, thirty armed men, their faces blackened, raided the Custom's warehouse in Eyemouth and carried off barrels of spirits and sacks of tea that had been impounded a month before. It is a scene worthy of Robert Louis Stevenson.

As a way of defeating the smugglers, the Scottish judge and philosopher Lord Kames advocated the abolishing of duty on tea and suggested replacing the duty with an innovative tax on the very act of drinking tea rather than purchasing it.[16] Pointing out that 'In Holland, a person is prohibited from drinking tea without license, for which he pays a yearly sum', Kames proposed that every tea drinker be registered and 'be subjected to a moderate tax, proportioned to his mode of living'. A family with a coach with two horses, for instance, would pay more tax than a family without a coach, and the more horses and liveried servants a household had, the more it would have to pay for the privilege of drinking tea. Kames may have been an enlightenment genius, but his progressive scheme for a higher tax on the better-off fell on deaf ears.

In 1784 Prime Minister William Pitt ended the rollicking smuggling saga by reducing the tea tax to its lowest-ever level of 12.5 per cent and put the smugglers out of business at a stroke. To make up for the loss of revenue, Pitt hiked up the Window Tax. Presumably, impecunious Scottish tea drinkers bricked up their windows and drank in the gloom.

Writing thirty years after the scrapping of tea tax, Sir Walter Scott tells of the demise of the smuggling scam:

> In those halcyon days of the free trade, the fixed price for carrying a box of tea, or bale of tobacco, from the coast of Galloway to Edinburgh, was fifteen shillings, and a man with horses carried four such packages. The trade was entirely destroyed by Mr. Pitt's celebrated commutation law, which, by reducing the duties upon excisable articles, enabled lawful dealer to compete with the smuggler. The statute was called in Galloway and Dumfriesshire, by those who had

thriven upon the contraband trade, 'the burning and starving act'.[17]

With the smugglers defeated, the East India Company's monopoly was once more intact and, within a year, Britain's tea consumption doubled. Even when Pitt later raised the tea tax to 90 per cent, to pay for the war against Napoleon, smuggling it was a thing of the past and failed to reassert itself.

The demise of smuggling wrested away from Scots what control they ever had over the supply and price of tea. Laws discriminated against dealers not based in London, and London merchants enjoyed the privilege of being able to store tea they had bought in John Company's warehouses and use that tea as security to raise credit to buy more. This 'critical-mass' of money and privilege made London the UK's undisputed tea capital. It rankled with the Scots merchants who were used to dealing with their friends in Gothenburg, and it rankled with the more entrepreneurial of them that they could not buy tea directly from China and ship it into Scottish ports. Among such merchants was Glasgow's dynamic Kirkman Finlay.

Born in the Gallowgate in 1772, Kirkman Finlay was the second son of James Finlay, a merchant who founded a company in 1750 to import rum and sugar from the West Indies. James Finlay & Company then moved into exporting cotton goods to Europe. Kirkman was educated at what is now Glasgow High School, where he had a reputation for being clever but 'a mischievous dog', and at Glasgow University. It was an exciting era for a bright young man with an eye for technology and a business brain. James Watt had patented his steam engine and, in 1776, Adam Smith had published *An Inquiry into the Nature and Causes of the Wealth of Nations*. Adam Smith had been a professor in Glasgow and the city's merchants claimed Smith as one of their own.

I remember . . . about the time of the appearance of *The Wealth of Nations*, that the Glasgow merchants were as proud of the work as if they had written it themselves; and that some of them said it was no wonder that Adam Smith had written such a book, as he had the advantage of their society, in which the same doctrines were circulated with the punch every day.[18]

No doubt, the Scottish merchants' copies of *The Wealth of Nations* were well-thumbed where Smith had written that the public:

over and above being excluded from the trade, must have paid in the price of the East India goods which they consumed, not only the extraordinary profits which the Company may have made upon the goods in consequence of their monopoly, but for all the extraordinary waste which the fraud and abuse, inseparable from the management of the affairs of so great a company, must necessarily have occasioned.

Kirkman Finlay grasped the opportunities of both industrialisation and free trade. He bought cotton mills and, in 1813, presented the Glasgow Chamber of Commerce's petition against the renewal of the East India Company's monopoly to both Houses of Parliament. Such a monopoly was, stated the petition, 'an infringement of general rights in having appropriated for the benefit of the few, advantages which were the property of all'. That year, an act was passed abolishing John Company's monopoly of the India trade but leaving the lucrative China tea trade firmly in its hands.

James Finlay & Company was quick to get in on the India act. In 1816 it sent the 600-ton *Duke of Buckinghamshire* – the first trading vessel to leave the Clyde for Bombay – to lay the foundations of a permanent trading presence in India. The following year, the company sent a ship and agent to Calcutta and then on to Canton to explore the possibilities of trade with China. It is believed that this venture opened Kirkman Finlay's eyes to the opportunities of the tea trade.[19] While Finlay sold cotton goods to China, the East India Company monopoly still rankled, and in 1830 Finlay, as chairman of the Chamber of Commerce, joined in a petition at the House of Commons protesting 'against the renewal of any part of the monopoly as being an infringement of the constitutional rights belonging to every British subject to a free participation in every branch of commerce in which capital can be beneficially employed'.

In 1830, after more than a decade-long campaign by tea dealers, the Edinburgh Chamber of Commerce and Manufacturers issued a manifesto against the East India Company's monopoly. In 1833 parliament gave way to the pressure and stripped the Company of its trading rights. Months later, a three-masted ship was launched in Greenock, proudly named the *Kirkman Finlay* and sailed for Canton. As for the man whose name the ship carried, a contemporary noted, 'He had been one of the keenest and ablest opponents of John Company's monopoly, and as soon as the door was thrown open, he pushed in and led the way for others.'[20]

From Bombay, Kirkman's son, Alexander Struthers Finlay, traded between India, Britain and China on his father's behalf. Letters from father to son, written over three years from 1835 and held in Finlay & Co.'s archive, are the first evidence that the Glasgow company had entered the China tea trade. It is a trade Kirkman was optimistic about, as a letter to his son in Bombay shows.

I am inclined to think that even the markets in the States may be obliged to apply to London this next year for Tea; and that the cargoes for that market will find buyers at fair prices. Everything depends on the quality coming, the quality purchased, and of course the prices paid being moderate – but if all of these join, I never knew anything promise better than Tea & Silk during the year 1838.[21]

In 1842 Kirkman Finlay died, just short of his 69th birthday, at Castle Toward, the Gothic Revival pile he had built for himself in Argyll. He had served as an MP, Lord Provost of Glasgow, and Rector of Glasgow University, but it was as an enterprising merchant that he was best remembered.

He was a born merchant, with the eye to see the profit and the nerve to force the risk; and if sometimes he was too careless of the risk for his own profit, others reaped where he had sown. He opened up new markets for us, he showed us novel combinations and ventures on a scale we had not been used to, and he spread the infection of his own spirit.[22]

In the half-century up until 1833, during which the East India Company had enjoyed the 'exclusive privilege' of importing tea from China, Britain's consumption of tea doubled. Tea had been the Company's top-selling commodity and the mainstay of its revenue. Its much criticised monopoly, however, had been strictly regulated. It had not only to annually import enough tea for the nation's needs, but also to stock a year's supply in its warehouses against the vagaries of the supply chain and the interference of Britain's enemies. The Company couldn't fix the price, as the tea was to be sold quarterly at public auction, allowing the market to control the final cost to the customer. Modern commentators have argued that the company's record was 'one of public responsibility, sensitivity to consumer demand, and responsiveness to its changes.'[23] But the free-trade zeitgeist of the era held monopoly to be inefficient, wasteful, corrupt and costly.

The East India Company played a crucial role in establishing the British Empire in India and expanding its interest in China and elsewhere in Southeast Asia. It had more revenue, ruled over more people and had a bigger army than the British state, but it became a victim of its own success. With its monopoly broken, traders in Leith and Glasgow, and the English ports of Bristol, Hull and Liverpool, were free to trade directly with China and sell as they pleased. Old certainties vanished overnight and new opportunities and dangers arose. The Scottish company Jardine Matheson was quick to react. Already established in Canton, it dispatched its vessel, the *Sarah*, with the first cargo of 'free tea' to London. Edinburgh's Andrew Melrose was also quick off the mark. He was one of a group of seven merchants who first imported tea from China directly into the port of Leith. Their new ship, the *Isabella*, sailed for Canton in December 1833, returning in April 1835 with 7,000 chests of tea.

The East India Company's control of China tea might have been broken, but there was still a mighty monopoly in place – that of the xenophobic Celestial Empire. It closely guarded the secrets of growing and manufacturing tea, and the thirsty British hated that. Enter a remarkable Scottish botanist and adventurer – Robert Fortune.

CHAPTER 3

Take Things Coolly and Never Lose Your Temper

It was November in the Year of the Tiger. In China, the British and the Chinese clashed once again over the contentious poppy. The Chinese had taken deep offence. That year, 2010, marked the 150th anniversary of Britain's final victory over China in the Second Opium War. To their Chinese hosts, the Remembrance Day poppies the visitors were wearing symbolised China's humiliating defeat and the enslavement of tens of thousands of its people to the opium poppy in the pursuit of Western profit.

The Chinese have long memories for such affronts, but when Prime Minister David Cameron and MPs George Osborne, Michael Gove, Chris Huhne and Vince Cable were asked to remove their poppies, they refused. Given that they were in China to drum up business for Britain, you might think that they would have been more sensitive. They weren't. But then Britain has a long history of insensitivity to the Chinese point of view. Historically, the Chinese came to think of all *fanquis* (foreigners) as 'white devils' or 'barbarians', but they did differentiate between them. The Portuguese were infamous for their lust for women, the French for their lust for war, and the British for their lust for money.[1]

Nineteenth-century China had a wealthy economy and was potentially a vast market – and the free-trade-obsessed British wanted part of the action, including the right to sell opium and to buy tea. When the Chinese emperor ordered the seizure of the traders' opium, the British went to war, using the industrial slaughtering-power of the most powerful navy in the world to crush China's resistance. Into these complex and volatile politics plunged some remarkable Scottish tea men.

In Cockney rhyming slang, 'tea leaf' means 'thief'. In one sense it neatly describes Robert Fortune, the self-made 'lad o' pairts' from the Scottish Borders who outwitted the Chinese military and civil authorities to smuggle precious tea plants out of the insular and secretive Celestial Empire. But Fortune was a truly remarkable man – bold, physically tough and with the inquisitiveness gene in spadefuls.

One of nine children of a 'hedger', an agricultural estate worker, Robert was born in 1812 in Edrom, a village in Berwickshire. The house has long gone, but the building which held the parish school still stands. Under teacher George Peacock, Robert received what is believed by today's Dunse Historical Society to have been a good early education in a wide range of subjects.[2] Unsurprisingly for a child of a rapidly expanding family in a humble cottage, he spent a good deal of time outdoors, where he received an alternative education that would stand him in good stead during his career as botanical explorer: 'I little thought that the knowledge I acquired in climbing for the nests of wood pigeons and rooks, when my more sober elders consoled me with the prophesy that I would break my neck, would turn out so useful as it afterwards did,' he recalled.

There is little in today's 'health & safety' culture that a

Victorian plant-hunter would recognise. Fortune took storms, extreme temperatures, disease, lengthy separations from his loved ones, the risk of arrest, robbery and pirate attacks all in his stride. Even after years of arduous travels 'the celebrated Chinese traveller' was described by Irish-born diplomat and diarist Robert Hart as 'a fine stout, healthy looking man'.[3] The young Fortune became an apprentice gardener in a local estate but, able and ambitious, soon found work at Edinburgh's botanical gardens and then at the Royal Horticultural Society in London.

In 1842 the First Opium War ended with the signing of the Treaty of Nanking and the ceding of Hong Kong to Britain. The treaty ports of Canton, Amoy, Foochow, Ningpo and Shanghai were also opened to foreign trade and there was an international scramble to ransack China. The Horticultural Society decided to send Fortune there to collect botanical specimens. In July the following year, after a four-month voyage, he arrived in the pestilential nightmare that was Hong Kong. Recording temperatures that reached 94°F (33.44°C), he described 'that malignant disease called the "Hong Kong fever," which has baffled medical skill and carried hundreds to the tomb'. He reported that the disease had killed the greater part of a detachment of soldiers and that two of his fellow passengers had gone 'to that undiscovered country from whose bourn no traveller returns'. Doctors advised new arrivals to 'leave the island and fly to Macao'. Disease was not the only danger. 'The town swarms with thieves and robbers, who are only kept under by the strong armed police lately established,' wrote Robert, who predicted, 'Viewed as a place of trade, I fear Hong Kong will be a failure.' Nevertheless he thought that 'the botany of the island possesses a considerable degree of interest'.

Fortune travelled the coast, visiting Amoy, Ningpo, Chusan Island, Shanghai and Portuguese Macao, but believing the south to have been already scoured by botanists, he was anxious to travel north and inland. That summer and the following summer, he pushed further afield to 'visit several parts of the country, which were formerly sealed to Europeans, and which contained subjects of much interest'. Fortune's book *Three Years' Wandering in the Northern Provinces of China* is crammed with observations about Chinese life, customs, religion, attitudes, geography and natural history, but – like most Westerners in China – he was fascinated by tea.

> There are few subjects connected with the vegetable kingdom which have attracted such a large share of public notice as the tea-plant of China. Its cultivation on the Chinese hills, the particular species or varieties which produces the black and green teas of commerce, and the method of preparing the leaves, have always been objects of peculiar interest. The jealousy of the Chinese government, in former times, prevented foreigners from visiting any of the districts where tea is cultivated, and the information derived from the Chinese merchants, even scanty as it was, was not to be depended upon.[4]

At his time, Western opinion was divided as to the origins of black and green teas, with some believing that the only difference was in the mode of preparation, while others maintained that black tea was made from *Thea bohea*, while green tea came from *Thea viridis*. Fortune himself had arrived in China believing that the teas came from different varieties. But at Foochow, a black-tea-producing area in Fokien Province, he made a discovery. 'Great was my surprise to find all the plants on the tea hills near Foochow exactly the same as those in the green tea districts of the north. Here were then green tea plantations on the black tea hills, and not a single plant of the Thea Bohea to be seen.'

Fortune took samples to compare and proved that the colour of tea was an outcome of processing, not of variety. While tea obsessed the British, Fortune was on an expedition with much wider interests; his paymasters wanted specimens sent home of all that was exotic, economically or medically promising, beautiful or undiscovered. Even for the resourceful, hardy and bold, plant-hunting in China was a challenge. The Opium War had left the Chinese simmering with resentment and suspicion. Europeans weren't allowed to stray from the confines of the treaty ports and they were discouraged from learning Chinese. Trade had to be conducted through interpreters, who were thought to be dangerous and dishonest.[5] Even when British diplomats negotiated their way into Peking, Fortune notes that they 'were so fettered and watched by the jealous Chinese that they saw little more than their friends who remained at Canton'.

When Robert Fortune's imagination was fired up, even the obstacles that daunted British ambassadors couldn't dampen his passion to explore. Chinese gardeners in Shanghai had whetted his appetite to visit the botanical treasure of the city of Soo-chow (modern Suzhou). Fortune recalled:

It is the Chinaman's earthly paradise, and it would be hard indeed to convince him that it had its equal in any town on earth. In addition to other attractions, I was informed by the Chinese nursery gardeners at Shanghae that it contained a great number of excellent flower gardens and nurseries ... I was, therefore, strongly tempted to infringe the absurd laws of the Celestial Empire, and try and reach this far-famed place.

Foreigners were limited to a journey out of Shanghai of not more than twenty-four hours and the western branch of the

Huangpu River was forbidden to them altogether, despite this ban being a breach of the Treaty of Nanking. Chinese boatmen were terrified of the mandarins, the powerful bureaucrats of the empire, and Fortune could only get a vessel by keeping its crew ignorant of the length of their journey and their destination, while his Chinese servant reassured the men that Fortune was 'perfectly harmless'. Navigating the labyrinthine canal network by compass, Fortune waited until he was twenty or thirty miles from Shanghai before admitting to his servant where they were heading and promised him a five-dollar bonus if he could persuade the boatmen to take them. The servant's persuasiveness, and the doubling of the crew's fee, did the trick. It may be that the boatmen agreed with Fortune's self-belief that he was a master of disguise. To disguise himself convincingly as a Chinaman, Fortune had to acquire a 'queue', or pigtail, a Manchurian hairstyle that had been imposed on the conquered Han people in the seventeenth century. By the time of the Quing dynasty the wearing of a pigtail was compulsory for all Chinese men except priests – failure to do so was treasonable.

> I was, of course, travelling in Chinese costume; my head was shaved, I had a splendid wig and tail, in which some Chinaman in former days had doubtless been extremely vain, and upon the whole I believe I made a pretty fair Chinaman. Although the Chinese countenance and eye differ considerably from those of a native of Europe, yet a traveller in the north has a far greater chance of escaping detection than in the south of China, the features of the northern natives approaching more nearly to those of Europeans than they do in the south, and the difference among themselves being also greater.

Fortune, however, soon had cause to quote (or slightly mis-quote) Robert Burns:'The best laid schemes of mice and men gang aft agee.' One night, as he lay asleep, a thief crept aboard and stole both his European and his Chinese clothes and set the boat adrift from its mooring. The journey was delayed until his servant could buy Fortune another Chinese outfit.

Soo-chow has been described as 'the Venice of China' and was the hub of a canal network that the Chinese had been building since the fifth century BCE. A major trading centre, it lay beside the Grand Canal, the oldest and (at more than 1,100 miles) the longest canal in the world. Fortune thought it 'A noble canal, as wide as the Thames at Richmond'. The Scot believed that he was the first 'Englishman' to have entered 'the most fashionable city of the Celestial Empire'. His disguise even fooled the dogs. 'These animals manifest very great hatred to foreigners, barking at them whenever they see them, and hanging on their skirts ...'

Soo-chow did not disappoint, and Fortune was able to visit nurseries and buy new and valuable plants, including 'a white *Glycine*, a fine new double yellow rose, and a *Gardenia* with large white blossoms like a Camellia. These plants are now in England, and will soon be met with in every garden in the country.' Today, the classical gardens of Suzhou, the product of a 2,000-year-old landscape gardening tradition, are a UNESCO World Heritage Site, as is the ancient Grand Canal which runs through the city.

Returning to Shanghai, Fortune had to step ashore in his Chinese clothes. 'I was not recognised by a single individual, although I walked up the street where I was well known, and even my friend Mr Mackenzie, with whom I was staying, did not know me for the first few minutes after I sat down in his room.' In Hong Kong Fortune busied himself, preparing his plants and seeds to be shipped to England. He divided them into three or four batches, sending them on separate ships to split the risk of losing the lot. The plants were packed in 'Wardian cases' and transported on the ships' decks. A decade earlier, English botanist Nathaniel Ward had revolutionised botanical exploration when he discovered that plants could survive long voyages if packed in tightly sealed glass containers, protected from the climates they endured on the voyage. Plants that had been sent to Ward from Australia in these cases had reached London in perfect condition after eight months at sea, surviving storms around Cape Horn. Today, the Chelsea Physic Garden proudly exhibits such a case in honour of Ward and the many explorer-botanists who used his invention.

Fortune travelled to Foochow on the estuary of the River Min – a journey on which he had witnessed fishing with cormorants, collected specimens, and further confirmed his belief that black and green teas were made from the same species. When his botanical researches were completed, he arranged a passage to Shanghai on a junk. The Chinese captain told him, 'I hope your gun is a good one and that you have plenty of powder and shot ... we are very likely to be attacked by the *Jan-dous*, who swarm amongst the islands.' *Jan-dous*, explained Fortune's servant, were pirates. Fortune dismissed the threat and, being feverish, took to his bed as the junk left the mouth of the river. That afternoon he was awakened by the captain and pilot with the news that a number of *Jan-dou* junks were closing in on them. Fortune checked his gun and pistols and went on deck.

> By the aid of a small pocket-telescope I could see as the nearest junk approached that her deck was crowded with men; I then had no longer any doubts regarding her intentions ... I knew perfectly well, that if we were taken by the pirates I had not the slightest chance of escape; for the first thing they would do would be to knock me on the head and throw me

overboard, as they would deem it dangerous to themselves were I to get away. At the time I must confess that I had little hopes of being able to beat off such a number, and devoutly wished myself anywhere rather than where I was.

Fortune tells that the captain, pilot, native passengers and sailors busied themselves by hiding their valuables before dragging up baskets of small stones from the hold that 'were intended to be used instead of fire arms when the pirates came to close quarters'. He found his servant dressed in rags, explaining that the pirates would only take prisoner those who looked as if they had money and could pay ransom for their freedom. Despite Fortune's junk having every inch of sail up, and doing seven or eight miles an hour, one of the pirate junks got close enough to give her a broadside, throwing Fortune's ship's crew into panic. Most ran below deck, but Fortune threatened to shoot the two helmsmen if they deserted their post. After several more broadsides, the Scot noticed that the pirate captain could not bring his guns to bear without putting his helm down and bringing his junk at right angles to his prey's stern. Crouching in the stern, Fortune let the pirate ship get close.

> I raised myself above the high stern of our junk; and while the pirates were not more than twenty yards from us, hooting and yelling, I raked their decks fore and aft, with shot and ball from my double-barreled gun. Had a thunder-bolt fallen amongst them, they could not have been more surprised. Doubtless, many were wounded, and probably some killed. At all events, the whole of the crew, not fewer than forty or fifty men, who, a moment before, crowded the deck, disappeared in a marvellous manner; sheltering

themselves behind the bulwarks, or lying flat on their faces. They were so completely taken by surprise that their junk was left without a helmsman; her sails flapped in the wind; and, as we were still carrying all sail and keeping on our right course, they were soon left a considerable way astern.

A second *Jan-dou* junk now came alongside Fortune's vessel and, as soon as it came within twenty or thirty yards, the botanist 'gave them the contents of both barrels, raking the decks as before' and dropping the helmsman and several others. The attack was thus beaten off and, as Fortune's junk drew away from the pirates, his shipmates' courage returned.

Now was the time for my heroic companions to come from their hiding-place, which they did with great alacrity, hooting and yelling as the pirates had done before, and, in derision, calling on them to come back and renew the fight. The stones, too, were now boldly seized and thrown after the retreating junks, reaching to almost a tenth part of the distance; and a stranger who had not seen these gentry before would have supposed them the bravest men in existence. Fortunately the pirates did not think proper to accept the challenge.

Fortune was, of course, writing for publication and money, but the derring-do nature of his pirate tales rings true. It was only two years since the death of 'pirate queen' Ching Shih, who had terrorised the South China Sea in the early decades of the century as the commander of the Red Flag Fleet of more than 300 pirate junks and 20,000 followers. The story of Westerners beating off pirates with modern firearms is borne out by the account of another pirate attack on the Pearl River in 1852 that tea-trader William Melrose sent to his father in Edinburgh.

> I have little news to give you. The only interesting thing here was an attack by pirates made on a boat at the Bogue in which were four young men of our community who had gone down there shooting. They were boarded by thirty pirates when at anchor and at dinner. Mr Dent, a young Mr Anderson from Edinburgh, McGregor, a Glasgow man, and a Mr Oakley were of the party. As soon as the cry of the pirates was raised, young Anderson seized a gun and looked out, saw a pirate lighting a fire pot to throw at them and shot him dead on the spot. The row then commenced; fire pots were thrown in numbers, spears and so on. But the four foreigners stood firm with their double barrels and shot coolly at the most conspicuous in the row. The pirates were not to be intimidated; they stood firm throwing their spears and making rushes forward until no less than eight of them were shot dead and lastly their leader, when they went away swearing that they would soon be back again. The four had a lucky escape.

At Shanghai, Fortune was nursed back to health, then he set off for Hong Kong, where he dispatched eight Wardian cases of plants to England. He himself sailed from Canton, with eighteen cases of 'the most beautiful plants of northern China' tied down safely on the exposed poop deck of the *John Cooper*.

Failing a journey to the classical gardens of Suzhou, Robert Fortune-hunters can visit the Chelsea Physic Garden, four acres of beauty, tranquillity and botanical enchantment in the heart of London. The job of head gardener there was Fortune's reward for his successful explorations. His annual salary was £100, a family house, coal to heat it and the right to grow vegetables along the bank of the Thames. Founded in 1673 by the Worshipful Society of Apothecaries to grow medical plants, the Chelsea is the third-oldest botanical garden in Britain, after the University of Oxford's (1621) and the Royal Botanic Garden in Edinburgh (1670). When Fortune took it over, he 'found it overrun with weeds, the botanical arrangements in confusion, the exotic plants in the houses in very bad health and generally in a most unfit state for the purpose for which it was designed'.

Undaunted and energetic, he got to work, overseeing the building of two new greenhouses, introducing a more scientific ordering of plants, accurately naming medical specimens and creating a tank for aquatic plants which is still in use today. Over the centuries, urban development has nibbled away at the edges of the garden, as the Chelsea Embankment and the Royal Hospital Road were built, so just less than the original four acres of beautiful and fascinating garden remain, and they are Grade-1-listed by English Heritage. The Chelsea Physic Garden remains a 'secret' haven in frantic London. I was shown around by Donatella, a knowledgeable volunteer who pointed me in the direction of the Tea Garden, where grows not only *Camellia sinensis* but also many of the hundreds of plants that tisanes – or herbal teas – can be made from. Specimens of some of the nearly 190 plants that Fortune introduced to Britain, of which 120 were previously unknown, also pay tribute to the adventurous Scot. Fortune's introductions include the golden larch, the Chusan palm, the white wisteria, many tree peonies and azaleas, the winter-flowering jasmine and that ubiquitous ornament to ice-cream, the kumquat. Many of them bear his name, *fortune*.[6]

Britain's thirst for tea – and reluctance to pay China in silver for it – would soon put paid to Robert's time on the Thames. The East India Company had lost its China tea monopoly, but it controlled huge swathes of northern India, where botanists were convinced tea could thrive. Once such man was William Jameson, a Leith-born, Edinburgh University-educated doctor who had turned to botany in India and was superintendent of the Saharanpur Botanical Garden in North India. His experiments convinced the East India Company to invest heavily in tea, but what was needed were the finest possible plants available, not the poor-quality specimens that had already escaped from behind Imperial China's bamboo curtain. In 1835 George J. Gordon, who had previously worked for merchant company Macintosh & Company, had been sent by the East India Company to collect seeds and plants from the coast of China, in clear breach of Chinese law and at great risk to his own life and liberty. But it is likely that Gordon had been fobbed off with seeds from the nearest gardens and had not collected the prize specimens that the British desired. A new, more tenacious plant-hunter was required.

In 1847 Robert Fortune's *Three Years' Wanderings in the Northern Provinces of China* – with its tales of disguises, pirates and derring-do – had been published. It was the perfect CV for the man to penetrate deep into northern China and steal the secrets of tea and the most prized tea plants. The Indian author Shashi Tharoor suggests that in sending the 'secret agent' Robert Fortune to China to steal tea the British invented industrial espionage.[7] It is a theme that was gleefully taken up by the tea company Twinings, whose advertising pastiche of the 'down the gun barrel' James Bond poster featured a figure wearing a sporran and a coolie hat. In 1848, on William Jameson's advice, Fortune was commissioned to return to China and bring home not only the finest varieties of tea plants, but also skilled tea workers and the tools of their trade. 'It was a matter of great importance to procure them from those districts in China where the best teas were produced,' Fortune wrote. Once taken from China, the plants would be planted in Britain's north-west provinces in India in an attempt to break China's ancient monopoly.

In June that year Fortune sailed for China, arriving in Hong Kong eight weeks later. On his last visit six years previously it had been 'a barren island, with only a few huts upon it, inhabited by pirates and fishermen'. He now reported that the British merchant-princes had built grand houses with fine gardens for themselves around its harbour and that a pretty English church was rising on the hillside. Another sea journey took him to Shanghai, more than 800 miles to the north-east. It was the most northerly of the five treaty ports. Fortune had predicted that Shanghai would overtake Canton in importance. Approaching the city, he found 'a forest of masts, not of junks only, which had been so striking on former occasions, but of goodly foreign ships, chiefly from England and the United States of America'. Scottish traders like Jardine Matheson and Gibb, Livingston & Company were quick to seize opportunities in this boomtown, acquiring sites on the malodorous riverbank that would become the world-famous Bund.

From Shanghai, Fortune plotted his expedition to the Hwuy-chow tea district 200 miles inland. It was a place forbidden to foreigners. His mission would have to be in secret and in disguise. If rumbled, he faced being torn apart by an angry mob still smarting from the humiliation of the Opium War, or of being arrested, imprisoned and possibly beheaded by the authorities. Despite the dangers, he ruled out simply hiring Chinese agents to collect plants for him, believing that they would palm him off with the very first tea plants they came across. 'No dependence can be placed upon the veracity of the Chinese,' he wrote. 'I may seem uncharitable, but such is really the case . . .'

His East India Company budget was modest, even stingy,[8] so Fortune's expeditions were small-scale. He hired two servants who agreed to travel with him. They were Hwuy-chow men, but the Scot 'had but little confidence in either'. Once again he dressed as a Chinese trader and the waist-long pigtail that he had kept from his previous adventure was braided into his own hair. Local boatmen had been severely punished for taking Europeans inland to the silk district, so a boat was hired in the name of his servant, Wang, who would also be his translator. The other servant, an older man referred to only as 'the coolie', was resentful of Wang's seniority and somewhat of a liability. Fortune found that the coolie had blabbed to the crew that an 'Englishman' was the passenger and more money had to change hands before they would sail. His cover blown, Robert boarded in Western clothes, only changing into his Chinese garb the following day. Wang was laid up with fever, so it was the coolie who shaved Robert's head. 'I suppose I must have been the first person upon whom he had over operated, and I am charitable enough to wish most sincerely that I may be the last.'

On 22 October Fortune's boat approached the suburbs of Hang-chow – the modern city of Hangzhou – where, he believed, the Chinese natural antipathy to 'barbarians' was intensified by the need to conceal a regime of 'squeezes' – tax extortion on foreign trade in breach of the Nanking treaty. Fortune thought that he made 'a pretty good Chinaman' as he walked through the streets, but as soon as his boatmen had been paid off they blabbed that their passenger was a foreigner. Luckily an old tea-seller who didn't despise a good customer procured a sedan chair to take him onwards. There he would travel, on an open seat in the middle of two long bamboo poles, with a small crossbar to rest his feet. To Fortune's dismay, the chair bearers didn't take him around Hang-chow but through the heavily guarded gates into the walled city. Once there, they set him down and told him they were going no further and that another chair would take him the rest of the way. Fortune's two chair-carriers had, however, already spent some of the money that was due to pay the second shift of bearers on tea and tobacco for themselves. A street brawl broke out between the two pairs. Wang and the coolie were nowhere to be seen.

> The situation in which I was now placed was rather critical, and far from an enviable one. Had it been known that a foreigner was in the very heart of the city . . . a mob would have soon collected, and the consequences might have been serious.

Robert Fortune revealed his mantra for such occasions: '"Take things coolly and never lose your temper" should be the motto of everyone who attempts to travel in China.' He sat tight in the sedan chair until the fight died down, then offered to make up the shortfall. Satisfied, the new bearers then shouldered their burden and jogged on. Stopping at an inn on the banks of the Green River, Fortune felt it safer to go hungry rather than eat, as, being out of China for three years, his awkward use of chopsticks might have given him away. His servants, who had mysteriously rematerialised as soon as the sedan chair fracas was over, secured him a place on a boat, where he slept after 'an exciting and adventurous day'.

Fortune was able to pass himself off as a Chinaman among the twenty passengers until his coolie, a 'silly, talkative fellow', found the weight of the secret intolerable. Wang informed his master: 'That coolie he too much a fool-o; he have talkie all that men you no belong this country; you more better sendie he go away, suppose you no wantye too much bobly.' Fortune translates the pigin word 'bobly' as 'disturbance'.

Much of the time the boat was being slowly pulled upstream by as many as fifteen men and Fortune had time to botanise along the way. The borders of China's provinces were guarded by soldiers from either side of them and these guards bore those on the other side 'little good will'. The mutually hostile guards reminded Fortune of 'our own border clans in feudal times'. When two attractive and well-dressed young women joined the boat, they sat at Robert's side chatting happily to each other. 'Had these pretty damsels known that a "barbarian" was seated at their side, how astonished and frightened they would have been!' At an inn an inquisitive traveller, whom Fortune thought had detected something unusual in his appearance, was told that the mysterious stranger only spoke the Court dialect and couldn't understand his inquisitor.

Fortune was now at an altitude where tropical shrubs and trees were unknown, and the flora was similar to that found in parts of northern India or England, although he dismissed the possibility of tea being grown in Britain. At the Hill of Sung-lo, which Fortune describes as where green tea was traditionally first discovered, he botanised every day that there wasn't torrential rain, collecting seeds, examining the vegetation and learning everything he could about the cultivation and manufacture of green tea. Much to their disgust, Wang and the coolie were dragged along as well to carry back the specimens. 'Chinamen generally have a great aversion to long walks,' wrote Fortune, 'and my men were no exception to the rule.' He had to be careful that they didn't lag behind, then claim that they'd lost him as an excuse to return to the inn.

Returning to Shanghai, Fortune carefully packed his precious specimens into Wardian cases to be shipped to Hong Kong and then on to Calcutta, where they arrived in excellent condition. He had long been perplexed as to why seeds sent to the West from China usually failed to germinate on arrival. Like others, he assumed that the Chinese boiled the seeds they sold 'in order that the floral beauties of China should not find their way into other countries, and that the trade in seeds be injured'. In Canton he asked a Chinese dealer he was on good terms with what the secret of successfully exporting seeds was. 'Burnt lice,' said the old man in what sounds like a racist Chinese-restaurant joke. Fortune explains the Chinese propensity for substituting the sound of 'L' for that of 'R', and that seeds mixed with burnt rice husks weren't eaten by maggots. As Mr Aching, the Chinese seed dealer, said: 'S'pose me no mixie this seed, worms makie chow-chow he.'

Fortune was obsessed with getting plants from the very best black tea districts of China to India, and to do this he needed to gather them himself. His destination was the Bohea Hills. In mid-May he left the treaty port of Ningpo in a boat he had hired and was quickly swept upriver by a favourable wind and tide. Despite the progress, Fortune was in low spirits. His guide was not dependable, and his journey would be long and take him through unknown and dangerous territory. On board his servant produced his Chinese clothes and told him it was time to change his 'outward man'. In a mirror he scarcely recognised himself.

When the river became un-navigable he travelled by sedan chair. Coming in the opposite direction were long trains of coolies loaded with tea bound for the Western market. Conditions were often harsh and Fortune admitted that under normal circumstances they might be 'discouraging'. 'I never expected to find my way strewed with luxuries,' he recorded. 'The only way was to make myself comfortable as the circumstances would admit of.' A renowned Victorian plant-hunter he might have been, but his Scottish Border peasant roots stood him in good stead.

At last, Fortune beheld one of the grandest sights he had ever seen – the Bohea Hills: 'Never in my life had I seen such a view as this, so grand, so sublime.' Known today as the Wuyi Mountains, the range is a beautiful UNESCO World Heritage site with winding valleys, subtropical forests and peaks rising to over 2,000 metres. The botany did not disappoint. The ravines were rich in bamboos, Chinese pine, a beautiful *Hydrangea*, a species of *Spiraea* with red flowers and a fine variety of *Abelia*. He dug up plants of all these species and – cajoling and sometimes threatening – got his servants to carry these 'weeds of no value' several hundred miles to Shanghai. Fortune notes with satisfaction that they were perhaps the first plants in Europe brought directly from the Bohea Hills.

On Fortune's arduous journey south he encountered beautiful scenery, a mountain storm and filthy inns, eventually reaching Tsong-gan-hien, a large town in the midst of the black tea area of Fokien, where the Canton Chinese who traded with the Europeans bought their tea. Arriving on a blistering hot day at a celebrated Buddhist temple among the Woo-e-shan Hills, Fortune was warmly received by the high priest who offered tobacco and tea as a sign of welcome. 'The tea soon quenched my thirst and revived my spirits.' With Fortune unwilling to enter a conversation that might reveal his origins, a new servant, Sing-Hoo, told their hosts that Fortune was from a far country 'beyond the great wall'. It was his usual way of explaining Fortune's silence and putting off the curious. Unfortunately, Sing-Hoo himself attracted the inquisitive, by boasting of his own importance and telling strangers that his master was a great mandarin from Tartary.

Sing-Hoo, who 'had been a great traveller in his time', had been to Peking. The temple's priests found his tales interesting and talked freely with him, referring to Westerners as *Kwei-tsz* – the devil's children – so it was well that none of the holy men saw through Fortune's deception. Leaving the temple, after three days of hospitality, to explore further, Fortune noted, 'As we threaded our way amongst the hills, I observed tea-gatherers busily employed on all the hill-sides where the plantations were. They seemed a happy and contented race; the joke and merry laugh were going round, and some of them were singing as gaily as the birds in the old trees about the temples.' At one tea garden he procured 400 more young plants, wrapped the roots in damp moss and then covered them with oil-paper to shade them from the sun 'and also the prying eyes of the Chinese, who, although they did not seem to show any great jealousy on the point, yet might have annoyed us with impertinent questions.'

Fortune's servant Sing-Hoo had a knack of attracting trouble. One night at an inn – 'not so respectable as I could have wished' – Fortune was woken by a ruckus in which the angry voices of his servant and chair-bearers could be heard. He threw on clothes, went to investigate and found Sing-Hoo being attacked by eight or ten men, including his chair-bearers. Sing-Hoo had his back to the wall and was keeping his attackers at bay with a large smouldering joss stick by poking it at their faces. 'The whole scene brought vividly to my mind Bailie Nicol Jarvie's fight with the red hot poker, so admirably described by Sir Walter Scott,' Fortune recalled.

The Scot ran to his room to fetch his small pocket pistol, but found it rusted and useless. Eventually he managed to break up the fight and learned that it was caused by Sing-Hoo trying to cheat the chair-bearers out of part of their fee – about a shilling. The following morning, Sing-Hoo's reputation had got around and no bearers or coolies would work for them; he himself had to shoulder Fortune's luggage on a bamboo pole and carry it through torrential rain. Around August, Robert reached Shanghai. 'Although I had been eating with chopsticks . . . I had not forgotten the use of knives and forks, and I need scarcely say I heartily enjoyed my first English dinner.'

Once, while in Darjeeling, my wife and I collected a pocketful of tea seeds, in the belief that a tea bush would be an interesting talking point in our Islay allotment. Not a single one germinated. Had I read Robert Fortune at that time, I wouldn't have bothered bending over to pick them up. Living tea seeds are difficult to transport. In August 1848 Fortune sent large quantities of tea seeds from China to India. He used all his expertise as a botanist and plant-collector – packing some in loose canvas bags, others in small packages, and still more mixed with dry soil in boxes. No doubt he tried packing some seeds in 'burnt lice' as he'd been advised. Mostly they died. Fortune reflected: 'Tea seeds retain their vitality for a very short period of time if they are out the ground ... hence the great difficulty of introducing these valuable trees into distant countries by seeds.'

The following year he solved the problem. He planted some fine mulberry plants from one of China's best silk regions in a Wardian case. Fortune then sprinkled freshly gathered tea seed over the earth around the plants, covered them with half an inch of soil, watered them, sealed the case and packed it off to India. What the Chinese port authorities saw was a case containing legally exported mulberry plants, not one with forbidden tea seeds. At the receiving end of this inventive scheme was Dr Hugh Falconer, the Forres-born superintendent of the Calcutta Botanical Garden. Falconer reported, 'The young tea-plants were sprouting around the mulberries as thick as they could come up.' Fortune sent more Wardian cases sown with tea seed and learned that not only had the seeds germinated by the time they got to Calcutta, but that the young seedlings had successfully been transported to the foothills of the Himalayas for planting. British India now had the finest tea plants that China had once exclusively possessed.

Fortune was now confronted with a task that he felt to be more difficult. He had learned during his travels in China that processing tea requires human skill, experience and great care. Somehow he had to lure expert Chinese tea manufacturers to

India. Fortune knew that a shipload of emigrants from Amoy and Canton had recently left for California and that it would have been easy to recruit men from the coastal region, but it was skilled workers from the inland, high-quality tea gardens that he required. Fortunately, a trader friend lent him his comprador, a highly respected Chinaman who agreed to find and hire men with the necessary skills. It was a tricky job. The punishment for illegal emigration was torture and flogging, not only of the emigrants themselves but of their families as well.[9] Fortune took off on another tea-hunting expedition and returned to Shanghai in late December to find that the recruitment of men and the purchase of equipment – ovens, pans and rolling tables – had been achieved 'far beyond my most sanguine expectations.'

Eight Chinese had been hired on three-year contracts with good pay.[10] On the day of their departure a large boat ferried them from the Shanghai quayside to the mouth of the river, where the ship *Island Queen* was at anchor. The emigrants and their friends on shore, hands clasped, bowed to each other many, many times as the vessel pushed out into the stream. The following morning, 16 February 1851, Captain MacFarlane of the *Island Queen* set course for Hong Kong. From there, the P&O steamship *Lady Mary Wood* took them on to Calcutta, the capital of British India, where they arrived after a month of travel. Despite the journey, the young plants and the Chinese tea workers were flourishing. The Chinese tea monopoly was irrevocably broken.

The ending of the East India Company's monopoly over the China tea trade in 1834 ushered in a new era on the high seas. The Company's large, lumbering vessels had never had to compete with other shipping lines to get tea to market, but the new free market changed that. There was now a scramble to get the new season's tea home from China ahead of rival merchants, so as to sell it at the best price. This race brought the design and construction of sailing ships to a peak of efficiency and beauty. Tea clippers, small, sleek ships that could 'clip' along at fifteen knots or more, lopped weeks off the time that the tubby, heavily laden Indiamen took. The first clippers built for the China trade were American, but in 1850, when the US clipper *Oriental* docked in London after sailing from Canton in just ninety-seven days, British shipbuilders – or more precisely those on the Clyde and in Aberdeen – took notice.

In fairness, shipbuilder William Hall of Aberdeen had been ahead of the game, scandalising his rivals by experimenting with model ships in a glass tank to produce a new shape of bow that would cut through the water. The acute 'Aberdeen bow', or 'clipper bow', first sliced through the sea in 1839 when the Hall Brothers, William and James, launched the *Scottish Maid*, a two-masted wooden schooner with a raked stem and a carved female figurehead. The *Scottish Maid* was the prototype for clippers to come. Hall Brothers went on to build many such ships for the opium, spice and tea trades, including the *Torrington* and *Stornoway* for Jardine Matheson. The *Stornoway* was named after the main town on the Hebridean island of Lewis, as James Matheson had bought the island a few years earlier.

Shipwrights on the River Clyde, where most of Britain's clippers were launched, innovated too – building frameworks of iron ribs which were then clad with timber planks, making the vessels robust but light. Most were three-masted, carried vast amounts of sail and were beautiful. Perhaps the most handsome of all was the *Ariel*, one of about twenty built by Robert Steele & Company at Greenock. She was nearly 200 feet long from her knife-like stem to her yacht-like counter stern. Her deck was completely flush and, as a sacrifice to speed, her crew lived in cramped forward quarters. Low in the water and with her bulwarks only rising to three feet above her deck, she was a greyhound of a ship, although vulnerable to being swamped by a following sea.

In 1861 an annual £500 bonus was offered to the ship that first made it from China to London with late April's new tea crop. By 1866 the Great Tea Race from China to London had become a national fixture in which the finest ships, skippered by the most skilful captains, competed. In May that year sixteen tea clippers were loaded at Foochow's Pagoda Anchorage on the Min River, about twelve miles from the open sea. Lighters brought about 12,000 chests of tea to each vessel in a four-day loading marathon. The chests were stowed carefully to give each ship what its captain thought would be its best trim. The Glasgow-owned, Liverpool-built *Fiery Cross* had won the previous year, but a new vessel, *Ariel*, was that year's favourite. Captains scrabbled for every advantage of wind, tide and influence with the Customs officials and tug skippers as the clippers hauled anchors.

To the delight of the press, it was a classic race with a nail-biting finish. The leading ships had left Pagoda Anchorage on the same tide and once out to sea their skippers had driven them hard, setting up to 30,000 square feet of canvas to take advantage of every wisp of wind. High up among the spars, each ship's crewmen spent days and nights adjusting, trimming, setting and resetting about forty sails. What a sight that must have been. I have seen many illustrations of clippers, but the nearest I've got to feeling the thrill of the race was when making a documentary series on a trawler for BBC Alba. One afternoon, aboard the *Audacious* north of Shetland, we sailed through the Tall Ships' Race on its way to Scandinavia. I'd seen many tall ships before, but only close to shore and carrying very little canvas. That day more than a dozen vessels were scudding along under full sail. With a stiff breeze on my face and a North Atlantic swell churning my stomach, it was easy to imagine that I'd entered a time warp and had been transported to the mid-nineteenth century.

After 14,000 miles and ninety-nine days at sea, three of the Great Tea Race ships of 1866 arrived at London on the very same tide, the winning *Taeping* docking just twenty-eight minutes before *Ariel*. For *Ariel*'s captain, John Keay of Anstruther, it must have been a bitter blow because *Ariel* had been ahead when the two ships were taken in tow by stream tugs, but because of the height of the tide *Taeping* had made it into her dock first. It could have been a contentious result but the *Taeping*'s owners agreed to share the prize with the *Ariel*. The James Finlay-owned *Serica* had arrived just an hour and fifteen minutes after the *Ariel* – to the vexation of its fiery Scottish skipper, Captain George Innes.[11]

The real winner of the race was Greenock's Robert Steele & Company, which had built all three of the leading vessels. The victorious *Taeping* was owned by Fife man Alexander Rodger of Cellardyke (where a street is named after him) and skippered by Donald MacKinnon of Tiree in the Inner Hebrides. MacKinnon is commemorated to this day at An Iodhlann, Tiree's cultural centre, as much for his role in saving the steam ferry *Chieftain's Bride* from sinking between Tiree and Mull as for winning the Great Tea Race the previous year. Benefiting from the close finish of the three clippers – and the sudden arrival of 45,000,000 pounds of fresh tea – was the tea-drinking public. The glut dropped the price by fourpence a pound, bringing the highest grade down from four shillings to three and eightpence.

In 1869 *Cutty Sark*, the most famous tea clipper of all time, was launched from Scott & Linton's shipyard, where the River Leven meets the Clyde. The fact that she is still available to explore as part of the Royal Museums, Greenwich, is a tribute to the skill of her builders. But the year of her launch was a fateful one for tea clippers. It was the year the Suez Canal opened – slashing the length of the journey from China to London. The canal was much more suitable for steamships that year on year were replacing sail. *Cutty Sark* spent little time in the tea trade; she made her reputation on the Australia wool run, on which, in 1884, she completed the New South Wales to London run in just 83 days, lopping twenty-five days off the previous record.

The clippers of Aberdeen and the Clyde enjoyed just two decades of exhilarating history before the final triumph of steam, but the communities that built them got a whiff of the profits of the opium/tea trade-off and created the most beautiful sailing ships ever launched.

When Robert Fortune had entered Hong Kong harbour on the Peninsula and Oriental Steam Navigation Company vessel *Braganza* in August 1848, an affable but serious-minded young fellow Scot was also aboard. William Melrose was the thirty-one-year-old son of an entrepreneurial Edinburgh merchant – one of several Scottish businessmen who had speculated on cashing-in on the end of the East India Company's China monopoly.

Melrose described his fellow passengers as 'all nice quiet people', but despite this collective reticence it is almost certain that the two men met on the journey. They had both left Southampton on board the P&O steamer *Ripon* for Alexandria, Egypt, on 20 June, on the first leg of a highly efficient mail route between Britain and China. They made the same ninety-mile, twenty-two-hour desert crossing from Cairo to Port Suez, and then took the wooden-hulled paddle steamer *Bentinck* to Ceylon before boarding the *Braganza* for Hong Kong. Both men were Scots, both had been in China before, and both their lives were inextricably bound up in tea. Given that ships like *Bentinck*, on which they were for twelve days, only took 102 passengers, the two were in constant close contact. But Robert Fortune and William Melrose were cut from very different cloth. The self-made and adventurous botanist and plant-hunter may well have found the scrupulous and well-brought-up young trader rather dull company. But while William's writings about China were mainly business letters to his father, and not to be compared to Fortune's best-selling page-turners, William's correspondence gives us fascinating insights into the tea trade with China and the role of Scots in it. The editors of Melrose's letters[12] describe his account of the China tea trade following the 1839–42 Opium War as 'unparalleled'. William's letters, written without thought of publication, not only reveal trials and tribulations of working in this volatile industry, conducted in an unfriendly political environment, but also the thoughts, hopes and fears of a young mid-Victorian Scot seeking to make his way, please his father and enrich the family firm.

The founder of that family firm was Andrew Melrose, the son of a Penicuik tenant-farmer-turned-vintner. Andrew first sold tea behind the counter as an apprentice to leading Edinburgh grocer Robert Sheppard. After eight years, the enterprising twenty-three year old opened his own shop in the city's Canongate. Today Melrose Tea – owned by Typhoo, which is a subsidiary of Indian conglomerate the Apeejay Surrendra Group – cites the 1812 opening of that shop as its foundation date. Andrew married Margaret Dickson in 1814 and over two decades fathered six sons and five daughters. His business was also fruitful and in 1823 he bought a country home in Lasswade, now Pittendreich estate. Andrew's second son William, born in 1817, was apprenticed to his father when he was fifteen. It was an exciting time for Scotland's tea men, with the end of the East India Company's monopoly of trade in sight.

Andrew secured a position for William with Ewart, Maccaughey & Company, his London tea broker. William learned the secrets of the tasting cup – daily slurping, judging and pricing countless 'chops' (or parcels of tea of the same quality). In 1842 William had the opportunity to travel to the heart of the tea industry, as taster and buyer for Jamieson How and Company, a Glasgow firm that traded British cotton and Indian opium for China tea.

When twenty-five-year-old William first arrived in Canton, the First Opium War had only just ended. The atmosphere was tense as well as hot and for the foreign 'barbarians' life was confined, claustrophobic and, for the large part, men only. Foreigner traders were restricted to the tiny footprint of the Thirteen Factories on the banks of the Pearl River. Straying out of the enclave was illegal and dangerous. Chinese were forbidden to teach foreigners their language under pain of death. An American missionary's Chinese language teacher always brought a shoe with him so that he could pretend to be a cobbler if they were discovered together, while the teacher of Scottish missionary Robert Morrison always carried poison with which he could end his own life and avoid torture if discovered.[13]

William lived and worked in House Number 3 of the Old English Factory, where he spent his days tasting and buying a range of teas at a price that he hoped would turn a profit in Glasgow, Leith and Liverpool. Speaking no Chinese, he had to haggle with a handful of Chinese merchants, known as the co-hong, through local interpreters who were not necessarily on his side. William was one of about 200 red-faced 'white devils' of the Thirteen Factories. Most were British, many of them Scots, and Americans, Arabs and Parsees made up the rest. The 'factories' lay on a narrow strip along the Pearl River, but they were not places where things were manufactured. Rather they were *hongs*, or warehouses with offices and accommodation, where the *fanquis* worked, ate, slept and socialised. The term 'factory' came from *feitoria*, the Portuguese word for trading post.

The foreigners' comfort, health and friendships were under constant strain in the hot and overcrowded quarters. Relations with the Chinese were tense and, only weeks after William arrived in Canton, rioters burned three of the factories. It took hundreds of Chinese soldiers to save the other buildings and restore order. When riots broke out again in July 1846, hundreds of Chinese chanting 'Kill the foreign devils!' attempted to set fire to the factory William worked at. His father warned him that the Celestial Empire 'may be the residence of the Son of Heaven: it is a very far cry from being heaven, although it may be perhaps a short cut to it'.

The ban on white women in the treaty ports condemned young men to enforced celibacy. Or did it? While the foreigners were walled off from the city, the boats on the river offered a variety of services, other than dining and laundry. The diaries of Irish-born diplomat Robert Hart are remarkably raunchy for their time. In October 1854 he noted 'some of the china women are very good looking: You can make one your absolute possession for 50 to 100 dollars and support her at a cost of 2 or 3 dollars a month.' The same month he wrote 'a couple of China Women have been peeping in through my windows. I hope I may be able to control myself properly here. Many temptations surround me; let me be a man "tenac proposit" [presumably *tenax propositi*, firm of purpose].'[14]

Hart, who went to China at the age of nineteen and rose to become inspector general of the Chinese Maritime Customs Service and the most influential Westerner in Quing dynasty China, was long tortured by lust and loneliness.[15] In 1857 he took a Chinese woman, Ayaou, as a mistress and had three children by her, Anna, Herbert and Arthur, all of whom he loved and cared for. But in August 1864 he recorded in his diary, 'Temptation to get a concubine is very strong, I must confess: Nothing bothers me so much as my liking for women.' The randy Irishman can't have been the only Celt, or Saxon, to succumb to the lure of Chinese women, but there is no hint of such distractions in William Melrose's letters to his Presbyterian father.

In the spring of 1846 William fell dangerously ill, but it wasn't until early the following year that he was fit enough to travel home. 'I left China as thin as anyone could be reduced to, almost ... desperately thin and yellow and weak, as you may guess I was lying in bed a whole summer and one of the hottest I can remember.' After eighteen months at home, Melrose completely recovered and in 1848 was drawn back to China by the lure of profitable trade. On his voyage to Canton he sailed with the same captain and purser he had met when he was invalided home, but who 'would hardly believe I was the same person'. With his health restored, William was confident. 'I feel like an old campaigner now,' he told his father. 'This time I will have much more chance of keeping my health excepting accidents or casualties occur, which God forbid.'

On the desert crossing from Cairo to the Port of Suez he had met two old Canton colleagues coming in the opposite direction while travelling home. They only spoke for a few minutes, but the pair gave William a copy of the *China Mail* and passed on the trading news. William wrote to his father from Aden: 'Low price in China and stocks getting low at home. I think some good may be done in them.'

Arriving back in Hong Kong, he wrote, 'It is astonishing the quickness with which one can travel now, 54 days and you make what used to be one of the most tedious and longest voyages.' William was benefiting from the steam-driven revolution in which a fast and efficient mail system was drawing Britain's expanding trade and empire together. The Peninsular Steam Navigation Company had been founded, by a Shetland sailor and a London ship broker, to provide fast and efficient communications between Britain and Spain and Portugal. But in 1840 the company was incorporated by Royal Charter as the Peninsular and Oriental Steam Navigation Company and given the government contract to provide the mail service to Egypt. With the short desert crossing and coaling stations in Aden on the Red Sea, P&0 was, within two years, able to serve India and then further extend its routes to Ceylon, Penang, Singapore and, by 1845, Hong Kong.

Robert Fortune recalled the 'busy and exciting scene' that awaited the arrival of the *Braganza*, as a flotilla of boats pulled alongside to take off passengers, goods and mail. 'There were two which presented a most striking appearance. They were very long and narrow, and were each propelled by fifty oars. They had been built by the English and American merchants to convey news to Canton on the arrival of the mail.' Being first with the news about the state of the markets at home gave dealers in Canton a distinct advantage, so large sums of money were given to the crew who reached Canton first. 'They ploughed the water like two enormous centipedes,' said Fortune, who later wrote that within a few years steam had invaded the quiet waters of the Pearl River and replaced the sweating crews of the 'centipedes'.

Arriving at Canton in August to resume his trading career, William Melrose was immediately frustrated that he had not arrived a month earlier when, he told his father, 'I feel sure I could have made a good deal of money both for you and myself.' A cautious dealer, he was relieved to see that the 'restless speculation' he had witnessed on his previous trip, had subsided. 'People have been so severely bit lately that I do not think that they will ship unless they can lay them down a good margin. The trade altogether here seems much more healthy and legitimate.' He had also arrived at a time when the market was highly competitive.

William was quick to let his father know that he'd wasted no time getting to work. 'I assure you I have had a busy time of it since I arrived, I have been tasting and comparing until I was almost sick and my mouth sore. I was so much behind the other tasters here that I found I had to work pretty hard to make up to them, as they had tasted and knew all the chops in the market intimately.' Developing a discerning palate was vital to a trader, as the 'chop' system was abused by the unscrupulous. While on his explorations, Robert Fortune had learned that boxes of tea often left the interior without chop names on them – leaving the salesman at the port of export to add a chop name of good repute before passing it on to European dealers.[16] William was also haggling, organising shipments, selling bills of credit, gathering intelligence, keeping meticulous records and corresponding with his father and John Simpson, his father's junior partner. It has been calculated that in just two and a half months William sent £24,000-worth of tea from Canton on seven separate ships. The tea was packed in chests each containing about 170 pounds.

Although constantly busy, William looked after his health. When business was quiet, he would take ship to Macao, the Portuguese colony ninety miles to the south. 'I hate to stay in Canton when there is no business to occupy one's time . . .' he wrote.

> I am going to take a trip down to Macao and get some shooting. I would like a change. At any rate, two months I think now quite long enough in this hole, although before I did not use to think eighteen months too long – experience teaches fools . . . Macao is greatly improved. They have a new governor there

who knows well how to treat with the Chinese, and instead of being liable to insults and being plundered when a mile away from the town, you are now able to walk four or five miles with perfect safety.

The potential for conflict with the Chinese was ever-present, even in Macao. On Christmas Day 1848 he wrote to his father telling him that the Portuguese governor had 'lately made it now quite safe to walk or ride out for miles in the country'. Only eight months later he reported, 'The poor governor of Macao was murdered the night before last and his head cut off by some Chinamen.' The assassination was a result of mounting tension over the status of Macao between the Chinese and Portuguese governments, and William clearly believed that the killers had some official backing. 'It is thought that the Chinese authorities had offered a reward for his head, so they [the assassins] carried away his head with them. He was a very clever man but very hot tempered and obstinate; and the Chinese being very obstinate, they have kept Macao in hot water nearly since he first became governor.'

The Chinese and the Europeans were mutually suspicious of each other. Robert Fortune thought that the Chinese 'have no idea of telling the truth unless it suits their interests to do so; in fact I often used to think that they rather preferred lying unless it was against their interests'. And although missionaries had converted some Chinese to Christianity, William Melrose doubted their faith.

I may be speaking rashly but I would not trust much to their belief in it. I don't think they understand it. The basis of the Christian religion is affection and love, and I think the Chinamen have so little of these feelings and put so little value on them that it must take a long time to make them understand the

principal feature in our religion: Our Saviour making a voluntary sacrifice of himself for love. I think a
'nigger'; a much more hopeful subject for conversion
than a 'Celestial'. The nigger has some heart and
feeling about him, though not very strong; but the
Chinaman is very apathetic to anything like fine feeling, and you must give him a new heart before you can
make much of him, I think.

Although William could relax in Macao with his closest
friends in China, the Scottish Doctor Wilson and his wife,
political volatility was not the only danger to Westerners.
William reported:

You may remember about seventeen months ago the
Governor who was here then was murdered by the
Chinese. A new one was sent out and some vessels of
war. The new one had hardly been here a month until
he died of cholera, and only some days ago one of
their frigates blew up, the magazine having exploded,
and about 200 (!) people killed.

William was always alert to the market and January 1849
found him requesting more funds from his father in order
to get a head start over their rivals in the new season. 'If new
Congous open low next year, I could have a cargo off to Leith
in a small vessel before Jardine's knew anything about it. I think
from some hints I have got that Bristol is a good port, it might
be worthwhile inquiring about it.'
     Jardine Matheson dominated the China trade. The scale
of their operation, and the speed and regularity of their ships,
gave them a fine-honed understanding of the market. William
paid close attention to their dealings. 'There may be some
truth in the report of a short crop. I know that Jardines firmly

believe in it. Mr Edger told me so the other day and it was Jardine himself who told him so confidentially.'

Dirty tricks were often used to put other traders off the scent of a good deal. When tea quality and price were favourable, the race was on to get the first cargo unloaded in Scotland. 'Getting into the Clyde before any other vessel is very much in its favour, and if you can hoist them up a bit, may do pretty well,' he advised his father. William thought it 'only a ruse' when a ship's captain assured him that the sailing ship *Queen* was not bound for the Clyde. 'That I very much doubt as I know their tea taster intimately and he told me she was going to the Clyde,' he reported. Where traders from the 'out-ports' (i.e. not London) may have had an advantage was in the detailed knowledge of what their local customers liked. William was quick to catch on to the opportunities:

> Now that I see there is such a difference of taste betwixt them . . . I think something might be made of it, and I am now in favour of a cargo either to Leith or Glasgow or both. When I say favour, I mean I think it likely teas might be bought in China, sent to these ports and leave a better profit than any that could be bought and sent to London, because the kinds that please the Leith people may be had much cheaper here in proportion than these that please the London people, and most likely if they please would fetch a good price.

Buying for specific markets gave Melrose a competitive edge. Telling of one chop that had not found favour in London, Melrose wrote: 'One or two people here laughed at me when I bought it and have ever since asked me with a sneer what the "malty burnt one", as they call it, had sold for. Of course, I keep them in the same opinion still; the worse they think of it the better, as we may get something of the same kind all the cheaper next time.' Tastes in tea, like those in clothes, went in and out of fashion, and William was often left to second-guess the market. He thought that a shipment of bright, lightly flavoured teas leaving Canton for the Clyde 'don't appear to me the tea for Scotland unless the taste has changed greatly, which may be the case'. Green tea was also out of favour in Glasgow.

The end of the East India Company monopoly and the rise of the free traders, anxious to get their tea to market, sometimes produced gluts that brought prices down. The spring of 1849 was, William thought, 'one of the most difficult seasons to invest to any advantage that I have ever known. The prejudice against the tarry flavour has made everyone run on the kinds free of it and raised their price above their value ...' A year on, William was still struggling with the question, 'What is tarry?':

> ... it is difficult to tell what may be called tarry at home. I don't think No 3 is in the least tarry. It has a little burnt Pekoe flavour, perhaps a little smoky ... and this year, being warned so strongly against tar and there being so few real Pekoe Souchong flavour, I find it rather difficult navigating and am very timorous in buying anything not of Souchong kind.

Not all William's decisions turned out to be wise or profitable. In May 1850 he wrote:

> Since my sojourn in China this last time I cannot recollect of a month that I have written in such low spirits as I fear as I must write this month. Your business letters bring me intelligence that all the Canton Gunpowders I have bought may turn out unsaleable. I hope not, but still it would be a terrible thing. I have

been counting up all the profits we have made, commissions and everything, and should they turn out unsaleable, we would be worse than when we began.

The Gunpowder – tea twisted into shot-like pellets to keep the leaf from light, air and moisture – had not yet been shipped from Canton. In late September William could report that 'by hook and by crook and hard work' he had sold most of it on.

William believed that the dealers belonging to the greater and longer-established firms had sneered at him when he first arrived in Canton, dismissing him as a mere dabbler. Two years into his second venture into the business, he was confident enough of his abilities and achievements to write to his father, 'Within the last two years the sneer has amazingly softened down; and I might, I think, if I like, now indulge in a sneer at some of them, of course this is betwixt ourselves.' Enterprising, but canny, opportunistic but cautious, the young Scot had learned to read the China tea leaves. In a letter to his father he may have misattributed Shakespeare's line from *Julius Caesar*, 'There is a tide in the affairs of men . . .' to Byron, but he understood the simile as applied to the tea trade. 'We must try to leave off just at the beginning of the "ebb" if possible, for an ebb is sure to come some time after a flood tide. As soon as I see any symptoms of it taking place, I am going to break all my tasting cups and go home.'

Six months later, in May 1851, William was still fretting about the state of the China trade, claiming that there was 'no trade so dangerous' and recalling that several trading houses that had started up in the past few years 'with mighty great ideas' had folded. 'I don't think I will stay much longer,' he wrote. Three months later he was still complaining. 'I don't know what to make of this season's operations at all; I feel at my wits' end about it.' The unpredictability of the supply, cost and quality of tea, and the fluctuating exchange rate and consumer demand, were exacerbated by the length of time it took to correspond with Edinburgh – two months for a letter to get there and another two for the reply to arrive. The delay caused occasional 'flyting' with John Simpson in Edinburgh. On one occasion, Simpson criticised him for not having gone to Shanghai to buy a tea that wasn't available in Canton; he said that he himself would have been remiss if he had failed to take the train to London in order to fulfil an order of beer not available in Edinburgh. William replied:

> So you compare a voyage to Shanghai to a ride in a railway coach to London – a voyage of 800 miles along the most dangerous coast in the world where, if you do happen to be wrecked and escape drowning, you are sure at least of being killed. Read about the crews of the *Nerbudda* and the *Ann* and others. Read the *China Mail* about six weeks back only, about the crew of the *Larpent* on her way to Shanghai – only two men were saved of the whole crew, although all escaped shipwreck to be shot in the water, or beheaded on shore. And this you compare to starting after comfortable supper and a bottle of ale with your head wrapped up, all ready for a nap in a railway carriage with seats as soft as a feather bed. I am afraid you will find a trip to the north an *autre chose* or in English 'another pair of shoes', against the monsoons especially.

William was able to rent an old Hong merchant's house on the river and delighted in its cool breeze. 'I think it will be one of the coolest houses in Canton,' he told his father. His life in Canton was certainly not riotous, although he did ask his father if he thought an Edinburgh Princes Street wine merchant might send him seventy dozen bottles of beer and twenty of porter. 'It is almost my only beverage here ... That quantity would last me a year at least ... at the rate say of three bottles a day for self and friends.' He was horrified when some Americans attempted to rent the premises next door to use as a billiard room. 'They would be there at all hours half seas over and making a terrible noise.' William eventually did a deal with the Chinese owner to rent the place himself rather than 'be bothered with them'.

During much of William's time in China, the Celestial Empire was being shaken to its foundations by the Taiping Rebellion, a mystically minded peasants' revolt. Three years into the rebellion William wrote to his father:

> There seems little doubt now that the rebels or patriots are a formidable body, and Chinamen who laughed at them as fools before now appear to think they are very dangerous ... from all accounts the rebels are making great progress and many [I] think will interfere with the tea crop for next year.

William was more explicate in a letter written the same day to Mr Simpson.

> Scu, the governor of Canton, has been taken by the rebels and put to a lingering death. The city of the district of Woolpack where the fine Congous came from has been taken, and the Chinamen say the place is in such a commotion that no teas will be had from there this next season.

On top of the rising political situation, there was the ever present problem of violent crime and piracy. The East India Company's ships usually travelled in convoy, carried cannon and armed their crews, but lone ships were vulnerable. In 1847

Walter Lowrie, a respected American missionary, had been thrown overboard and drowned when pirates attacked the boat he was travelling on in the Bay of Chapoo.[17] In February 1852 the captain and officers of the *Herald* were murdered by their Manila-recruited crew while taking tea to Leith for one of the Melrose family's rivals. William wrote from Macao:

> Were it not for the loss of life, we might be glad of it rather than otherwise and, I suppose, so might the shippers as, if they are well insured, they have gone to a good market. I did not know the captain; his poor wife must have suffered dreadfully. I hope they will hang all these Manila men, cold-blooded rascals they must be.

The case was appalling. One night, in the Sunda Strait between Java and Sumatra, the mutineers murdered the *Herald's* officer on watch and threw him overboard. They then burst into Captain Lawson's cabin, killed him with an axe and raped his wife. The other mate and ship's carpenter were killed, and the steward and Bengali servants were butchered over the following few days. The mutineers then stripped the *Herald* of all small valuables, took to the lifeboats and scuttled her. Mrs Lawson begged to be taken with them but was locked in a cabin and went down with the ship. The mutineers landed on the Java coast, where their possessions aroused suspicion and they were interrogated by the Dutch authorities. Three men – claiming they had been compelled to join the mutiny – confessed. Ten of the crew were executed.[18]

A year later William wrote to his father from Hong Kong about the routing of pirates by the Royal Navy paddle-steamer *Hermes*.

> She captured five junks and brought home about

seventy people. I went off to see the junks yesterday … I saw lots of shot holes in them; they appear to have been well peppered. They made an attempt some days ago to attack the *Nymph* coming from Shanghai with $200,000 but she sailed too quickly for them; as soon as she came to Hong Kong, she reported what she had seen of the pirates and immediately a steamer was sent out after them. One of the officers of the steamer dined at Murrow's yesterday and he said the pirates fought well; and although not a life was lost amongst the steamer's men, that it was owing to good luck as a good many of the pirates' shots came near them and struck them in the bow and in the paddle box. One junk would not give up but fought it out to the last although asked to give up the fight, so they had to sink her.

In May 1853 William wrote from Penang that he was on his way home; he predicted that the next season 'will be a speculative and dangerous one'. He was right. Within a few years, major China trading houses were collapsing. William never returned to China. In 1856 he married 'ravishing beauty' Eliza Laura Bella Stedding and settled down to live comfortably on his small fortune. The couple's happiness was short-lived. After a lengthy illness William died in 1863 at forty-six years of age. In China he had twice been laid low by serious illness and it may be that his quest to bring tea home to Scotland shortened his life. The tea that bore the name of his father's shop in Edinburgh's Canongate can still be drunk.

When William was in China, the Celestial Empire supplied nearly all the world's tea. Today, the tea that William so assiduously dealt in has largely given way in Scotland, and much of the rest of the world, to the black teas of India, Ceylon and Africa. But something of China remains in every cup we drink – the very name 'tea'. While India and the Middle East drink *cha* or *chai*, we use an anglicisation of the Amoy dialect word for the drink, *te*, because that's where it was first shipped to us from. Hilaire Belloc wittily professed to be appalled by this Oriental intrusion into the English language. 'What is the Latin for tea? Is there no Latin word for tea? Upon my soul, if I had known that I would have let the vulgar stuff alone.' Of course, there is a Latin name for tea that recognises the drink's origins – *Camellia sinensis*, the camellia of China.

CHAPTER 4

The Days for Gathering Rupees

When we last saw Robert Fortune, he was steaming towards India on the P&O ship *Lady Mary Wood*, accompanied by eight hand-picked Chinese tea workers and sixteen Wardian cases sown with tea seeds. In March 1851 he reached Calcutta, where he and his more than 12,000 healthy seedlings lodged with Dr Hugh Falconer at the city's botanical garden. Falconer and some of his friends were curious to see how tea was manufactured, so Fortune ordered his workers to unpack their implements and set up a little oven. The Chinese were astonished. 'How can we make tea without tea leaves?' they asked Fortune. He explained that the gentlemen wanted to see 'the mode of manipulation only' and that the resulting brew 'was to look at, not to drink'.

And so the surreal charade of making undrinkable tea began. The Chinese fanned out to collect leaves that looked like tea – Fortune notes that they chose *Pongamia glabra*, a member of the pea family – and proceeded to roast them in pans, roll them on bamboo mats and roast them again while tossing them with their hands until they were perfectly twisted and dry. 'The samples were so like the teas of commerce, that nineteen person out of twenty would never have suspected them to be anything else,' boasted Fortune.

Fortune and his Chinese were ordered by the Indian government to take a steamer through the remote Sunderbans – where he heard blood-curdling tales of woodcutters being consumed by Bengal tigers – up the Ganges to Allahabad, then to travel by bullock cart to Saharanpur, thirty miles from where the land rises steeply to become the Himalayas. The town boasted an impressive and unique botanical garden. India's other scientific gardens, at Calcutta and Bangalore, were tropical and unsuitable for temperate plants like tea.

In 1817 the East India Company had engaged yet another botanically minded Scot to found the garden at Saharanpur to cultivate plants suited to this northern, cooler outpost. The site chosen was the pleasure garden of a local nobleman and the task of turning it into a place of scientific enquiry was given to Dr George Govan, a son of Cupar in Fife, who was the town of Saharanpur's thirty-year-old civil surgeon. George Govan is a sadly neglected figure in Scots–Indian history, being eclipsed as a botanist by the dynasty of Scots who followed him as the superintendents of the garden he founded: John Forbes Royle, Hugh Falconer and William Jameson.[1] Today, Saharanpur in Uttar Pradesh is second only to Calcutta among India's botanical gardens.

When Robert Fortune pitched up at Saharanpur with 12,838 tea plants it was on Leith-born William Jameson's watch. Jameson had been a twenty-seven-year-old graduate of Edinburgh University's medical school when he took over Saharanpur and had also been put in charge of the government tea plantations in the area. Fortune thought Saharanpur 'a valuable establishment, and exceedingly well managed by Dr. Jameson and the excellent head gardener, Mr Milner'. But even remote and northern Saharanpur, at under 900-feet elevation, was too hot for China tea plants to thrive, so from there they were transported to a nursery which had been set up near Mussoorie and Landour, British-founded hill stations that lay at about 6,000 or 7,000 feet. Fortune tells that he and Jameson visited the nurseries – not a job for the faint-hearted:

> The country was very mountainous, and there were no traces of cultivation for many miles on this part of the journey. A long train of Paharies or hill-men carried our tents, luggage, and provisions. Dr. Jameson and myself rode on ponies, while Mrs. Jameson, who accompanied us, was carried in a jaun-pan, or kind of light sedan chair. In many places our road led along the sides of precipices which it made one giddy to look down, and had we made a single false step we should have fallen far beyond the reach of earthly aid.

On that expedition Fortune noted with doubtless satisfaction that many of the plants he encountered were identical to those he saw in the Bohea Hills. Tea country was tea country, whether in China or India. In his book *A Journey to the Tea Countries*, Fortune apologises for devoting a chapter aimed at 'the man of science and the merchant' and warns that 'it may not contain much of interest to the general reader'. But from the chapter's observations on the soil, temperature and drainage in the great tea regions of China we can see that Fortune recognised the potential for growing the precious plant in British India. Tea, he observed, thrived on the sloping sides of hills, or on well-drained flat ground at high altitude, with plenty of summer rain. This could have been a description of India's tea-growing regions of the future.

To Fortune's delight he found thriving plantations based on seedlings he had previously sent to India. Also acclimatising well were his Chinese manufacturers, who quickly settled into farm cottages where 'everything was done to add to their comfort in a strange land'. The Chinese gathered to see him off, handing him packets of letters to post home for them. 'I confess I was sorry to leave them,' he wrote. 'We had travelled together for a long time, and they had always looked up to me with the most perfect confidence their director and friend.'

By the time Fortune arrived in India with his seeds and his Chinamen, the Scottish invasion of the subcontinent was well underway. George Bogle, the well-connected son of a Glasgow tobacco lord and an aristocratic lady who was descended from the early Stewart kings, was the diplomat whose expedition opened up British relations with Tibet. Writing home in 1771, he observed, 'There are now so many of my countrymen here that I am, every now and then, meeting with an old acquaintance.'*

The rising tide of Scottish influence did not recede. Nearly a century later, the Radical English politician Sir Charles Dilke wrote:

> ... the Bombay merchants are all Scotch. In British settlements, from Canada to Ceylon, from Dunedin to Bombay, for every Englishman that you meet who has worked himself to wealth from small beginnings without external aid, you find ten Scotchmen. It is strange, indeed, that Scotland has not become the popular name for the United Kingdom.[2]

The 'Scotification' of India would have a profound influence on the history of tea.

---

* Coming from a long line of Ayrshire quarrymen and peasants, I was surprised and tickled to discover that George Bogle's uncle on his father's side was my times-six great-grandfather.

The botanical garden in Calcutta, now the Acharya Jagadish Chandra Bose Indian Botanic Garden, and previously the Royal Botanic Garden, is one of the largest and best-stocked in the world. It was a cradle of the tea industry and a hotbed of Scottish scientific enterprise. The great Joseph Dalton Hooker, who followed his father as director of Kew Gardens – and who knew a thing or two about botany – declared, 'Amongst its greatest triumphs may be considered the introduction of the tea-plant from China . . . the establishment of the tea trade in the Himalaya and Assam is almost entirely the work of the superintendents of the gardens of Calcutta and Saharunpore [sic].'[3]

Although born in Suffolk, Joseph Hooker was raised a Scot in Glasgow and Helensburgh. His father, Sir William Jackson Hooker, became Regius Professor of Botany at Glasgow University when Joseph was just three and remained in post for twenty-one years. Precocious Joseph started attending his father's lectures at the age of seven and attended Glasgow High School before studying medicine at the city's university. The family spent a lot of time in Helensburgh 'so that the children may have country air and liberty', wrote Sir William. The young Joseph spent a lot of time rambling and botanising in the nearby Highlands and on Arran. He was a hardy soul and on one occasion walked twenty-four miles from Helensburgh to Glasgow rather than wait for the morning steamer up the River Clyde and miss his first lecture. It was an ideal upbringing for a man who would undergo rigorous travels in Antarctica, India and the Himalayas, North Africa, the Middle East and the American West.

Joseph Hooker was not the only man with a Scottish medical degree to make his mark on India. Time and time again while researching this book I encountered references to Scottish doctors in India who mixed their 'day jobs' with botanical and scientific research. They were true grandchildren of the Scottish Enlightenment – curious about everything and driven to explore, record and understand. Some became significant figures in the cultivation of tea in India.

Employment abroad was a common choice for young Scots doctors. In the second half of the eighteenth century, Scotland – with only a tenth of the United Kingdom's population – produced more than 85 per cent of British doctors.[4] The renowned medical schools in Glasgow and Edinburgh were turning out more graduates than their country could employ and at one time half of the assistant surgeons appointed by the East India Company were Scots. For many of them botany, or 'natural science', was a hobby verging on a passion.

Hugh Falconer, the Forres-born superintendent of the Calcutta Botanical Garden, for whom Robert Fortune put on the pantomime of making 'tea' from the leaves of trees, was a pioneering geologist, botanist, paleontologist and paleoanthropologist. He had trained as a natural scientist at Aberdeen University, before studying medicine in Edinburgh, where he was also taught geology by Professor Robert Jameson, who tutored the young Charles Darwin. In 1830 Falconer took what was to become a typical passage to India for bright young Scots – on an East Indiaman, serving as an assistant surgeon. He joined John Company's medical service in Bengal, but his work on fossils quickly won him a reputation as a serious natural scientist. Within two years he was made superintendent of the Saharanpur Botanical Garden, where he was encouraged to explore the possibility of growing tea in India. His work as a tea pioneer has been largely forgotten, but visitors to the north-east of Scotland can still enjoy the fruits of his ceaseless curiosity about the natural world. During his time in India, Hugh Falconer sent tons of fossils back to the Natural History Museum in London, but a fascinating selection of them found their way to Forres, where he and his brothers (one of them had been a Calcutta merchant) set up a museum in a fine Victorian building that can still be visited today.

The main 'forcing bed' of Indian tea, Calcutta's Royal Botanical Garden, was first laid out in 1787 and from the beginning was a largely Scottish concern. Its founder was Robert Kyd, an Angus-born man who may have studied medicine at Edinburgh University but joined the army of the East India Company at eighteen as an ensign in the Bengal Engineers. Kyd, who rose to become a lieutenant colonel, was a passionate amateur botanist whose hobby was to gather and tend a vast collection of plants in his own garden at Shalimar near Howrah across the Hooghly River from Calcutta. When a sea captain arrived from China in 1780 with a few specimen tea plants, Kyd planted some in his garden but clearly had ambitions to work on a much larger scale.[5] Kyd also planted the seed of a scheme for a botanic garden in the imagination of Bengal's governor-general, Sir John Macpherson, who was a fellow Scot and son of the manse from Sleat on the Isle of Skye. Kyd's sales pitch was that the garden would be a nursery raising 'stock for disseminating such articles as may prove beneficial to the inhabitants, as well as to the natives of Great Britain, and which ultimately may tend to the expansion of the national commerce and riches'.[6] Macpherson was convinced and in turn persuaded the East India Company. A site was cleared and the Calcutta Botanical Garden took root on the fertile alluvial plain of the Hooghly River.

Early successes included the cultivation of teak and spices. Sago from Malaya and dates from Persia were also experimented with, as foods that could supplement the local diet during times of famine. Kyd wanted India to grow tea commercially and became the staunchest ally of Sir Joseph Banks when the great English naturalist argued in 1788 that the East India Company support growing tea in India. But John Company jealously guarded its China tea monopoly and the Banks/Kyd proposal was ignored. Despite this setback, Robert Kyd's work at the botanic gardens was fruitful. Within two or three years, 4,000 plants were growing under his watchful eye.[7] Today the garden he founded covers 270 acres and is home to 1,400 species.

On Robert Kyd's death in Calcutta in 1793 another Scot, William Roxburgh, took over the gardens. Kyd's desire to be buried beneath his favourite avocado pear tree wasn't met, but Roxburgh paid him the compliment of naming a newly identified tree after him, *Kydia (Kydia calycina)* of the family Malvaceae.

William Roxburgh, an Ayrshireman, was born in 1751 on an estate near Symington where his father worked (although there is speculation that William may have been the natural son of a local aristo). He followed the now-familiar route to India of a medical degree at Edinburgh University followed by the post of 'sawbones' on an East India Company ship. As well as surgery, Roxburgh had studied botany under John Hope, who is recognised as the founder of Edinburgh's Royal Botanic Garden. Roxburgh became John Company's botanist in Madras, working on the cultivation of sugarcane, indigo and sago as potentially useful crops. His achievements in India revolutionised the economy and social history of Dundee, as it was he who first recognised the potential of a coarse Indian vegetable fibre and even gave that fibre its name. In a letter of 1795, to the Company's Court of Directors, he wrote about 'jute', an anglicised form of the word 'jhout', 'jhot' or 'jhut' used by the native Odisha gardeners he employed. Roxburgh encountered jute when he was searching for a substitute for European hemp that the Company's ships could use for cordage and sacking.[8] Up to 30,000 workers in Dundee would eventually be employed in spinning jute.*

---

* Most were women. Their frequently unemployed menfolk were known as kettle bilers (kettle boilers) – those who stayed at home and made tea.

Roxburgh collected plants from all over India and developed a herbarium, a classified collection of dried specimens that still exists today in the archives of the Botanical Survey of India. His books *Hortus Bengalensis* (1814) and *Flora Indica* (1832, published 17 years after his death) were for many decades the definitive works on Indian flora. Roxburgh is regarded as 'the father of Indian botany'.

In 1814 Roxburgh was succeeded by another Edinburgh-trained surgeon-naturalist, Francis Buchanan, or Buchanan-Hamilton (he adopted his mother's maiden name when he inherited her Callander estate). Buchanan-Hamilton had also wielded a scalpel as a ship's surgeon before travelling widely throughout India, collecting plants and making a significant contribution to the study of the country's natural history before being driven back to Scotland by ill health.

Buchanan-Hamilton was succeeded by a protégé of William Roxburgh's, the Danish-born doctor Nathaniel Wallich. But even Wallich fits into the 'Scots medic' category, as his MD was awarded by Aberdeen University.[9] Wallich was superintendent at the Calcutta Botanical Gardens for thirty years and made a significant contribution that was much praised by Joseph Hooker. He survived cholera, but for a long time suffered from declining health and left India for London in 1846, when Hugh Falconer took over the gardens, doubling up as professor of botany at Calcutta's medical college and playing host to Robert Fortune, his Chinese tea men and sprouting seeds.

At this point a serious question has to be asked. Were Robert Fortune's efforts, adventures and privations in China actually worth it? He most certainly introduced fine Chinese tea plants and expertise into British India – but the plant had been growing under the turned-up Imperial noses of the British all the time they had occupied Bengal. For all their genius, rapacity and desire to wrest the tea monopoly from China, they had failed to notice that a native sub-species of the treasured *Camellia sinensis* grew wild in the forests of the Brahmaputra Valley in Assam.

Assam was part of the Empire – not the British, but the Burmese Empire. In 1824, believing that Burma threatened British Bengal, the army of the East India Company invaded Burmese-occupied Assam, expelled the Burmese army and, for good measure, occupied a slice of Burma itself – finally conquering the entire country in 1885. Assam was now John Company's to do with what it liked. It installed a puppet king and five years later dethroned him, taking complete control over the potential tea-growing Brahmaputra Valley.

Even before the British invasion of Assam, Edinburgh-born adventurer Robert Bruce, a former major in the Bengal Artillery and something of an adventurer, was exploring the region in search of trade and had penetrated beyond the eastern frontier of British India. In 1823 he ventured into the Ahom Kingdom of upper Assam. At Rangpur, the capital, Bruce met Maniram Dewan, a native nobleman, who told him of the existence of indigenous Assam tea being used by the Singpho tribe. Deep in the jungle Bruce discovered the Singhpo preparing the leaves of a tree with oil and garlic, eating them as a vegetable and drinking an infusion made from them. Bruce realised that the trees resembled the tea bushes he had seen in the Calcutta Botanical Gardens. It was an astute observation, for in the jungle tea trees grow to enormous heights with leaves only at the top and difficult to see from the ground.

Anthropologist Alan Macfarlane suggests that the trees Bruce discovered may be the true root-stock of *Camellia sinensis* and that the plant may first have evolved in the highly biodiverse jungles of the eastern Himalayas. From there, he argues, tea was traded by tribal people into the settled population of China, who then began cultivating it.[10]

The Singpo were reluctant to reveal the source of the valuable plants, but, while Bruce was sitting cross-legged, smoking a pipe and negotiating with Beesa Gaum (a 'gaum' is a clan chief), the gaum's envious eye fell on Bruce's gun. A deal was struck: the gun for the location of the precious trees. In the jungle, the gaum ordered tea to be brewed, which Bruce thought was not unlike China tea. Back in the village, the guam shared the locations of more tea trees in exchange for money and opium. Bruce left the jungle with seeds and plants, convinced that he had discovered a native Indian tea that would replace the China brew on the tea tables of the Empire. He sent his samples to David Scott, the North-east Frontier's officer-in-charge, who forwarded them to Calcutta. Robert Bruce received neither a reply nor recognition for his discovery, for he died later that year.

Robert's younger brother, Charles Alexander Bruce, took up the cause. Nathaniel Wallich, at the Calcutta Botanical Gardens, now examined the leaves and seeds that Bruce had gathered and, while he recognised them as a camellia, he failed to spot that they were *Camellia sinensis*. For several years Charles Bruce's arguments, that the plants his brother had discovered were a variety of tea native to Assam and worthy of cultivation, fell on stony ground.

In 1834 Lord Bentinck, the governor-general of Bengal, formed a Tea Committee to explore the possibility of growing the crop in his domain. The committee's members were sceptical, but Bentinck insisted that an attempt be made. By now Charles Bruce had been joined by others who had recognised that wild tea flourished in Assam. Andrew Charlton, a lieutenant of the Assam Light Infantry, had sent plants from his remote station at Sadiya to Calcutta only to have his carefully gathered specimens rebuffed as inferior camellias. The scientific establishment had set its mind against the botanical enthusiasm of army upstarts like Charlton and Bruce, living in the wilds of Assam. How wrong they were. But, as Robert Burns said, 'facts are chiels that winna ding'. On Christmas Eve 1834, eleven years after Robert Bruce's discovery of tea in Assam, the Tea Committee issued a report that would have a profound impact on both India and Britain:

> It is with feelings of the highest satisfaction that we are enabled to announce to his Lordship in Council that the tea shrub is beyond all doubt indigenous in Upper Assam, being found there through an extent of country of one month's march within the Honourable Companie's territories from Sadiya and Beesa to the Chinese frontier province of Yunnan, where the shrub is cultivated for the sake of its leaf. We have no hesitation in declaring this discovery ... to be far the most important and valuable that has ever been made in matters connected with the agriculture or commercial resources of this empire.
>
> We are perfectly confident that the tea plant which has been brought to light will be found capable under proper management, of being cultivated with complete success for commercial purposes, and that consequently the object of our labours may be before long fully realized.

The previous month Dr Wallich had re-examined leaves, fruit and blossoms of the native plant. Reversing his assessment of a decade previously, he declared the plant to be tea. *Camellia sinensis var. assamica* had arrived. One can almost imagine the spectre of Major Robert Bruce wailing 'I told you so!'*

---

* The American writer Gore Vidal argued that 'I told you so' were the four sweetest words in the English language.

It certainly must have given great satisfaction to his brother Charles.

The following year a scientific commission led by Nathaniel Wallich journeyed for four months from Calcutta to Sadiya in Assam, the most extreme North-east Frontier station of the British Raj, travelling on foot, by bullockcart, elephant, boat and 'express canoe'. Charles Bruce joined them as their guide and took them to five jungle locations where wild tea grew in great profusion. Bruce described the tea in its natural state: 'It struggles for existence among so many other trees, that it becomes tall and slender, with most of its branches high up. The largest Tea tree I ever met with was twenty-nine cubits high (approximately fifty feet), and four spans round [approx. three feet]; very few I should say attain that size.' It was the very size of the trees that Robert Bruce had discovered that made even knowledgeable people sceptical about whether they really were tea plants.

> With respect to the Assam plant some botanists and practical gardeners find it difficult to believe, and with much show of reason, that a tree of from thirty to forty feet in height, and eight inches in diameter, can be of the same species as the diminutive tea plant of China and Japan. Yet it is affirmed to be identical by competent botanists, and otherwise scientific men, sent expressly to determine that doubt. But whether the Assam tea tree be a distinct species or not, it is evident that the form, height, and circumstances under which it was found, are those of a forced and unnatural growth. 'When the surrounding jungle was cut down,' says Mr. Bruce, 'the long slender stems of the tea tree seemed hardly capable of supporting their own weight.'[11]

Dr William Griffith, one of three scientists on the Tea Committee, reported that his two colleagues disagreed about the origins of the tea they found in Assam. Geologist John McClelland thought the Assam tea was an indigenous plant well suited to 'the shade of dense forests and a gloomy and excessively humid atmosphere', while Dr Nathaniel Wallich decided that the plant had probably originated in China and needed to be cultivated at a higher altitude to produce the 'more valued and superior teas'. For a long time scientists argued whether the wild plant could ever be made to be as good as the long-cultivated China tea; Dr Wallich argued the Assam tea could be just as good, but the Tea Committee ruled that no wild plant could match one that had been cultivated for centuries and decided to develop 'the China plant and not the degraded Assam plant'. Hugh Falconer was on the side of China tea, which perhaps explains his enthusiasm for the vast haul of seedlings that Robert Fortune turned up with in Calcutta in 1851. For years British India concentrated on developing the Assam tea industry based on imported stock from China. Tea planter David Crole later noted 'thus did these scientists unwittingly bring about the introduction into the province of a curse that at one time seemed as if it would prove as disastrous to Assam as ever the *Phylloxeravastatrix* has been in France or the *Hemileia vastatrix* in Ceylon'.*[12]

This wasn't the only blunder of the Tea Committee. The ten-acre site of the first experimental plantation in Assam was probably the worst location they could have chosen. The soil laid down by the river was rich, but beneath it lay a sandbank, which was certain death for a tea plant's taproot. Crole recalled:

---

* Crole is referring to insects which devastated grapevines in France in the late nineteenth century, and the leaf rust that affected coffee production in Sri Lanka, almost completely destroying the industry by 1890.

'In a short time the kindly Brahmaputra flowed over the site of this, the first tea garden in Assam, and buried in its water a lamentable failure.'

Despite having no training in botany, Charles Bruce was made superintendent of the government-led project to develop tea in Assam, winning support for the post from Dr Wallich. Essentially Bruce was an adventurer. Strong-minded, hardy and resourceful, he was at home amid the jungles of Assam and their native peoples. His early life reads like the pages of the Patrick O'Brian series of Aubrey/Maturin Napoleonic war novels. Born in 1793, Charles became a midshipman at sixteen, took part in two naval battles against Napoleon's navy, was taken prisoner, marched across Mauritius at bayonet point and incarcerated on a prison hulk until the island was captured by the British. He then commanded a troopship during the British defeat of the French in Java. In 1824, when British rule over prosperous Bengal was threatened by Burmese invasion, Bruce commanded gunboats against hostile native clans. He recalled, 'It was my good fortune that year to go against Dutta Gaum and his followers, who threatened to overrun our frontier, and it was my good fortune to expel him twice with my gunboat from two strong positions.'

China tea did not thrive well in the intense heat of Assam, but at Sadiya, in the extreme north-east, Charles created a nursery of native tea bushes that in 1836 produced a decent cuppa that won the praise of the Tea Committee. That year Charles Bruce wrote a short treatise with a very long title, *Black Tea as now Practised at Suddeya in Upper Assam by the Chinamen Sent Thither for that purpose, with Observations of the culture of the plant in China and its growth in Assam, by C.A. Bruce, Superintendent of Tea culture.* Despite this, Bruce has some interesting things to say about growing it in the hot climate of India.

I have taken great numbers of Tea plants from the jungles, brought them 4 to 8 days journey to my own house, and planted them in the sun, that is, without any shade; during the first six months the half of them died, at the end of the year about one quarter of what I had originally brought only lived; at the end of the second year there were still less; those that did live threw out leaves and blossoms, but the fruit never came to perfection.

Charles also gave us the name for what might have been called 'tea farms' or 'tea plantations'. He was the first person to use the expression 'tea gardens' and wherever the British planted tea thereafter they called their cultivations 'tea gardens'. Although not a botanist, Charles combined instinct, close observation of wild plants and trial-and-error to produce tea that even Lord Auckland, the viceroy, liked. Now the game really was afoot.

On 6 May 1838 it was announced that eight chests of Bruce's Assam tea, about 350 pounds, had been shipped to London. A few months later amid 'much curiosity' the East India Company auctioned the first ever tea from Assam – three cases of Assam souchong and five of Assam pekoe. Bidding on the first case of souchong began at five shillings a pound and was finally knocked down at twenty-one shillings. The first case of pekoe – 'after much competition' – went for twenty-four shillings a pound, with 'every broker appearing to bid for it'.

The *Asiatic Journal* reported that a Captain Pidding had been moved to buy all eight cases 'by the public-spirited motive of securing a fair trial to this valuable product of British Assam'. The quality of a second shipment was thought to be higher and one broker, Messers Twining & Co., declared, 'Upon the whole, we think that the recent specimens are very favourable to the hope and expectation that Assam is capable of producing an article well suited to this market ...'

That it took so long for the Assam plants to be recognised as tea seems extraordinary, but the Bruce brothers had to battle against deep-rooted China tea snobbery and vested interest. Tea historian William Ukers wrote tartly: 'For ten years indigenous India tea begged for recognition, only to be met with cynical indifference; and when the recognition came, how halting, how half-hearted it was!'

Now aware that there were two varieties of teas, and unwilling to have to trot out the Latin names for them, people dealing in tea adopted the word *jat*, meaning 'type' or even 'caste', and referred to the Assam *jat* or the China *jat*. Unscrupulous Chinese dealers helped popularise the Assam *jat* when it became known that China tea was often adulterated with common hedgerow plants and worse. Gunpowder green tea had even been found to have been substituted with real gunpowder mixed with gum, pale Prussian blue dye, turmeric and sulphate of lime.[13] After this scandal the public flocked to buy unadulterated tea, even though it came from a new territory and had a robust flavour that needed to be tamed with a splash of milk or, as Mrs Beeton recommended, mixed in the pot with a little China tea.*

Charles Bruce had never doubted that Assam was potentially great tea country and was certain that the dense jungles of the Brahmaputra Valley were rich in the precious plant. He himself had discovered huge tracts of tea trees 'growing absolutely so thick as to impede each other's growth'. From Jaipur in 1839, he wrote:

> I feel convinced the whole of the country is full of tea.
> Again, in going farther to the south-west, just before I
> came to Gabrew hill, I found the small hills adjoining

---

* Braithwaite's of Dundee, the more-than-a-century-old speciality tea shop, still sells a lovely China/Darjeeling blend.

it, to the eastward, covered with tea-plants. The flowers of the tea on these hills are of a pleasant delicate fragrance, unlike the smell of our other tea-plant; but the leaves and fruit appear the same. This would be a delightful place for the manufacture of tea, as the country is well populated, has abundance of grain, and labour is cheap.

Bruce was visionary in his belief that Assam was a region where the wild plants his brother had discovered could be cultivated, but he doubted if the Assamese were up to it. A by-product of Bengal's production of opium for the Chinese market had been wide-scale addiction among the men who grew it. Bruce wrote:

> That dreadful plague, which has depopulated this beautiful country, turned it into a land of wild beasts, with which it is overrun, and has degenerated the Assamese, from a fair race of people, to the most abject, servile, crafty, and demoralized race in India. This vile drug has kept, and does now keep, down the population; the women have fewer children compared with those of other countries, and the children seldom live to become old men, but in general die in manhood; very few old men being seen in this unfortunate country, in comparison with others. Few but those who have resided long in this unhappy land know the dreadful and immoral effects, which the use of Opium produces on the native. He will steal, sell his property, his children, the mother of his children, and finally even commit murder for it.

Addiction, warned Bruce, had not only destroyed the Assamese, but would also enslave the immigrant labour now pouring into the region to pick and manufacture tea. Bruce urged 'our humane and enlightened' government to slash production of the poppy, but Britain long continued to import China tea paid for in Bengal opium. Addicted Indians and Chinese was the price paid for every cup.

The tea trade with China, however, was going off the boil. Within a generation or so, Assam was tamed for the cultivation of the native tea and the deep, dark, malty brew won the hearts of the British, overthrowing China's 200-year-old monopoly. Soon, more than two million acres of Assam were under tea bushes, with more than one and a quarter million people cultivating them. The long-ignored *assamica* had become one of the greatest wealth creators in the British Empire. In his 1946 essay *A Nice Cup of Tea*, George Orwell was able to say confidently, 'Anyone who has used that comforting phrase "a nice cup of tea" invariably means Indian tea.'

If only the Brits had been quicker to observe the habits of the Singpo people of Assam, the need to smuggle destructive opium to China – and the two wars that that caused – could have been avoided. Although, as Arthur Herman points out in his book *How the Scots Invented the Modern World*, had that been the case, 'Hong Kong, Asia's premier commercial city and modern China's window on to the capitalist West, would not exist'. Robert Bruce had not lived to see the discovery he made in the jungles of the Brahmaputra Valley recognised as tea. His brother Charles wrote that he himself had 'little thought that I should have been spared long enough ... to see the day and thanked God for so great a blessing to our country'. He went on:

> Should what I have written on this new and interesting subject be of any benefit to the country, and the community at large, and help a little to impel the tea forward to enrich our own dominions, and pull down

the haughty pride of China, I shall feel myself richly repaid for the perils and dangers and fatigues, that I have undergone in the cause of British India Tea.

It took many years for the Tea Committee to put its faith in India's native *Camellia sinensis var. assamica* over what was now being referred to as 'the miserable China variety' and the bastard hybrids it engendered. Eventually many planters came to understand that the 'Indian plant is improved in hardihood by a dash of the China plant in it'. Tea author Edward Money further argued that Indian tea, grown with a mere trace of Chinese in it, 'is as superior to pure China tea as gold is to silver'.[14] The airy Himalayas, however, proved more suitable for China plants, and today about 75 per cent of the cultivars of that region are *Camellia sinensis var. sinensis*, with the remainder *Camellia sinensis var. assamica*.[15]

From this we can see that, in fact, Robert Fortune's trials and tribulations were not in vain.

In 1871 Charles Bruce was presented with the Royal Society of Arts' Gold Medal for his pioneer cultivation of the indigenous tea plants in Assam. He died that year aged 78 at Tezpur on the banks of the Brahmaputra in Assam, where he is buried in the Christian cemetery. Today the economy of Tezpur depends on the tea gardens that surround it. Meanwhile, back in Scotland, artisan tea is being grown by Charles Bruce's great-great-great-granddaughter, Susie Walker-Munro. We shall encounter Susie and her tea bushes in a later chapter.

In 1840 the East India Company sold its gardens to the London/Calcutta-based Assam Company and this new enterprise embarked on a steep and bumpy learning curve. Believing that 'every man with a pigtail' knew how to grow and manufacture tea, the Assam Company imported labourers from Singapore, who were so 'turbulent, obstinate and rapacious' that they had to be deported.[16] The company also persisted for years in growing the China *jat* rather than the native Assam one. It was not until 1856 that the company paid a dividend. Eventually, however, enormous profits were made and by 1907 the Assam Company had produced 1.17 million pounds of tea and had yielded dividends of £1.36 million – a 730 per cent return on capital![17] Assam tea went down particularly well in Scotland. 'Generally speaking,' wrote one dealer, 'the London tea blender sends his strong Assam blends into Scotland; Darjeeling and Travancore into Yorkshire; Ceylons and certain of the China teas into the southwestern counties; reserving Indian and Ceylon blends for London and the eastern counties.'[18]

The growing reputation of Assam tea for tasty profits as well as full flavour prompted a land grab. Any claims of the indigenous people were swept aside. The land was parcelled out to whites and thousands of acres of primeval forest hacked down for planting. The government of Bengal offered free land to planters under very simple rules. A tract of jungle was given freehold to anyone who would agree to clear 10 per cent of it a year. And so by clearing just twenty acres a year, a man could own outright a 200-acre tea estate in a decade. Even when the government began to auction land, prices were low. 'These were the good old times in tea,' commented tea planter Samuel Baildon.[19]

Colonel Richard Keatinge, the Dublin-born chief commissioner of Assam, who had won the Victoria Cross suppressing the Indian Mutiny and securing the Imperial gravy train for Britain, extolled the virtues of the land grants: 'They will give every man a chance of obtaining an independent position and leave the field open to the hard-working man as well as to the capitalist.' Conditions for such entrepreneurs were primitive, unhealthy and dangerous. In his 1877 guide for young men coming to India to start work on plantations, Samuel Baildon recalled the old, hard times.

> Seeing a European once a month was very frequent: planters tables were seldom furnished as they are now ... there were no steam communication on the Brahmapootra, and country boats took an indefinite period to come and go to Bengal. Few doctors or good houses; most men doctored themselves, and sometimes lost their lives in so doing. Scarcely any roads: only beaten jungle tracks, such as frequently no horse could travel, for after the death of the Rajah the great roads in Assam got into jungle. Grumble as much as we will, these are civilized times, so to speak. The unopened country and low living induced fever and sickness generally, and although in many instances, money was not scarce, the smallest luxury could hardly be obtained. Yet these were the days for gathering in the Rupees!

William Ukers, in his magisterial 1935 work *All About Tea*, paints a miserable picture of the lonely young planter's life.

> A tea planter's bungalow in those days was a rather pathetic sight. There was a stove, a platform bed of split bamboos, a table, a box which did duty as a chair, and a medicine shelf. This last was really the principal article in the furnishings, as it provided the essential without which no tea planter could be expected to survive; for in order to survive, the planter's health code demanded 'quinine every morning, castor oil twice a week, and calomel at the change of the moon ... Here removed from all his friends, stripped of

every luxury, he breaths a miasmatic air, is exhausted by a perpetual vapour bath, but bears it all.'

Ukers quotes an old Assam tea planter recalling the daily, unhealthy grind 'from week to week, till it was time for the trip home to recruit, or else for rest in the grave'. Some planters made good money, many others found early graves, but the primitive, dangerous and uncomfortable conditions did little to deter succeeding generations of young men from becoming tea men. Very many of them were Scots. When Englishman Peter Banyard joined the Scottish agency of Begg Dunlop in 1934, his new boss in Calcutta wrote that he thought Banyard was 'OK' but added 'couldn't you have found a Scot?'[20]

Wherever they came from, the planters' lives were hazardous ones. The Finlay's archive contains a chilling note from 1908 about Mr A.W. Strachan, an assistant manager at Goombira Estate.

20th August 1908

We much regret to inform you that Mr Strachan has been the victim of a very unfortunate accident, having been very severely mauled by a tiger, and it has been found necessary by Drs Silvester and Burkitt, who were both attending him, to amputate his right arm and also his left leg below the knee.

Strachan was hospitalised in Calcutta before being shipped home, first class.

Wild elephants were no respecters of the planters' lives or land rights and continued to trundle along their ancient migration tracks even after the jungle had been cleared. As recently as 2018 three tuskers on the loose from a nature reserve caused mayhem on Assam estates, crushing tea bushes and labourers' quarters.

As well as vast tracts of dense jungle, wild animals, cholera, malaria, dysentery, smallpox and typhoid, Assam challenged European planters with another serious problem – the Assamese. Native to this land, they had no desire to buckle down to an entirely new way of life in which their traditional freedom was bought for the tiny wage paid for the monotonous job of plucking tea. Nor, as Charles Bruce had discovered, would they allow their nimble-fingered women to work in tea gardens. Instead of using local labour, the tea gardens had to import indentured coolie labour from other regions. Poor, illiterate, unorganised and far from home, these men, women and children were ripe for exploitation on an obscene scale.

John Carnegie arrived in India in 1866 after an abortive attempt to make his way in China and was soon joined from Scotland by his brother Alick. Their letters home, now in the British Library, make startling reading.[21] As dutiful sons, their correspondence was fond and gossipy, but their letter are also starkly revealing about the attitude of the white tea masters to their indentured coolie labourers. Both Carnegie brothers got jobs in Begg & Dunlop tea gardens and Alick's first task was to deliver indentured coolies from the steamer which had brought them from Calcutta to the Assam plantations where they would live and work. Alick wrote home to his parents: 'We had awful work driving the coolies, we drove up and down the line and had to shove them on exactly as nigger drovers in America.' John wrote to his mother, 'we have 500 coolies on board, the dirtiest brutes in creation swarming with lice and one had cholera last night, what with coolies musquitoes and lice I shant be sorry when this is at an end which wont be for 12 days yet.' Later in the letter, which seems to be written over several days, he notes casually, 'Two coolies died thus morning of cholera that's the obituary.' From Tezpur, high up the Brahmaputra River in the tea garden region of Assam, John wrote to his mother:

... all together we have 360 coolies going to different places and of these 59 died of cholera before we got to Tezpur ... coolies die awfully fast here they were all Bengal coolies and they stand the climate here even worse than Europeans there were 3 dead here since arrival and that only four days.

Unknown thousands of indentured coolies died as they were transported in appalling conditions to the plantations. Once there, they were virtual prisoners, had to endure atrocious living conditions and very often weren't paid the going rate for their labours. Planters exercised arbitrary justice over those they thought to be slacking. In desperation, some coolies fled the tea gardens and took their chances in the hostile jungle. In April 1866 Alex Carnegie reported:

I was woken at one o'clock in the morning three days ago by the news that 7 coolies had run off so the manager who was here at the time sent his servant on a horse to the stations he had to take my gun loaded with ball to keep off the tigers & bears & leopards that come out of the thick jungle at night and lie about the roads, or rather the foot paths, for there are no roads up here except one and that one is fully ten miles away ... four of the coolies were caught, and brought in this morning. They got a great mauling from the [Sardans] overseer and are put to double work for the next month, at least I said so today but in about a week I will let them do the same as the rest, it is an awful bore when they run away.

As well as punishing coolies, it was the estate manager's job to try and keep them alive. John Carnegie describes 'dosing' two sick ones, an old man and a girl, that were brought to him for treatment: 'they both died however about an hour ago and I have seen the bodies carried into the jungle where the jackals will have a feast on them tonight, the man was not worth much but the girl was a good leaf plucker her father and mother both died on the river on the way up she was an imported coolie.'

Picking tea required nimble fingers and about half the workers in Assam tea gardens were women, giving the planters a self-reproducing workforce. Historian Jayeeta Sharma's scholarly investigation into conditions contains material that might come from Conrad's *Heart of Darkness*:

> Since the planters had the right to private arrest, any coolies that would escape were subjected to severe punishment. Frequent instance of flogging a recalcitrant worker to death, rubbing pepper into the sexual organs of female coolies, and other equally vile forms of torture have been recorded in various archives and first-hand accounts.[22]

Sharma goes on to tell not only of the flogging, and even killing, of coolies, but of fragmentary, anecdotal evidence of sexual exploitation by the white masters of female coolies and of the illegitimate children born as a result.

Hundreds of thousands of Indians were ruthlessly exploited in tea gardens, so that their white masters could make vast fortunes, and Britain and her colonies sip tea at a reasonable price. It was an exploitative regime that lasted beyond Indian independence and the eventual takeover of tea gardens by Indian companies and managers. Our bold, hardy, resourceful and entrepreneurial Scottish tea men were not all exactly moral paragons possessed of progressive and humanitarian instincts. In *Burmese Days*, the great English writer George Orwell wrote an angry anti-imperialist diatribe of a novel, revealing the racism and general awfulness of the white Brahmins. Orwell served during the 1920s in the Indian Imperial Police (when Burma was ruled as part of British India). There he came to detest the despotism, snobbery and racism of the Empire but recognised that these faults were by no means only 'English' ones. In *Burmese Days* he has his teak planter protagonist John Flory declare, 'The British Empire is simply a device for giving trade monopolies to the English – or rather to gangs of Jews and Scotchmen.' Is this Orwell speaking, or just his fictional character? Either way the sentence reveals an antagonism to the disproportionate number of Scots lording it over the natives.

Orwell's lifelong hostility to Scots – which only softened after he had moved to the Hebridean island of Jura to write *Nineteen Eighty-Four*– may have been formed by his experience of Scots planters and officials who had set themselves up in Burma as *pukka sahibs*. Mr Macgregor, the deputy commissioner in *Burmese Days*, is 'good-hearted' but essentially dull and pompous, while one Scot is described as 'an old Scotch gin-soaker' who describes natives as 'dirrt', and another is a loutish Glasgow electrician called Macdougall who was sacked for drunkenness and was 'only interested in whisky and magnetos'. Orwell later defended his novel from claims that he had 'let the side down', saying 'much of it is simply reporting what I have seen'.

For many young Scotsmen a career in planting was an exciting and rewarding alternative to the restrictions of life at home. The hardiness and spirit of adventure among them is exemplified by the career of Dugald McTavish Lumsden, a Peterhead boy who, at 22, took up a post at a tea estate at Tezpur in Assam. Inspired by the part-time local army units of his homeland, he set up a volunteer cavalry unit and eventually formed Lumsden's Horse, a 250-strong force that sailed from Calcutta in 1900 to take part in the Boer War. Not all Scots, however, were made from the rugged planter mould. Many more prospered in tea while seldom leaving Calcutta. Tea auctions began there in the early 1840s and the city rapidly became the tea capital of India, as brokers and merchants dealt in the leaf that came from up-country.

Kolkata, as historic Calcutta is now known, and its suburbs are home to nearly fifteen million people. But before the arrival of the East India Company in 1690 it had been nothing more than a handful of little villages scattered around the east bank of the Hooghly River. Despite the area's torrid summer heat and drenching monsoon season, the English recognised its potential as a trading port. By 1712 Fort George had been built to protect the interests of the now politically United Kingdom from the Nawab of Bengal and the French. The infamous 'black hole of Calcutta' resulted from a brief occupation of the fort by the Nawab's forces before they were driven out by the army of Clive of India. The city became the headquarters of the Company and the centre of its opium trade with China. At the centre of the centre lay Dalhousie Square, named for the Scottish governor-general of India from 1848 to 1856.

Calcutta was a city of contrasts: Imperial opulence and eye-watering wealth side by side with abject poverty; a city of Anglican and Presbyterian high-mindedness and a hell-hole of opium dens, arrack-shacks, nautcheries and pox-palaces; a place, said the novelist Amitav Ghosh, 'where Europe hides its shame and its greed'. By the 1830s opium accounted for one-fifth of the entire revenue of British India.

During Lord Dalhousie's reign, Calcutta and India were awash with Scots, many of them young men employed in the Writers' Building by John Company, but others serving in the army, in commerce, as missionaries, forest managers or police-men and in the business of tea. Dalhousie Square has now been renamed B.B.D. Bagh, the initials standing for the names of three martyred Bengali freedom fighters who assassinated a hated police inspector of prisons in the Writers' Building in 1930. But you can still stroll in Minto Park, Urquhart Square, Duff Street, Kyd Street and Elgin Road.*

In the 1850s Calcutta was mushrooming, partly due to the rise of the jute industry. Bengal had a virtual monopoly over raw jute production and the coarse fibre, whose value had first been recognised by William Roxburgh, now bound up the city's fortunes with those of Dundee and Scotland, where it was first woven. While sandbags are usually associated with the First World War, it was the Crimean War in the 1850s that stimulated the demand for plentiful and cheap sandbags and it became cheaper to build factories in Bengal and make them there.# The first Bengal jute mill, with machinery from Dundee, opened in 1855, and by the First World War there were thirty-eight mills around the city employing 1,000 Scots and 184,000 native workers.[23] Calcutta was now both a trading and manufacturing city, with Scots at the heart of it.

Two Scots firms, Andrew Yule & Co. and James Finlay's, were leaders in the jute business. Professor Tom Devine points out that in 1813 fourteen out of thirty-eight major trading concerns in the city were essentially Scottish.[24] At the same time, Scots engineer George Turnbull, a native of Luncarty in Perthshire and a protégé of Thomas Telford, was building the 600-mile railway line to Benares (now Varanasi), and India's greatest train station, the giant twenty-three-platform Howrah Station in Calcutta.

---

*   My wife and I had an outstanding meal at Kewpies, a family-run Bengali restaurant in Elgin Lane.
#   A key redoubt at the Battle of Inkerman was 'The Sandbank Battery'.

Scots were so ubiquitous in the city that they even had their own cemetery. It is now a sadly dilapidated and vandalised ruin. When we visited, its caretaker was Norman Hall, an Indian whose grandfather, he told us, 'was born and died in Scotland'. My wife and I wandered round the shattered tombstones, quickly finding one that read:

In Memory of Robert Anderson,

Dessoi Tea Estate, Assam,

Who died in Calcutta on 3nd June 1933

The stone was broken and lay on the ground. Norman said that he often had to call the police to deal with drunks, drug addicts and thieves looking for dressed marble. Nevertheless, we were rewarded with glimpses of a long-gone era when Calcutta was a magnet for the adventurous from the length and breadth of Scotland.

Calcutta is far from the great black-tea growing areas of Assam and Darjeeling, but it is the commercial capital of the industry all the same. Tea from plants descended from ones cultivated in the city's botanical gardens in the nineteenth century is sold in the city's auction houses in the twenty-first. The most venerable of Calcutta's tea agencies, Gillanders, Arbuthnot & Co., was set up in 1819 by Scotsman Francis Mackenzie Gillanders, backed by his wealthy uncle, the Leithborn merchant and slave-trader John Gladstone, father of a future British prime minister. Gladstone had amassed a fortune, partly through his plantations in Jamaica and Guyana. When Britain abolished slavery in 1833, Gladstone made another fortune − about £9 million in today's terms − by being compensated for the loss of his slaves. Deprived of his captive workforce, he then hired indentured labourers from India whom he treated no better than the 2,500 men, women and children he had once owned. The Indians were procured for Gladstone by his nephew Gillanders, who described them as 'hill coolies', having 'few wants beyond eating, sleeping and drinking' and being 'more akin to the monkey than the man'.[25] In 1824 Gillanders was joined by David Ogilvy, another of Gladstone's nephews, to form Gillanders, Ogilvy & Co. When Ogilvy retired, Captain Arbuthnot joined and the company became known as Gillanders, Arbuthnot & Co., with their head office at 8 Clive Street, Calcutta. It dealt not only in tea but also in jute, timber, oil, construction, engineering and railways – with bases in Bombay, Madras, Karachi, Lahore and Delhi. Today, the company is involved in textiles, engineering and tea. The Indian owners have seen no reason to drop their company's overtly Scottish name.

Walter Duncan was another Scot who made the journey from Glasgow to India and from textiles to tea. After founding a cotton business in Calcutta, Walter, now joined by his brother William, set up companies under the names Walter Duncan & Co. in Glasgow and Duncan Brothers & Company in Calcutta. Within a few years the pair made tea their main business. By 1890 they owned twelve tea gardens and more than nine square miles of bushes. Walter died in 1900, but Duncan's continued to thrive. By 1923 the company's sixty estates covered more than seventy-seven square miles and produced nearly 14,000 tons of tea a year. In 1951 Duncan Brothers Limited was taken over by the Indian Goenka family and, although it is now part of a massive and diverse company, its Scottish origins are still clear in its current name, the Duncan Goenka group.

Balmer Lawrie & Co. Ltd is another still-thriving Indian company that was founded in Calcutta by two Scots, Stephen George Balmer and Alexander Lawrie. The two men tossed a coin to decide which of their names came first in their new company's title. The business was set up to blend and export tea, although it soon diversified into banking, shipping and manufacturing. Today the company is India's biggest maker of steel barrels. In September 2013 Virendra Sinha, the company's chairman and managing director, announced that tea manufacturing was incurring losses and that it was ceasing production. A 165-year-old tradition ended.[26]

By the beginning of the twentieth century, McLeod & Co., founded in 1887, was one of the largest tea agents and traders in Calcutta, with an imposing HQ in Dalhousie Square. By the time William Ukers published *All About Tea* in 1935, McLeod's had interests in forty tea estates covering 34,313 acres. It also dealt in coal, rubber, indigo, shipping and railways.

Andrew Yule & Company was formed by the eponymous Stonehaven man. After seeking his fortune in Manchester, Andrew – lured by tales of colonial trade – moved to India, where he quickly established the Hoolungpooree Tea Company, followed by Andrew Yule & Co. in Calcutta in 1866. That company's early interest was cotton spinning. Although Bengal had an ancient tradition of hand-spinning, Yule introduced industrial mills to the region, a process that had previously only been carried out in Bombay. Yule was quick to see where money could be made and was soon dealing in jute, cotton, coal and tea. His brother George* and their nephew David then came out to India to make it truly a family firm. Today Andrew Yule & Co. Ltd is a manufacturing and industrial conglomerate, largely owned by the Indian government.

---

* In 1888 George Yule became the first non-Indian to serve as president of the Indian National Congress, the political party which would eventually lead India to independence. It had been founded three years earlier by Allan Octavian Hume, an Imperial civil servant and distinguished ornithologist, who was the son of Montrose-born Joseph Hume, a radical Scottish doctor and MP.

In 1824 the Scots David Jardine and Charles Skinner founded textile company Jardine, Skinner & Company in Bombay to import cotton goods from Manchester and Glasgow and export indigo, silk and later jute. In 1844 the company moved to Calcutta to trade in tea, opium and timber. It had close ties with Jardine Matheson & Co. of Hong Kong. David Jardine was a nephew of Jardine Matheson's co-founder William Jardine. Such bloodties were common among the Scots in India and elsewhere throughout the Empire. Sons followed not only fathers into trading companies and plantations but also uncles and more distant relations, or at least enjoyed their patronage to get started. William Jardine wrote to a nephew seeking employment: 'I can never consent to assist idle and dissipated characters however nearly connected to me, but am prepared to go to any reasonable extent in supporting such of my relatives as conduct themselves prudently and industriously.'

Did this Caledonian kin-network develop because men like Jardine often came from a relatively small middle class in a little country where bonds of blood and friendship were easily maintained?* Or was it because Scots, who were latecomers to British Imperial India, had to forge their own colonial network to compete with their larger neighbours? Whatever the case, kinship ties brought many thousands of Scots to India and helped them prosper. Duncan MacNeill, an orphaned nephew of Campbeltown-born businessman and ship-owner Sir William MacKinnon, was given a leg-up by his uncle and sailed to Calcutta to join the Scottish tea company Begg,

---

* Even today, when Scotland's population is far greater than it was in William Jardine's time, I use the expression 'Scotland the village!' when I encounter connections between disparate people that I meet who turn out to be connected to people I know or am related to.

Dunlop & Company, but eventually left to found MacNeill & Co., which included tea and shipping in its portfolio.

These Scottish companies frequently favoured 'their ain folk' and the tradition of recruiting 'creepers' (trainee planters) from Scotland, particularly from the North-east, was quickly established and continued even after Indian independence.

In 1962 twenty-year-old John Davison had dropped out of university and was mucking-in at his uncle's farm when he saw an advert for 'trainee tea planters' in the *Press and Journal*. An interview with a retired tea man in Aberdeen led to a further interrogation at the London headquarters of the Inchcape Group, an old company founded by Scots (a Mackinnon and a Mackenzie) in Calcutta. The fact that Inchcape was as interested in John's outward bound qualifications and farming background as they were in his school qualifications reveals that the planter's life was still an arduous one.

Six weeks later, having signed away five years of his life, Davison sailed for Bombay.[27] After just a night there, he spent three days and nights crossing India to get to Calcutta by train. Davison recalls his first days with the Inchape subsidiary McNeill & Barry Ltd: 'I spent a week in Calcutta getting "kitted out" with crockery, cutlery, bed linen, etc ... all the while accompanied by a head office "wallah" to guide and look after me. I also got to know a few head office personnel but particularly a young Englishman who "educated" me in the ways of the company. I learned that my first posting was to Nangdala Tea Estate in the north-east of West Bengal, very close to the border with Bhutan.' Nangdala, in the high-quality producing region of the Dooars, had been founded by McNeill's in 1923.

It was the young Scot's first time outside the UK, but the slums, poverty, beggars, litter, noise and overcrowding that he witnessed in Calcutta didn't dampen this enthusiasm for this 'adventurous fresh start'. Flying to Siliguri in the foothills of the Himalayas he was met by Dulal Moitra, the fellow assistant manager that he'd share a bungalow with, and the pair began a four-hour journey on rutted and dusty roads in a battered 1940s Austin with 'suspicious brakes' and a radiator that needed frequent refreshing.

John's first manager was a fatherly veteran of the Burma Railroad under whom the green young assistant learned the basics before being transferred after three months to the Maijan estate on the south bank of the Brahmaputra in Upper Assam, the third-largest estate in the world. With 2,000 acres under bushes and a workforce of 2,000 it produced 1.22 million kilos of tea a year. The workers and their families lived in villages scattered round the estate, close to the bushes they tended. At the top of the tea tree was Mr Munro, a superintendent in charge of several company gardens, who lived in the 'White House', a palatial two-storey building with Doric columns and an extensive garden. Like Munro, most of the management were Scots. Munro, along with the garden's general manager and factory manager were Maijan's *burra sahibs* (big bosses), while John Davison, who was the assistant factory manager, and three garden assistant managers were its *chota sahibs* (small bosses). The most senior Indian on the plantation was the estate doctor.

John had a two-bedroom bungalow with a large sitting/dining room and a veranda. The cook-house was in a separate building (in case of fire), and while John paid for the cook himself the company provided him with a bearer (a sort of butler who served him his meals), a sweeper (cleaner), a day watchman and a night watchman. 'So you can see I was well looked after,' John recalls. It sounds like a luxurious lifestyle for a twenty-year-old university drop-out, but during the March to early November plucking season the factory ran continuously and John could only snatch very few hours out of every twenty-four to eat or sleep. Convivial evenings in the planters' club became distant memories. After one such season, John was moved from the factory to a garden and was able to down a few *chjota pegs*, after enjoying golf and tennis at the club.

John was transferred to Rajghor, a garden that included a clonal research unit to further develop Assam's teas. It was ideal tea country, hot and humid with an average 240 inches of rain a year. The swollen Brahmaputra would swallow up areas of bushes every rainy season. Leaches infested the garden and John learned to burn them off his legs with cigarettes. Cobras were common and the workforce would refuse to enter the bushes until the 'snake walla' had dealt with them. Hookworm thrived where the workers relieved themselves among the bushes; the worms burrowed into the skin of the next person to pass by and entered their bloodstream. John was hospitalised by such an infection.

Assam was about as far from the swinging sixties as any young man could get. The estate had a single telephone, but the connection even to Calcutta took hours to make. For some, the planting life was just too hard, too isolated and too restricted. John recalls that a fellow new-boy had only got as far as his hotel in Calcutta before fleeing home. The expectations of the baby-boom generation had forced the company to reduce the length of the first tour of duty from five to three years. John spent his first leave in Hong Kong, where he met and courted Margaret, a young Australian. The couple married and returned to John's estate in Assam, where Margaret settled well into the role of a planter's wife. But times had changed. Young Indians were now claiming their right to exploit their nation's resources and the Hindi heard in the tea gardens was increasingly native and not the hard-learned variety spoken in a Scottish accent. 'Last in, first out' was the company's rule and the young couple 'sadly' left India in 1967 for a new life in Australia.

Ian Davidson, brought up on an Aberdeenshire dairy farm, was another of that last generation of planters from Scotland's

North-east. A meeting with a family friend who was 'in tea' at Aberdeen's Atholl Hotel – the 'local' for retired planters or those home on leave – set the young engineer on course for the Balijan Tea Estate in Upper Assam in 1964. Ian was plunged into the manufacturing monsoon season where he worked fifteen or sixteen hours a day in hot, humid weather.

The end of the busy season found Ian more frequently at the long-established Panitola club, which had excellent sports facilities and a busy bar. Life was good. Ian fished on the Brahmaputra and went shooting in the jungle. He recalls, 'There used to be river parties where we took our bearers etc & had tiffin on the riverbank and met other planters. Pink gins come to mind!' Coming home to Scotland to marry his fiancée, Lilian, Ian then returned to India with her. They both loved the life there, but it was short lived. The white sahibs at Balijan were being systematically replaced by Indian managers and Ian was among the first batch slated to go. The Davidsons were devastated but, in one respect, lucky. On 6 June 1966 – 6/6/66 – India devalued the rupee by 57 per cent. Older planters with children in UK boarding schools and stacks of rupees in the bank suffered crippling losses. Ian and Lilian – in their twenties, without children and with skills that made them employable – were able to make new lives elsewhere. Ian Davidson and John Davison were thus among the last generation of young men to take part in the more-than-a-century-old tradition of chain-migration from the North-east of Scotland to the tea lands of the East.

While the journalist and author Neal Ascherson amusingly admits to his own failure to be admitted to such a Scots colonial network in Malaya in 1951, he writes insightfully about the 'authoritarian oligarchies' set up by Scots throughout the Empire.[28] Ascherson argues that such 'private partnerships', set up under Scots law, were interested in trade not territory and that their purpose was to make money, not to make the natives 'British'. Such companies could also tap into the surplus of capital that Scotland's iron, steel, shipbuilding and heavy engineering industries was producing. Scotland's private partnerships could compete and thrive in the British and global markets because they were 'certainly more flexible and serviceable than anything to be had at the time under English law'.[29]

The number, scale and longevity of the Scottish companies in Calcutta illustrate the depth and breadth of Scottish involvement – indeed, domination – of the Indian tea trade. When the Indian Tea Association was set up in 1881 to protect the interests of the British tea planters, its founding chairman was a Scot from Begg, Dunlop & Company, and his successor a Scot at Jardine, Skinner & Co. Needless to say the 'interests' that were protected were those of the owners and managers, not the estate workers, and the Association sought to control wages and conditions so as to maximise profit.

Resilient planters and wily traders were not the only Scots who made India's tea a global product. Aberdeen brothers William and John Jackson were returning from a tea garden in upper Assam when their ship broke down on a Brahmaputra sandbank. Using their enforced leisure to explore the country, they came across a Marshall portable steam engine with a self-contained boiler. William was entranced and became convinced that this sturdy machine was ideal for powering the tea-rolling machine that he had been busily constructing inside his head. Unable to find a suitable partner in Scotland, Jackson set up shop at the Britannia Iron Works of Marshall, Sons & Company in Lincolnshire. Jackson's first steam-powered tea roller began work at the Scottish Assam Tea Company's Heeleakah garden at Jorhat in 1872. Jackson also invented tea-sorting, drying and packing machines, revolutionising the previously labour-intensive processing of tea in India and Ceylon, bringing down the price to the consumer. Jackson's first machine cranked into action in 1872, when tea cost 11d a pound to produce. By 1913, 8,000 Jackson rolling machines did the work of 1,500,000 coolies and the price of tea had been cut to 2½ or 3d a pound. While a pound of tea had previously needed eight pounds of good timber, converted into charcoal, to dry it, Jackson's machines could run on any wood, grass or refuse.[30] Such innovation in India wreaked further economic destruction in China.

By 1888 Britain was importing more tea from India than China. China was to be destroyed as the prime tea producer for the Western world. The peasant farmers, porters with crates on their backs, agents and dockers that Robert Fortune and William Melrose encountered in China were thrown out of work, adding to the Chinese Empire's ills as the British Empire profited.

Despite successes in Assam with native Indian tea, planting the China *jat* in British India remained an obsession. The 20,000 plants that Robert Fortune had brought back from China had been carefully transplanted in India, and in certain terrains they flourished. Dr William Jameson was given permission to establish a tea nursery at Ayer Toli, near Byznath in the North-Western Provinces. He quickly realised that it was an ideal environment for the China *jat*. 'The cultivation of the tea plant is destined ultimately to change the feature of the hill provinces, and render them as valuable to the state, as those of the plains,' he reported. 'The finer kinds of tea plants, introduced by the government through Mr Fortune from the northern districts of China . . . have been distributed throughout the whole of the districts, and have yielded a large supply of seeds for the ensuing season.'[31]

Tea had now migrated from the low country of Assam and the Brahmaputra Valley to the foothills of the Himalayas.

The wild, jungle-cloaked hillsides began to be cleared to make way for the neatly terraced slopes of tea gardens. It had been the tenacious Scot John Forbes Royle who first proposed the north-west Himalayas as a possible tea-growing region. Royle had been born in India but educated in Haddington and Edinburgh High School before studying medicine and joining the East India Company as an assistant surgeon. He fetched up in Calcutta in 1819 and first travelled to the North-Western Provinces as a Bengal Army doctor, where he indulged his passion for botany and geology. His pastime became his profession when he became superintendent of Saharanpur Botanical Garden and became influential in economic botany – not least the recognition of the Himalayas as potential tea country. In fact, he was so obsessed with the idea that he wrote to the government recommending it in 1827, 1831, 1832, 1833 and 1834.

Tea was now spreading to the very outer limits of British India. It was in this contested and airy province that yet another adventurous Scottish doctor would sow the seeds for what would gain world renown as 'the Champagne of tea'.

CHAPTER 5

The Place of Thunderbolts

Assam is an unlikely parcel of land. Lying below the eastern Himalayas, it is only attached to the body of India by what is known as the 'Chicken's Neck', a fourteen-mile-wide corridor between Nepal and Bangladesh. Bangladesh, as part of Pakistan, was wrenched from former British India by civil war and bloody Partition, and India's old rivals, China and Myanmar, are too close to India for political and military comfort. Astride the chicken's vulnerable neck sprawls the vibrant city of Siliguri. As the gateway to remote north-east India it is an important transport hub and military base, and the two functions are closely intertwined.

We flew into Bagdogra Airport, an Indian Air Force base that hosts a civil enclave. It was an arrival of contrasts. On the runway, technicians tended armed fighter-jets while our guide greeted us with a deep *namaste* and garlands of flowers. The other passengers looked on with curiosity as to whom should merit such treatment. 'This must be what it's like to be Posh and Becks,' said my wife. 'More like John and Yoko,' I thought, showing my age, as a garland was slipped over my neck.

We had a long and winding road ahead of us, for our destination was not Assam but another great tea area – Darjeeling, the world's finest and most renowned. The two revered but deeply contrasting tea regions of India lie cheek by jowl. Siliguri, the gateway to the sultry Assam lowlands, is only just over 40 miles from airy and temperate Darjeeling. We made the journey partly by road and partly – just for the joy of it – by the famous toy train, the Darjeeling Himalayan Railway. We boarded at Ghum – at 7,407 feet, the highest railway station in India (about 3,000 feet higher than Ben Nevis) – but only after visiting the tribute to Scottish engineering that is Ghum's Rail Museum. The shiny brass plates on steam locomotives bear the stamps of the North British Locomotive Company's 'Atlas Works' and 'Queen's Park Works', both in Glasgow. The Scottish-built engines plied a Scottish-engineered track, as Gillanders, Arbuthnot and Co. – the enterprising Scottish tea house – had expanded and diversified enough by 1878 to take on construction of the line.

We checked into the colonial splendour of the Elgin Hotel, which had once been the summer palace of a maharaja and is now all oak floors, prints and photographs from the time of the Raj, with turbaned waiters who look as if they belong to that era too. There was an open fire in our room which, as it was February, was welcome. The next day we began to explore: the Peshok Tea Garden; the craft workshops at the Tibetan Refugee Centre; the Leaf & Life Tea Co-op; and St Andrew's Church, the foundation stone of which was laid in 1843, just three years after a pioneering Scotsman founded the town. Inside were plaques to Darjeeling tea planters: Alexander MacKenzie MacDonald, died 1874; Donald McIver Murray, died 1882; Robert Douglas Mackie, died 1931 ... and so on. When we visited, the church was apparently at the centre of a dispute between two Presbyterian sects as to which of them owned it. How very Scottish.

Darjeeling lies at a mere 6,700 feet in the 'lesser Himalayas', skulking beneath the jagged peaks of Kangchenjunga, the world's third-highest mountain. Sacred to Buddhists, the summit of Kangchenjunga may no longer be 'assaulted' by climbers, but many an attempt on Everest has been launched from Darjeeling, including that by the ill-fated Mallory and Irving in 1924. From the comfort of the town even just the sight of Kangchenjunga was enough to take our breath away. Darjeeling was built as Calcutta's hill station, a temperate place for enervated British officers and officials to escape from the ferocious summer heat of the city. Wandering around, the British influence is clear: the town square, colonial-style buildings, churches, a public school and a planters' club.

Before the coming of a handful of East India Company employees, the area's dense and sloping forests were only home to scattered tribal villages of – according to the botanist Joseph Hooker, who visited the region in 1848 – Lepchas, Moormis, Tibetans, Limboos and Mechis. The land had long been fought over by the Kingdom of Sikkim and the Gorkhas of Nepal but, by the beginning of the nineteenth century, the Gorkhas had got the upper hand. The Gorkhas, however, had made enemies of the British and the two martial races' conflicting ambitions brought about the Gurkha War of 1814. Defeated, Nepal was forced to cede the captured territory where Darjeeling now stands – not to Sikkim, from which they had taken it, but to the victorious East India Company. John Company later restored the land to Sikkim, but soon realised that *Dorje Ling* – 'the place of thunderbolts' – was highly desirable. Its climate was attractive, it would make an admirable sanatorium for the Company's soldiers and it was strategically important. The ridge was an eyrie from which to watch over Sikkim, and command trade and dealings with Nepal and Bhutan. The *dorje* of the place-name may refer to the mystic thunderbolts of Lamaist belief, but Darjeeling became a place from which British thunderbolts could defend the northern frontier of the Empire. A deal was done to lease land from the Chogyal, or 'righteous ruler', of Sikkim. The question as to whether this

'Deed of Grant' entitled the British to rule over the inhabitants who lived on the land, or just build houses on it, would
quickly become the source of friction – but, might being
right to the Honourable Company, Darjeeling had joined the
British Empire. Enter yet another Scottish doctor, Archibald
Campbell.

Archibald Campbell was born on the Inner Hebridean island
of Islay in 1805, the sixth of eleven children raised by parents
Archibald and Helen. Archibald senior was the tacksman of
Ardmore in the parish of Kildalton, on the ragged easterly
coast. A tacksman was a 'sub-laird', a gentleman who leased a
large area of a landowner's estate and sublet parcels of it to
lesser tenants, and Campbell was significant enough to serve
on, and in 1814 preside over, Islay's Stent Committee, a local
'parliament' of gentlemen who imposed taxes (or 'stents') on
the islanders for various public works.

Close to what was the Campbell home at Ardmore stands
Islay's famous Kildalton Cross, an eighth-century carved Celtic
masterpiece, and the ruins of the medieval parish church, beside
which the graves of Campbells of Ardmore can still be seen,
although the kirk where Archibald Campbell of Darjeeling
was baptised was in nearby Lagavulin. The register of births
for the parish suggests that Archibald and Helen Campbell
waited until 1821 to have their eleven children baptised, all
on the same day. Back then parish ministers were occasionally sloppy in their record-keeping and sometimes had to play
'catch-up', but, more commonly, a mass christening would take
place after a minister convinced the erring parents of a family
of unbaptised children to remedy the situation.[1]

Lagavulin was an important community, boasting merchants and a distillery (legal since 1816) that produces a

Right. A ubiquitous Indian tea stall. Latecomers to tea-drinking, Indians now drink more black tea than the rest of the world combined.

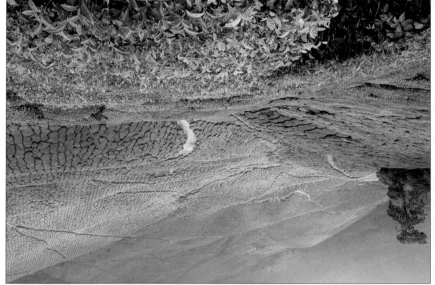

Right. The Scottish Cemetery, Calcutta. The last resting place of many a soldier, trader, tea planter and their families.

Below. A tea estate in the Western Ghats, on the border of Kerala.

A James Finlay estate manager and workers as they plant young bushes in the early 1900s. (Courtesy of James Finlay & Company)

Chests of tea are loaded onto bullock carts in the early 1900s. (Courtesy of James Finlay & Company)

A Wardian case at the Chelsea Physic Garden. These cases revolutionised plant-collecting.

Camellia sinensis in flower. (Jenni Minto)

A bamboo mountain travelling chair of the type used by Robert Fortune in China.

The tea-rolling process, as witnessed by Fortune in 1843.

Robert Fortune, who travelled in disguise in China and brought tea plants to the British Empire.

The river at 'Shanghae', described by Fortune as the great gate to the Chinese empire.

James Taylor's original tea bushes, planted in 1867 and still thriving at Loolecondera estate, Sri Lanka.

Field no. 7, Loolecondera.

A Walkers' tea roller in the Ceylon Tea Museum. John and William Walker worked for James Finlay & Company in Scotland before founding their engineering company in Sri Lanka.

Sri Lankan tea ready for export. (Jenni Minto)

Tamil tea pickers near Kandy, Sri Lanka.

The ruins of the house that James Taylor built for himself at Loolecondera.

James Taylor's grave in Kandy. His estate workers carried his coffin eighteen miles from Loolecondera to his final resting place.

Examining the records of the Garrison Cemetery, Kandy. Of 450 Europeans buried there, only eleven of them lived to be over fifty. Caretaker Charles Carmichael, a Sri Lankan of Scots descent, stands in the background.
(Jenni Minto)

James Taylor and Thomas Lipton. For countless working-class Scots 'tea' became Lipton's Ceylon tea – and Ceylon's tea was James Taylor's tea.

Mary Ann Imlah, 'Ma' Brown, the daughter of a Scots coffee planter from a Ceylon estate and wife of Henry Brown. (Courtesy of the Society of Malawi)

Henry Brown's grave in the rich, red soil of the Thornwood estate in present day Malawi, where the shoots of Africa's gigantic tea industry first sprouted. (Mexter Mfungulo)

Monica Griesbaum of Windy Hollow tea estate at Trinity Gask, near Auchterarder.

Author drinking tea with grower Susie Walker-Munro. (Jenni Minto)

Susie Walker-Munro, Kinnettles Farm, Angus. (Jenni Minto)

distinctive, complex and smoky whisky to this day. Gentlemen farmers there spent 'almost the whole of their time rearing good black cattle'. Cattle, horses and linen yarn were shipped out of the parish, and meal, salt, sugar and tea were among the goods probably landed at Lagavulin.[2]

Campbell of Ardmore had an heir (John, born in 1801) and a spare (William, born in 1803), so young Archibald would have to make his own way in the world. In this era Islay was haemorrhaging people, especially young men. Many went to the Lowlands for work, while others left for America and other foreign climes, but when young Archibald left Islay it was to study at Glasgow and then Edinburgh universities. The *Old Statistical Account* shows that there were two schools in Kildalton Parish at the beginning of the nineteenth century and it was one of these that gave Archibald the grounding that he needed to flourish. Although Campbell was of 'the better sort' of islander, he would have been a fluent Gaelic speaker and may well have dreamed of a *cupa tì air a deagh-tharraing* (a well-brewed cup of tea) on his arduous Indian journeys. Edinburgh University's records show that he graduated in medicine in 1827; his thesis (written in Latin) had been on *De Cynanche Tracheali* – spasmodic laryngitis, or croup, a condition seen mainly in children. Later that year Campbell joined the East India Company as an assistant surgeon. Archibald's father – no doubt pleased to see his third son gainfully employed – may well have echoed the words of Sir Walter Scott, who wrote around this time: 'India is the corn chest for Scotland where our poor gentry must send our younger sons as we send our black cattle to the south.'

June 1828 found young Campbell stationed with the elite Bengal Horse Artillery at Meerut, 'a strong corps of Europeans and natives', with which he served for four years before being appointed surgeon at Kathmandu in Nepal. The British Resident in Kathmandu was the foremost Oriental scholar

Brian Houghton Hodgson, a gifted naturalist and ethnologist. Hodgson inspired Campbell's passion for the Himalayas, while Campbell also impressed Hodgson with his intelligence and diligence. The following year the young Scot was made Assistant Resident. 'Resident' is an innocuous-sounding name for what was, in effect, a political puppet-master who imposed a form of indirect British rule. Campbell learned Nepalese and his work with Hodgson brought him praise from Lord Auckland, India's governor-general, for his zeal and ability, and the progress he had made in 'conquering Nipalese [sic] prejudices by means of medical skill and kindness.'[3] In 1893 the 'intelligent and zealous' Islayman was chosen to accompany a commission to investigate a five-year border dispute with Sikkim. The success of the mission was, according to a letter from the governor-general, 'mainly attributable to the judgement and address displayed by Dr. Campbell in the conduct of the delicate and difficult duties confided to him'.

In 1840 Campbell was made superintendent of the new British outpost at Darjeeling and was effectively responsible for playing 'the great game' in the region. Sikkim was bordered by Nepal, and the warlike Nepalese Gorkhas coveted the little state which depended on Britain for protection and Campbell's watchful eye.

> The importance of this post may be imagined when it is considered, that were it once given up, the Nipalese would take not it only, but the whole Himalaya extending to the extremity of Upper Assam, and thus secure to this bellicose race an almost impregnable position of many hundreds of miles in extent, from which they would have threatened all of Bengal and Assam whenever so disposed.[4]

Darjeeling lay a two-month journey by bullockcart, horse

and foot from Calcutta, but Campbell energetically began to develop his little mountain fiefdom in the British manner – building roads, European-style houses, a hotel and a bazaar. People from Nepal, Bhutan and Sikkim began to settle there and within a decade the population rose from fewer than a hundred to about 10,000. Like the Scottish doctors we encountered in the Calcutta Botanical Gardens, Archibald Campbell had a lively, enquiring mind and wide interests. He published papers on a vast range of subjects, including native languages, rural economy, the musical instruments of the Nepalese, earthquakes, the proboscis of the elephant, the elevation of the Himalayan peaks, the cultivation of tea . . . and many more.

The year after his arrival in Darjeeling, which was also the year of his marriage, Campbell planted tea of both the China and Assam *jats* in his garden at Beachwood in Darjeeling. Both that year's projects proved fruitful. He set Darjeeling on course to become the most prestigious tea country in the world, and the thirty-five-year-old's marriage to the twenty-year-old daughter of a fellow doctor produced twelve children, nine of whom outlived him.

His interest in botany was the likely catalyst for a close friendship with a distinguished visitor, the naturalist Joseph Hooker, who had been encouraged to explore Sikkim by Hugh Falconer of the Calcutta Botanical Garden and partly financed to do so by the British government. It is for his three-year plant-hunting expedition in the Himalayas that Hooker is most revered by botanists.

Hooker arrived in Darjeeling in 1848 only to find that the Raja of Sikkim hadn't given him permission to cross into his kingdom, so he used his time to study the local flora and get to know Campbell. The two men – both doctors with strong West Highland connections – had a lot in common. When Hooker did finally make his first visit into the mountains of

Sikkim, he returned to Darjeeling with eight porter-loads of specimens to be sent to Kew.[5]

In April 1849 Campbell wrote, in the governor-general's name, to the Raja of Sikkim, informing him that Hooker now wished to make a second and longer expedition to 'the loftier parts of Sikkim'. Grudging permission – much delayed – was eventually received and on 3 May Hooker and his party of forty-two, made up mostly of indigenous Lepchas and Sikkim-born Tibetans, left Darjeeling. Campbell, along with five sepoy guards and an interpreter, accompanied the group as far as Sikkim's frontier on the Great Rangeet River. The expedition's daily intake of rice was eighty pounds, equivalent to one man's load, and as it was difficult for extra provisions to reach the expedition Hooker was reduced to rationing each man to a pound of rice a day, sometimes less. He eked out the meagre allowance with a few ounces of preserved meats and occasionally 'splicing the main brace with weak rum and water'.

Despite the short rations, Hooker continued to explore into October and rejoiced to meet up again with his friend, who had undergone a trying journey from Darjeeling. Hooker thought Campbell looked 'much the worse for his trying journey'.

> I know no greater trial of the constitution than the exposure and hard exercise that is necessary in traversing these valleys, below 5,000 feet, in the rainy season: delay is dangerous, and the heat, anxiety, and bodily suffering from fatigue, insects and bruises banish sleep, and urge the restless traveller to higher and more healthy regions.[6]

Campbell was lucky to have made it at all. Just days before, while negotiating a narrow mountain track, the pony he had been riding had slipped over a precipice and fallen to its death – 'dashed to pieces', Hooker reported. Campbell had only saved his life by adroitly slipping from the saddle as soon as he felt the animal's foot give way.

Campbell was on a diplomatic mission and 'had proceeded to Sikkim with the purpose of bringing about a better state of affairs between the British government and that state than could be effected from Darjeeling'. He and Hooker had been instructed not to cross Sikkim's sensitive border with Tibet, but on 7 November 1849 they disobeyed that order. The writer Thomas Pakenham, who travelled to Sikkim in the footsteps of Hooker, believes the distinguished botanist 'behaved like a crazy sixteen-year-old' when he crossed into Tibet and provoked his and Campbell's arrest.[7] To Darjeeling historian Basant B. Lama, it was 'the ultimate travesty' and 'the proverbial last straw' in Sikkim's relationship with the Brits.[8]

Joseph Hooker wrote that the pair was roughly marched back into Sikkim by a mixture of Tibetan and Sikkim sepoys, and that the Sikkimese began to threaten Campbell:

> ... they behaved very rudely, and when still half a mile from the Sikkim frontier, jostled him and feigned to draw their knives, and one of them pointed a spear-headed bow to his breast. Campbell defended himself with a stick, and remonstrated with them on their rudeness; and I, who had nothing but a barometer in my hand, called up the Tibetans. The Dingpun [commander] came instantly, and driving the Sikkim people forward, escorted us to the frontier.[9]

However, Lama claims that 'Campbell in his anger flayed his fists at his "captors" and the Sikkimese guards in turn were compelled to physically restrain him'. While Lama is a doughty anti-imperialist, he may be stretching credibility by suggesting that a company of armed sepoys might have had much difficulty in restraining a middle-aged Scotsman. It also seems out of character for the politically astute Campbell, whose reputation was that he was 'liberal in his views on all matters and adverse to disputation though tenacious of his opinions'. On the border, Hooker writes, the Tibetan Dingpun explained that his jurisdiction ended there, saluted and left the Europeans in the hands of the Sikkimese. That night, Campbell left an overcrowded hut they had been billeted in to pitch tents. He had not long gone when Hooker heard a sudden cry for help.

> He had scarcely left when I hear him calling loudly to me, 'Hooker! Hooker! The savages are murdering me!' I rushed to the door and caught sight of him striking out with his fists, and struggling violently; being tall and powerful, he had already prostrated a few, but, a host of men bore him down, and appeared to be trampling on him; at the same moment I was myself seized by eight men, who forced me back into the hut, and down on the log, where they held me in a sitting posture, pressing me against the wall; here I spent a few moments of agony, as I heard my friend's stifled cries grow fainter and fainter. I struggled but little, and that only at first, for at least five-and-twenty men crowded round and laid their hands upon me, rendering any effort to move useless . . .[10]

Lama gives a different account of this struggle, in which 'the poor Sikkimese soldiers, unable to understand the English language, politely shoved a fully loaded hubble-bubble "Hookah" into Campbell's mouth. Pity they shoved it up the wrong end. They wanted to smoke the truth from him I suppose.' Such clear detestation of Campbell on Lama's part may call into question his version of events.

Hooker reports that he himself wasn't seriously ill-treated but that Campbell was bound hand-and-foot, beaten and tortured by having his neck bent to his chest almost to breaking point and having the cords around his wrists painfully tightened with a bamboo wrench. His life was then threatened with the ominous hand-across-the-throat gesture. The explanation given to Hooker was that the Raja was dissatisfied with Campbell's conduct during the past twelve years. Attempts were made to make Campbell sign documents limiting British powers over Sikkim, and the Dewan (prime minister) clearly believed that by taking Campbell hostage he could exert some power over the British. Hooker was offered his liberty but chose to remain with his friend. He eventually managed to contact Lord Dalhousie, the new governor-general of India, whom Hooker had stayed with on his way to Darjeeling. Dalhousie immediately dispatched a regiment to the border. This was too much for the Raja, who ordered the Dewan to release Campbell and Hooker. Hooker reported that when he first saw Campbell after his torture, 'He was sadly bruised about the head, arms, and wrists, walked very lame, and had a black eye to boot, but was looking stout and confident.' On Christmas Eve the two erring trespassers made it back to Darjeeling. In gratitude for the governor-general's intervention, Hooker later named the *Rhododendron dalhousiae* after him and named the magnificent *Magnolia campbellii* after his fellow captive, Archibald Campbell.

The escapade didn't turn out too well for the Raja of Sikkim. While the British government believed that Campbell was partly to blame for his own troubles, British prestige required a response. The following year the East India Company used the friction to justify the annexation of more than 600 square miles of the Raja's little country. After a short war with Bhutan, Kalimpong and the Dooars foothills, the narrow strip of land that ties Assam to West Bengal, were also added to 'Campbell's kingdom' – giving the Darjeeling area its current size and shape. As for the Dewan, Hooker reported that he '[is] disgraced and turned out of office, is reduced to poverty, and is deterred from entering Tibet by the threat of being dragged to Lhassa with a rope round his neck.'

Despite his trespassing escapade, Hooker's 1849 expedition had been a triumph and the success of it credited jointly to Hooker and Campbell:

> They were able to bring back important results, both geographical and botanical. Their survey of hitherto unexplored regions was published by the Calcutta Trigonometrical Survey Office, and their botanical observations formed the basis of elaborate works on the rhododendrons of the Sikkim Himalaya and on the flora of India.[11]

Hooker returned to Calcutta, arriving by boat at the botanic garden's *ghat* on the Hooghly River to be met by the hospitality of Dr Hugh Falconer. When he got to England in 1851, his father, William, had just been made the director of Kew Gardens, a post that Joseph himself would take over in 1865 and occupy for twenty years. Under William and Joseph Hooker, Kew became world-renowned. Campbell remained superintendent of Darjeeling for twenty-two years, during which time the settlement grew rapidly. He also saw his tea experiments flourish. In the airy Himalayas the China *jat* thrived as it had never done in lower climes.

> It was soon found that the plant throve readily at this altitude and others began to follow Dr. Campbell's example, seed being distributed by the Government by those who desired to cultivate the plant.[12]

Virgin forests were felled, the ground cleared and terraced, and the landscape familiar to modern visitors to Darjeeling began to emerge, with tea replacing natural vegetation except in high and remote areas, and a sharp decline in biodiversity. By 1856 there were thirty-nine tea gardens with 10,000 acres under cultivation. Today there are more than eighty tea gardens in the seven valleys of Darjeeling. Ones like Bannockburn and Glendale serve as working memorials to the Scots who first cleared, planted and named them.

In 1860, more than a decade after enduring his roughing up by the Sikkimese sepoys, Campbell led a small invasion of Sikkim to annex land and obtain 'satisfaction for insults and injures done to British subjects and for violation of British territory'. His ill-equipped force of just 130 men was surprised and routed, and Campbell fled back to Darjeeling with British prestige and his own reputation being dragged through the mud behind him. With the Indian Mutiny just two years in the past, such loss of face could not be tolerated by the British Empire and a force of 2,000 men, along with rocket launchers and a mountain gun, successfully conquered Sikkim with little fighting. At this stage, Britain had no desire to annex the country, but 'Restoring prestige demanded victory', concludes one historian of the region.[13]

The once-lauded Campbell was now out of favour, and in 1862 he left Darjeeling and retired to London, where he continued to take a lively and active interest in anthropology, the hill station he had founded, tea and Eastern affairs. In 1866 Joseph Hooker wrote to Charles Darwin requesting medical advice on behalf of Campbell's twenty-two-year-old daughter, who had been ill for several years. Helen Maria was now unable to keep food down and Hooker feared that she was 'at death's door'. Hooker was deeply concerned, telling Darwin that the girl 'was for 8 years under my charge while her parents were in India', so revealing the endurance of a friendship that he and Campbell had first forged in the Himalayas eighteen years previously.[14]

Archibald Campbell later moved from Notting Hill with his family to Slough, where he died in 1874. His obituary not only paid tribute to his efforts as a tea pioneer, but also as a player of the 'great game.'

> The ultimate result of his example will be the constitution of new English kingdoms in the healthy mountain regions of the Himalayas, which will become fresh centres of civilisation, barriers against Russia's aggressions, and safeguard against revolt on the plains. His active attention to the introduction of tea experiments in Darjeeling was at length rewarded by the establishment of an extensive culture, the produce which has obtained a distinct recognition in the London Market.[15]

So, what made Darjeeling so successful? In short, the soil, climate and altitude all conspired to make great tea. Tea needs sun – but not too much. The high Himalayas attract enough cloud to make sure that the plants are never frazzled. Tea needs rain – but not too much. Darjeeling gets around 150 inches a year, but the sloping gardens make sure that the roots of the plants are well-drained. As for the soil, Joseph Hooker commented that in the landscape's natural state 'it is difficult to conceive a grander mass of vegetation'. The slightly acid, organic-rich loam – carefully tended by planters and workers who know what they are doing – is ideal for growing fine tea. Tea bushes tolerate the cold, and a February morning expedition to Tiger Hill to watch sunrise over Mount Everest and Kanchenjunga provides a sharp lesson in how cold it can get. While the high-altitude chill had us shivering, it also deters many pests that plague lower tea regions.

Today Darjeeling produces just about 1 per cent of India's teas, with around 48,000 acres under cultivation which, as writer Jeff Koehler points out, is no bigger than the Queen's Balmoral Estate. At this altitude, growth is slow, which limits production but concentrates taste, yielding a complex, almost floral liquor that fills the mouth with flavour but doesn't require milk to tame it. It is the ideal accompaniment to the meal that bears the drink's name, afternoon tea. The tea is hand-picked, much of it is organic, some even biodynamic. Some bushes may be a century old and while these older plants are less productive, many tea drinkers believe them to produce deeper flavour. The plants themselves are mostly kin to Robert Fortune's *Camellia sinensis*, tea of the China *jat*, although there is some *assamica* on hand, and locally bred cultivars. Darjeeling's tea gardens have now branched out into tourism, offering tastings and accommodation. This has an interesting parallel in the whisky distilleries on Campbell's home island of Islay, where shops, cafés, branded clothing and souvenirs have now pimped-up what was once just thought of as an industrial process. Tourists also find that the climate that first attracted Europeans to the place of thunderbolts suits them well, particularly after visiting hot and steamy Calcutta.

Explorers, natural-history-obsessed doctors and pioneer planters have dominated these pages so far, but now it is time to meet a Scottish tea baron – one of the men who turned tea into gold.

Both the carrot and the stick drove Scots to the Indian tea party. The chaos caused by the outbreak of the American Civil War in 1861 turned the attention of the Glasgow business James Finlay & Company towards India. Its profits, not to mention the jobs of its large workforce, depended on finding an alternative source of raw cotton for the three water-driven mills that had been purchased early in the century by the company's founder, Kirkman Finlay: Ballindalloch Mill (on the River Endrick), Catrine (on the Ayr) and Deanston (on the Teith).

At the helm of the company at this time was Glasgow-born John Muir. In the year the Civil War broke out, Muir had joined Finlay's as a partner with a modest shareholding, but such was his zeal and vision that, by 1883, he owned it outright. While Kirkman Finlay had traded through Bombay in 1816, it was Muir who fully grasped the possibilities of the Indian trade, and between 1862 and 1901 James Finlay & Company opened branches in Bombay, Calcutta, Karachi, Colombo and Chittagong. Muir founded the Champdany Jute Company, which employed up to 5,000 workers in two Bengal mills, but his greatest business venture was tea. It started modestly with a small shipment of eighty chests of Indian tea from Calcutta to New York in 1872.

Ignoring the naysayers that surrounded him, Muir began boldly buying up tea gardens and quickly amassed a £4.6 million portfolio of companies that were ultimately managed from the firm's new headquarters at 22 West Nile Street – the Consolidated Tea and Lands Company (founded 1896), the Amalgamated Tea Estates Company (1896), the Kanan Devan Hills Produce Company (1897) and the Anglo-American Direct Tea Trading Company (1898). Finlay's had become one of the largest tea traders in the world, and it remains a staple part of the group's business. It currently has 27,000 hectares of land around the world under tea – an equivalent to more than 44,000 football pitches.

A strong Free Churchman, Muir was a generous philanthropist, supporting charities in India and Scotland, and his energy, wealth and influence allowed him to work for the city of his birth. For three years he served on Glasgow town council, before becoming lord provost in 1889. He was vice-president of the city's 1888 Great Exhibition, at which he ran the India and Ceylon section. He was a leading figure in the raising of Kelvingrove Museum and Art Gallery and knighted in 1892. Sir John Muir had looked East and steered Finlay's well out of its traditional comfort zone of spinning cotton in Scotland, but the company's official history admits 'the responsible heads of the firm in India were chary of plunging too deeply into this attractive but risky speculation'. But of Sir John it says, 'His foresight in expanding his Company's activities to tea in North and South India and Ceylon was not fully apparent until after his death. Where he had sown others have reaped in bountiful measure.'

While Sir John Muir took enormous financial risks, his planters risked much more. Opening up land for tea planting was a laborious and dangerous job. Sir Leybourne Davidson, who rose to become general manager of Finlay's South India estates, recalled his days as a young planter in Ceylon. The road to his estate led through a leech-infested swamp and rice fields through which he had to wade, waist-deep. Home was a thatched hut with a mud floor. There were no roads, only tracks, and transport was by coolie porterage. Very often food and supplies didn't arrive. There were earthquakes, cyclones and floods, and the threat of wild animals. Plantation life was one of danger, discomfort and disease.

Sir John Muir's demanding standards outlived him, and Finlay's expected high standards of commitment and efficiency from its managers. A thick leather-bound tome in Finlay & Co.'s archive at Glasgow University contains the handwritten reports by the superintendents on the conduct of the company's planters in the early years of the twentieth century. From it we learn that Mr Griffith was 'a sober, quiet fellow, not brilliant'; that Mr Fraser was 'a good man on a garden ... but does not shine at officework'; and that Mr MacLeod had been 'under the influence of liquor and unfit for work' (a charge he strenuously denied). Many of the entries deal with routine applications for furloughs, promotion, transfers between estates and requests for pay rises, but sometimes serious failings are revealed. The inability of one planter to stop coolies from absconding prompted this letter from the Calcutta office:

> We regret to inform you that we have for some time past received very indifferent accounts of your management at Tuskurri and especially your handling of the labour force. The loss of labour from the garden recently has been very heavy and we have therefore been compelled to arrange for an immediate change of management. We thereby give you notice of dismissal under Clause VIII of your arrangement and you will kindly arrange to vacate your quarters on the estate on or before the 30th inst. Mr Hickman will pay you three months salary in lieu of notice . . .

Scottish planters didn't only plant tea seed. Even after the Second World War, tea companies still had strict rules against anyone lower than a senior manager bringing a wife with him from Britain. It meant a lonely life for planters, isolated in their bungalows, far from friends or neighbours, and often cut off entirely during the rainy season. Well out of sight of missionaries, memsahib and other pillars of respectability, many planters found local women to sleep with from among their estate workers. While some strong and tender relationships were formed,* many women were subjected to virtual sexual slavery and were discarded, along with any children they had borne, when the planter was moved to another estate, returned home or transferred his affections to another. In the

---

* We shall examine such a case in the Ceylon chapter of this book.

tea gardens of Darjeeling, the fact that these fatherless children were a Scottish problem is implied by the fact the partial remedy was also a Scottish one – a Church of Scotland minister.

Dr John Graham had arrived in India, bound for Kalimpong and Darjeeling, as a missionary in March 1889. His task was to reach out to various tribes and peoples of Sikkim, Nepal, Bhutan and Tibet, but Graham soon encountered a 'lost tribe' – the mixed-race children of white planters and local women. Dr Graham recalled visiting planters' bungalows and seeing little light-skinned children being spirited out of sight of the padre sahib. Graham, who had plans to build an industrial school for Nepalese children, decided that it should also be open to the mixed-race children he encountered.[16] That school, Dr Graham's Homes, situated behind a metal gate in the form of a giant saltire amid beautiful grounds high above the bustling market town of Kalimpong, is still going to this day, although educating a much wider range of children.

In the early days of Empire, many whites took Indian wives, or *bibis*. The British Resident in Delhi, David Ochterlony, 'lived the life of a Mughal gentleman', and every evening paraded around Delhi followed by his thirteen wives, each on her own elephant. Scots were by no means immune to the charms of beautiful Indian women. James Achilles Kirkpatrick, British Resident in Hyderabad, fell in love with a Mughal princess, converted to Islam and transferred his loyalty from the East India Company to the Nizam of Hyderabad, whom he was supposed to be controlling. Ochterlony was the Boston-born son of a Highland Scot who returned to Britain after the American Revolution, while Kirkpatrick was the grandson of a Jacobite who fled to South Carolina after the 1715 rebellion. They were not alone in having Indian wives and mixed-race children. William Dalrymple discovered that in the 1780s more than a third of East India Company men left money and possessions in their wills to Indian wives and children.[17] But a cataclysmic event changed forever the relationship between white Brits and Indians.

The Indian Mutiny, or Rebellion, of 1857–58 was a patchy affair, with much of the country remaining calm and many Indian troops staying loyal to the Raj. But the atrocities carried out by both sides, during and after it, poisoned the British–Indian relationship. John Griffiths suggests that in the early pre-mutiny days of the tea industry the rapport between the white managers and their Indian workers was generally good, and that the Europeans mixed well with the native communities in which they found themselves.[18] The mutual fear and suspicion that followed the mutiny grew worse as Victorian values infiltrated East. In the mid-nineteenth century, steamships cut the journey time to India, and the opening of the Suez Canal in 1869 made the journey even shorter. The arrival from Britain of 'the fishing fleet' – marriageable, young women looking for husbands* – and the consequent rise of the *memsahib*, meant that 'never the twain shall meet' when it came to sexual and even social relationships between brown and white – at least not within the bounds of respectability. Whites were to become the new 'caste' – British brahmins, imposing their position at the pinnacle of the ancient Indian hierarchy, with the Indians now seen as an inferior and subject race.

To escape from the sweltering heat of the plains, the British created hill stations in the image of little English towns where brown faces were never those of senior army officers, rich merchants, professional men, intellectuals or high-ranking government officials, but of servants. At the heart of every hill station was 'the club'.

---

* Tea planter's wife Iris Macfarlane observed that quite a few of them were 'less than brilliant, the plump, the pimply and the plainly unmarriageable'.

... when one looked at the club – a dumpy one-storey wooden building – one looked at the real centre of town. In any city in India the European Club is the spiritual citadel, the real seat of the British power, the Nirvana for which the native officials and millionaires pine in vain.[19]

Even remote areas had such establishments where planters and their families could gather and socialise. Although 'whiteness' permitted admittance, the clubs operated a systematic snobbery not unlike the caste system. From governors down through senior army officers to 'box wallahs' (businessmen or shopkeepers), there was a clear hierarchy among the white tribe. But snobbish and racist though they might be, they were an oasis of familiar British comfort for men and women in the far corners of Empire. Iris Macfarlane, who would become an insightful writer, had high expectations of such a club when her husband, 'Mac', from a Gigha family in the Inner Hebrides, took over the management of an Assam estate in the 1940s, just after the war. After eight weeks on the estate the family piled into a newly acquired, but ancient, Hillman Minx and ventured out into the steamy afternoon.

As my crispness collapsed into damp, bedraggled disarray, I cheered myself up with the thought of the club. I pictured polished floors, flower arrangements, chintzy sofas, tea trays and iced drinks carried by servants in white coats and cummerbunds. I thought of a library, a card room, a children's playroom, I thought in fact of the clubs I had known on the other side of India where magistrates, forestry officers, policemen had mixed with doctors and colonels to talk about jobs and hobbies. Their wives sketched a bit, sailed skilfully, were keen gardeners and bridge players. The club for all its petty cliques and established racism was quite a civilised place. There was friendship and laughter and relaxation there.[20]

Iris was deeply disappointed. Instead of the 'interesting Empire Builders' she had known in more sophisticated clubs, here in Assam there was 'nothing but planters, all of a red-faced, thick-legged, sweaty Scottish variety'. The men went straight to the bar. The women, none of whom had brought children, sat on wicker chairs ... and sat ... and sat. What stood for conversation was a liturgy of complaints about their servants. One planter's wife advised Iris that the servants were 'a pretty primitive race here, not long down from the trees'. In her casual racism the un-named woman went even further than Kipling's *The White Man's Burden*:

> Your new-caught, sullen peoples,
> Half devil and half child.

When her children finally fell asleep, Iris said that she would fetch her husband. The coven of wives was aghast. No woman ever entered the inner sanctum of the bar, but waited patiently until their husbands emerged 'staggering a bit but ready to drive off to their gardens'. That evening Iris returned to her bungalow determined that this would be the last hot season she'd spend in Assam, but in fact spent twenty years in 'this beautiful, vibrant, exhausting, magical country'.

My own experience of 'the club' was quite different from Iris Macfarlane's, but similarly disappointing. The *Lonely Planet Guide* promised us 'day membership' of the Darjeeling Planters Club where we could relax in splendid wicker chairs, drink gin (with an appropriate dose of malaria-dispelling tonic) and play billiards. When we got there the club was open in all its Old World splendour – but was entirely deserted. No members, no tourists, no staff and definitely no gin and tonics. We wandered around the place, unchallenged, looking at trophy-heads on the wall and photographs of old Mount Everest expeditions. Eventually we settled down on the veranda, where we attempted to glimpse the snowy peak of Kanchenjunga through the cloud while listening out for faint echoes of ricocheting billiard balls and the Scottish accents of sweaty planters as they clinked glasses. Such was the might of Darjeeling tea that in this club – unusually – tea-garden managers were at the top of the hierarchical totem pole, ahead of army officers, Indian civil service types and railway men. There was even a hierarchy among alcohol. Beer was drunk up until midday, gin in the afternoon and whisky after sunset.[21]

Now that the British knew tea would flourish in India – and had the men, knowhow, technology and even the social clubs that were required to exploit it – they began to look beyond alluvial Assam and the foothills of the Himalayas. In the south-east of India lies Kerala, the modern Indian state that includes the ancient kingdoms of Travancore and Cochin. Travancore is today a major tea producer, and Scots – some of them East India Company soldiers – were the industry's founding fathers.

Writing in 1892, a forester working for the Travancore government credited one such Scot, Major General William Cullen, for first introducing the tea plant 'many years ago,'[22] and Scots remained the movers and shakers in Travancore tea up to and beyond Indian independence. They may have stayed to grow and manufacture tea, but it was war that first brought Scots to the region.

Standing beneath the walls of the great fortress of Seringapatam, 200 miles inland from Chennai, I began to understand the sheer, brute military power of the East India Company. In my head lurked the military statistics – 50,000 Company soldiers (the majority Scots and sepoys) engaged in a month-long siege against Tipu Sultan's army of 30,000 – but the cannonball-pocked walls and the gaping breach where General David Baird's men poured into the citadel turned the bare bones of history into a gut feeling of palpable power. The British had mustered there, in the final year of the eighteenth century, to destroy Tipu, 'the Tiger of Mysore', a warlike Indian ruler who had allied himself with the French against the Company's encroachment on his rich and powerful kingdom. For General Baird, a Haddington man, it was a grudge match. After a British defeat by Tipu's father, Hyder Ali, Baird had spent more than four years chained up with other captives in a Seringapatam dungeon. His mother is said to have remarked, unsympathetically, 'God help the chiel chained to our Davie.' The dungeon had become a whitewashed tourist attraction by the time I visited it, but it was a filthy hole during Davie Baird's incarceration.

Vain, rich and (according to British history) cruel and despotic, Tipu is today regarded by many Indians as a free-dom fighter and proto-nationalist who was martyred in the cause of anti-imperialism. The place on his battlements where he himself fought and died in the final onslaught – firing sporting guns that were loaded and handed to him by his servants – was marked with flowers, and I watched both Hindus and Muslims file reverently past his tomb, which lies within the walls. I was at Seringapatam to make a documen-tary about Lachlan Macquarie, the Ulva-born Scottish soldier who became governor of New South Wales and 'Father of Australia'. The diplomatic skills Macquarie had brought to his work in Botany Bay were honed during his nineteen years of service in India, which included a spell as military secretary to the governor of Bombay. Macquarie also fought against Tipu, as did many other Highland officers and men, including Colin Macaulay, who would play an important part in the transformation of Travancore jungles into tea gardens.

In 1789 Tipu had attacked the kingdoms of Travancore and Cochin – and, at the hands of the well-armed and disciplined Travancore army, suffered his first defeat. Travancore's highly able and enlightened king, Dharma Raja, was an ally of the East India Company and in 1795 signed a treaty that brought his kingdom under the Company's 'protection'. But Dharma Raja's death three years later brought an ineffectual sixteen year old to the throne – shifting real power into the hands of successive Dewans and British Residents. The first of these Residents was Colin Macaulay, a son of the manse and a grandson of the notorious Lewis clan-chieftain Dòmhnall Cam (among whose feats was the burning and partial destruction of Carloway Broch, which happened to be full of rival Morrison clansmen at the time). Colin Macaulay too had a colourful and dramatic life, having been chained up by Tipu in the black hole of Seringapatam along with David Baird. Macaulay served for thirty years in the Company's army, rose to the rank of general, spoke several languages, was a close friend of the Duke of Wellington and became an MP and an active anti-slavery campaigner. His role as Resident was to ensure that these areas remained favourable to British interests. British 'interests' kept changing. The more John Company got, the more it desired. At first it wanted a trading monopoly over Travancore's produce. Then it demanded a tax-free market for British manufactured goods that, for instance, put local cotton weavers out of business. Finally it sought a place for capitalists to invest money in mines and plantations. But on this occasion the frog knew that it was being slowly boiled. In 1808 Macaulay faced a revolt by the Dewan of Travancore and survived an attempt on his life. The following year Macaulay led 15,000 men in a successful campaign against the rebels.[23]

Another powerful Resident who bent Travancore to John Company's will was Seringapatam veteran John Munro of Teaninich, ninth of that ilk. Munro was born near Alness, in Ross and Cromarty, and at fourteen enlisted as a cadet in the Madras Army of the East India Company. He was promoted to captain in the wake of Tipu's defeat, but Munro was no ordinary sabre-waving warrior. He was an accomplished linguist and, as well as a handful of European languages, he had mastered Arabic, Persian and a number of Indian tongues. In 1810 he was appointed as the Company's puppet-master to Travancore and Cochin, and later Dewan to their Rajas. As such he was a major figure in the opening up of these states to British influence and to Travancore as an eventual major tea region. John had a number of children with native women, including Urban Vigors Munro, who went on to manage Travancore's teak forests. Urban was the father of John Daniel Munro, who founded the state's first tea plantation and is the true father of Travancore tea.

John Munro of Teaninich later married Charlotte Blacker, the sister of an Irish fellow-officer in Madras, and had six children by her, including Stuart Caradoc Munro, who became a tea planter in Ceylon. John Munro retired to Scotland as a major-general in 1819, buying Teaninich estate from his brother (and later inheriting the eponymous whisky distillery his brother founded). A devout Christian, he supported the breakaway faction at the Great Disruption of the Church of Scotland in 1843 and posed for a calotype by pioneer photographers Hill and Adamson as a study for Hill's massive painting that depicts 457 of the movers and shakers of the early

Free Church. Thus, he is the first significant Scot who put the tea in Britain to be photographed. His grandson, John Daniel Munro, would achieve even greater distinction as a tea man. Another extraordinary British puppet-master in Travancore was Major General William Cullen, who was Resident there for two decades from 1820. A professional artillery officer, and a veteran of the Napoleonic wars, Cullen was a man with a deep hinterland. He was the son of an advocate and the grandson of Dr William Cullen, a towering figure of the Scottish Enlightenment who had made Edinburgh University the Western world's leading medical school. Cullen had arrived in India as a nineteen year old and became fascinated by the country, devoting much of his time to the scholarly study of its life, beliefs and culture. Apart from his army service in France, he spent his entire adult life in India, choosing to retire there until his death at the age of seventy-seven. His respect for Indian ways did not go down well with Christian missionaries.

> The British Resident, General Cullen, who had occupied this important post since 1840, though kind and courteous in his manners, generous in his gifts, and scientific in his tastes, was completely under the influence of Brahman favourites, adopted their views, and saw no necessity for missionary labours, or the Christian instruction of the poor. He was thoroughly 'Hindooized' by an uninterrupted residence of nearly fifty years in India.[24]

Cullen was a keen amateur gardener and was prepared to experiment with crops.

> . . . a certain quantity of coffee, cinchona and tea is also grown and exploited. Coffee had been grown in the low country under the heavy shade of jacks and other

trees for many years before the success of the enterprise in Ceylon turned the attention of some Ceylon
planters to the suitability of the hills of Travancore
to the cultivation of that product. General Cullen, a
former Resident, has already opened experimental
gardens at Ashambu and the Velimala hills, and had
been successful, so that when Messers Grant and
Fraser came over from Ceylon in 1864 or 65 the future
success of the enterprise seemed quite assured.[25]

The future for Grant and Fraser did indeed seem assured.
They grew ambitious and began to clear jungle, take over exist-
ing plantations, plant coffee on a grand scale and raise money
from the Caledonian Bank and other investors in Scotland to
fund their expansion. But a devastating disease – an incurable
leaf rust that, as we shall see in Chapter 6, ruined the coffee
planters of Ceylon – now struck Travancore. This, along with
drought and mismanagement, brought the company almost to
collapse. An attempt to diversify into tea – the crop that would
save Ceylon – was to no avail. Perhaps it was just too little, too
late. In October 1897 the Scottish Indian Coffee Company
was voluntarily wound up. The Caledonian Bank eventually
wrote off £30,000 – the loss contributed to its decision to
merge with the Bank of Scotland in 1907.[26] Even for hardy
and ambitious Scotsmen, the life of a planter was fraught
with uncertainty and potential disaster. Meanwhile, the tea in
General Cullen's garden thrived.

I procured plants from Mr Haxam and put them
down in an experimental spice garden which I established some twelve years ago at some 1800 feet on a
hill in the south of Travancore at Oodagherry. They
are now trees of twenty to thirty feet high growing
vigorously; and I have four hundred plants procured

from their seed growing on another hill near the Tinnevelly frontier, at an elevation of 3200 feet. There can be no doubt, therefore, of the facility of its introduction, although from the moderate altitude and great atmospheric moisture of the localities, they may possibly be considered to grow more luxuriously than desirable; but which, of a defect at all, can probably be easily remedied by selecting ground more to the eastward and with less humid climate.[27]

Our base for exploring Kerala – much of the old Kingdom of Travancore – was Munnar, the old hill station that nestles in the rugged Western Ghats, the mountain range that runs parallel to India's Malabar Coast and the Arabian Sea. John Daniel Munro, the grandson of the former Resident, John Munro of Teaninich, was the first European to enter this tribal area, around 1870. John Daniel was the Raja of Travancore's superintendent for cardamom cultivation and was a habitual explorer. He may have entered the region to solve a border dispute and it is not far-fetched to imagine that he fell in love with this beautiful country and realised its potential. He reported 'tea and chinchona [the South American tree from the bark of which quinine is produced] would grow in some of the forests. There are large forests to the extent of many square miles available for these purposes, and there being the great inducement of good climate, it will doubtless not be many years before these fine hills get occupied . . . It only wants capital and energy to bring a large portion of this fine tract of land into cultivation.'

Munro was prepared to put his money where his mouth was. The territory was part of Travancore, but it was the *jenmam* (or birthright land) of the Poonjar royal family, an ancient and once-mighty dynasty that had fallen on hard times. Munro persuaded the impecunious royals to lease him nearly 230 square miles of the land and in 1879 launched the North Travancore Land Planting & Agricultural Society. At first it was coffee, cardamom, cinchona and sisal [a jute-like plant used for cordage] that were planted, but the experiments with tea were proving fruitful. In 1880 planter A.H. Sharp – a Scotsman, according to a Munnar tourist website – cleared twenty hectares of dense jungle and began to plant tea on what is now part of the Sevenmallay Tea Estate, the Tata Tea Company's largest in South India. As leaf rust began to destroy the region's coffee plantations, the new crop was introduced just in time. A witness reported that 'of late, the ravages of leaf disease have been very trying. Tea, therefore, is being largely planted as a second resource, and so far is doing well'.[29]

It was a truth universally acknowledged that the lives of tea planters throughout the empire were primitive and harsh, and the tea pioneers of Travancore were no exception. Their homes were thatched mud-and-wattle huts, surrounded by ditches to stop elephants stomping through them. Tigers were much more common than they are now, but even as recently as 2015 a Kerala tea-estate worker was killed by a man-eater.[30] Like the remedies available to their counterparts in Assam, self-medicated quinine and castor oil were about all the medicine available to Travancore planters. Yet there were men ambitious and dedicated enough to carve tea gardens out of the high forests, and the prediction that John Daniel Munro made in his *High Ranges of Travancore* came true. 'Capital and energy' triumphed. Soon, roads replaced wild elephant tracks, and in 1892 a post office appeared at Devikulam.[31] By 1894 there were about twenty-six estates in the High Range, and four years later Glasgow's James Finlay & Company joined the tea party and formed the Kanan Devan Hills Produce Company.

At the beginning of the twentieth century the town of

Munnar came into being as merchants opened bazaars close to a major Finlay's tea estate. When twenty-one-year-old Dick Tewson was posted there in 1937 his only luxury was a precious gramophone, although he was often too tired to listen to it and went to bed early, having worked outdoors all day in heavy rain. Social life revolved around the High Range Club in Munnar. During the holidays the club had the added attraction of girls from home visiting their planter parents, although never enough to go round.

> There was always the problems of girls to play with in competition with some thirty other lusty young bachelors in our High Range. Those who came out from School in England or Scotland had an endless choice of boy friends, generally stamped, sealed and approved by careful Parents! There was a song which went 'Too many outdoor sports and not enough parlour games'; the story of a Bachelor's life in a Planting District! Sometimes dusky maidens appeared and made rather pathetic noises outside the bedroom window. On investigation they were found to be terrible old bags from the nearby Estate; any port in a storm! There was an unwritten law which said 'leave the girls alone on your own doorstep.'[32]

James Finlay's was a major force in Travancore tea right up to the 1970s, when a joint enterprise, Tata Finlay, took over the production and marketing. In 1983 James Finlay's sold its shareholding to Tata, and Tata Tea was born. Today the Kanan Devan Hills remain a major tea-producing region of South India. Not as well esteemed as Nilgiri teas, they nevertheless produce dependable and good-value leaf. As in Assam, it is mostly India's native *assamica* that is grown in the south, with about 20 per cent *sinensis*.

In Munnar we hired a robust 4x4 and a seasoned driver to negotiate the monsoon-ravaged road and the thirteen hairpin bends that took us to the Kolukkumalai Tea Estate. Kolukkumalai means 'jagged peak' in the Tamil language, and at over 8,000 feet it is the highest tea estate in the world. The bone-jarring journey through this wonderful landscape was deeply rewarding. The estate straddles the mountainous border between Kerala and Tamil Nadu, and the terrain is so rugged that less than half of its 220 hectares is under tea, while the rest is uncultivated and a haven for native flora and fauna. The high peaks were shrouded in morning mist but, as it cleared, we had an eagle's-eye view over a contoured landscape blanketed green with tea bushes, through which rocks and crags loomed. High and remote, Kolukkumalai estate was only cleared and planted in the 1920s. Every bush, tool, sheet of corrugated iron, girder and machine was dragged up the mountain on a pony path or ropeway. The great steel beams that form the framework of the factory bear the words 'Lanarkshire Steel Company Scotland', and the ancient Moore's Patent Balanced Continuous Automatic Sorter was made by the Scottish-founded Balmer Lawrie & Co. of Calcutta, while the Michie's Patent Sifter was manufactured in Ceylon by David Kinloch Michie and his business partner, Walter Lamont of Helensburgh, at the Colombo Iron Works.[33] The Tubeless Empire Tea Drier was made by Marshall's of Lincolnshire, but was the invention of the Aberdonian William Jackson. The machines are old but 'never resting, never rusting', according to our guide, Saravan Kumar.

Britain's tea plantations in India were sold to Indian companies in the years after Indian independence in 1947. Finlay's planter, Dick Tewson, who had left his plantation for the army during the Second World War, recalled:

... after Demob in 1946 returned to that happy life

until 1967 when India had to give the chop to some of us Britons, after we had trained a cadre of young Indian Planters to take our place. We went through the traumas of Independence smoothly and without rancour. But the shock of giving up this good and happy career was painful.

No longer will you hear orders in the tea gardens shouted in Scottish – often Doric – accents. But 8,000 feet up in the clear air of the Western Ghats, the rattle of Michie's Patent Sifter still bears witness to Scotland's contribution to the history of Indian tea.

Apart from some tribal people in the very north of the country, the population of India were latecomers to tea. Their land may have been deforested to grow it, and their countrymen and women exploited to pick and process it, but it was a long time before the subcontinent's masses were invited to take tea. The produce of Assam, Darjeeling and Nilgiris tea gardens was for sending home to Blighty and it was not until the Great Depression of the 1930s and the downturn in sales that the growers thought of unloading their overproduction on Indians, whom they had ignored as potential customers for a century.[34] Even then, Gandhi condemned tea as unhealthy, arguing (incorrectly) that the 'tannin' in tea hardened the inside of your stomach the way it hardened leather in the curing process. Despite the Mahatma's warnings, Indians proved to have a mighty thirst and today drink more black tea than the rest of the world combined.

Robert Fortune would not have been surprised. In 1852 he lamented the fact that the Indian peasant 'has scarcely the common necessaries of life, and certainly none of its luxuries'. He compared their plight unfavourably to that of the tea-drinking Chinese peasant:

> Tea is his favourite beverage from morning until night; not what we call tea, mixed with milk and sugar, but the essence of the herb itself drawn out in pure water. Those acquainted with the habits of this people can scarcely conceive of the Chinese existing, were they deprived of the tea plant; and I am sure that the extensive use of this beverage adds much to the health and comfort of the great body of the people. The people of India are not unlike the Chinese in many of their habits. The poor of both countries eat sparingly of animal food, and rice with other grains and vegetables form the staple articles on which they live; this being the case it is not at all unlikely the Indian will soon acquire a habit which is so universal in China.

In this chapter I have touched on tea being the saviour of Ceylon after the devastation of its coffee economy by a fungal leaf disease. It is now time to meet the remarkable Scot who worked that magic.

CHAPTER 6

The Master Who Is God

In Sri Lanka, people welcome you with the greeting *ayubowan* – 'long life'. Modern visitors have a good chance of that, but for planters in the nineteenth century life in what they called Ceylon was often frighteningly short. At the British Garrison Cemetery in Kandy, I was greeted by a slight, elderly man whose job and passion is the maintenance of this resting place of white colonials. His looks, demeanour and accent are entirely Sri Lankan, but his name, Charles Carmichael, betrays Scottish ancestry, in which he takes modest pride. The cemetery was established shortly after the conquest of Kandy by the British in 1815, but with Sri Lankan independence was abandoned and reclaimed by the jungle. It may even have been used to keep elephants – certainly many of the gravestones were broken. As the country's 1998 half-centenary of independence approached, Charles was among the squad recruited to reclaim and restore the cemetery. He was then retained by the Commonwealth War Graves Commission and Friends of the Garrison Cemetery as the caretaker. Today, he is the acknowledged expert in the place and accords the same welcome to inquisitive travellers like myself as he did to Prince Charles in 2013. 'There are 163 graves here, in which were buried 450 people,' he told me as we wandered around the tombstones.

Then came his astonishing punchline: 'Only eleven of them lived to be over fifty. When they came here, there was nothing – only jungles and disease, no medicines.'

The Brits came to Kandy as invaders, so the earliest graves in the cemetery are of soldiers. Captain James McGlashan survived the Battle of Waterloo to face a lingering and painful death by cholera in 1817 at the age of twenty-six. Ensign Archibald Montomerie, an Ayrshireman, died at twenty of 'jungle fever'. Quarter-master Sergeant R.M. Gunn, of the 78th Highlanders, died at thirty-three, while Captain J.P. Lardy of the same regiment succumbed to fever at thirty-nine.

With the military conquest of Ceylon came its economic exploitation and the arrival of planters. The island – the size of Ireland and shaped a bit like the Paisley pattern 'teardrop' – is a luxuriant tropical garden where rice, coconuts and cinnamon thrive. The weather system that churns around its high mountains brings two annual monsoons that drench the land and ingenious irrigation ensures that today's tea plantations are productive all year round. Land was cheap, about £1 an acre, but it was dense jungle that needed to be cleared and burned before it could be planted.[1] From the beginning of the British era, Scots were prominent in both planting and engineering the infrastructure. 'The rough work of pioneering in the early days before there were district roads, villages, supplies, doctors, or other comforts of civilisation, was chiefly done by hard-headed Scots,' wrote John Ferguson, the Highland Scots editor of the *Ceylon Observer* and the *Tropical Agriculturist*. 'Men bivouacked in the trackless jungle with the scantest accommodation under tropical rains lasting for weeks together, with rivers swollen to flood-level and impassable while food supplies often ran short as none could be got across the wide torrents.'[2]

Robert Tytler, from Peterhead, had ventured at just fifteen to work on a sugar estate in Jamaica. Three years later, in 1837, he turned up in Ceylon to jointly manage a company that was developing coffee estates. He began methodically and scientifically testing new crops on the island, and he was the first person to plant cocoa there. He also initiated irrigation schemes and pioneered modern methods of coffee production. The 1840s were a boom time for coffee and Tytler's example drew many more canny farmers from the North-east of Scotland to Ceylon. So numerous were the North-easteners that the *Ceylon Observer* published articles in the Doric dialect. One such essay, titled 'How I Lost My Wattie', attributed to 'an Auld Scotchman' described coffee planting life in the 1840s. Issued in booklet form in 1878, it had been previously published in the newspaper. The 'Auld Scotchman' tells of a young Peterhead man's rise and fall in Ceylon. 'Tae be plain an practical,' he wrote, 'my widowed mither saul oot o' the fairm left us by oor faither, an £1,500 o' the proceeds comin tae my share, I determined wi this tae become the laird o' a coffy estate.'

The National Library of Scotland attributes the pamphlet to Peterhead-born planter Arthur Sinclair, of whom we shall hear more later. But whoever the 'Auld Scotchman' was, he had high hopes for life on his 'wattie', or coffee plantation, in Ceylon:

> I daresay aifter a there are few blyther spots on this bonnie earth than may be seen on the hills an straths o' Ceylon. Gie me a sma coffy wattie, free o' debt, in a fairish districk, an a fair crap upon't, a cosy bungalow, a cautie managing wife who never scouels, and bairns that never greet, an I seek nae mair.

But between the planting of coffee and the reaping of the rewards lay a lean time, and the 'Auld Scotchman' took out a mortgage with a company that spectacularly crashed.

> To mak a lang story short. The ancient and muckle resseckie house o' Messers. ---- & Co, had crumbled

doon like a great rotton jungle-tree in which nae mair
the birds coud big their nests, and my precious wattie
wi mony ithers was handed ower to the tender mer-
cies o' Messers. ----- & Co., Colombo . . .

The young Scots planters' expectations were high, but their
lives were often short. In Charles Carmichael's office-cum-
archive I discovered an early account of the Garrison Cemetery:

> In this lonely spot . . . lie many hundreds of kindly
> Scots, who, cut off in the very prime and vigour of their
> manhood, sleep the sleep which knows no waking,
> under the rank weeds and wiry grasses which cover
> their neglected graves. Many a sad tale of hardship,
> agony and pain, could the tenants of these nameless
> graves tell were they permitted to speak. Few of them
> had any kind friend or neighbour near to comfort
> them in their last sad agony, to place even a glass of
> cool water to their parched and burning tongue, or to
> speak a word of comfort to their often troubled mind.
> Left to the care of native servants, many of these
> young men died friendless and neglected in some
> distant jungle bungalow, from fever, from cholera,
> diarrhoea, or dysentery. The brandy bottle finished
> many of them, for, as Anthony Trollop justly remarks,
> there is no other solace at hand to cheer the loneliness
> of the wild jungle life . . . [3]

The death toll of young Scottish planters makes grim reading.
Martin Fraser of Laggan died at twenty-one, as did Abraham
Duncan, who had not been in the country long enough for
his name to be included in the *Ceylon Almanac*'s directory.
Margaret Jolly, the wife of Laurencekirk planter W. Bissett, died
at twenty-six, and David Moir of Laurencekirk at thirty-one.

David Bell, of Dundee, died at thirty-two, after less than two years in Ceylon. Alex Lumsden of Aberdeenshire died at twenty-two, and George Baxter Wilson, of the same county, of fever at twenty-one. Farquhar McDonald, the planter son of a Black Watch officer, lived to just thirty-two. Gray Scott Cargill died at twenty-seven, and his young niece, Dora Grey Thomson, at seventeen months. Jane Fraser, wife of William Grant, died on her husband's estate at thirty-one. Walter Ross Duff, of Rosshire, lived and became experienced enough to manage several estates, but died at forty. Cholera claimed James Urquhart at thirty-two. Robert Arnott, of Inverness, died at the Midlothian estate at thirty-three. Donald Bain of Kingussie perished at the same age, Henry Mackenzie at twenty-eight, and James Gibson of Pitlochry at twenty-six.

Disease was not the only contributor to the ranks of the Garrison Cemetery. Thomas McCall of Hamilton drowned while crossing to an estate by canoe during a flood, A. McGill died of sunstroke at thirty-six, and David Finlay died at thirty-eight when a house in Kandy collapsed on him. James Souter's gravestone says he died 'suddenly' at twenty-four – killed, Charles Carmichael tells me, by a cricket ball. John Spottiswood Robertson, the eldest son of one of the Deputy Keeper of the Records of Scotland, was one of seven Europeans known to have been killed by elephants between 1815 and 1833.

Snakes and leopards were a constant danger to natives and planters alike. In the last decade of the nineteenth century about 150 people a year lost their lives to wild animals. In 1924 a leopard was shot while devouring what was at least its twelfth victim; as recently as 2011, a thirty-one-year-old woman was killed by a leopard in Sri Lanka. Writing some years after the First World War, John Still recalls 'a grand old Highlander' who left his estate to shoot jungle fowl and wounded a monkey by mistake. Firing his second barrel to put the animal out of its pain, he found himself attacked by the whole tribe of monkeys and only just managed to get back to his estate before they tore him apart.[4]

It was into this intimidating world that, on 20 February 1852, plunged the sixteen-year-old Scot James Taylor.

James Taylor – destined to become 'The Father of Ceylon Tea' – was born in 1835 on an estate near the village of Auchinblae, close to Laurencekirk in Kincardineshire. As well as being renowned for its skilful agriculture, the district also cultivated a rich crop of coffee and tea planters, as Kandy's Garrison Cemetery testifies. James, or Jamie, was the oldest of four children born to Michael and Margaret Taylor. Margaret died when James was just nine. His carpenter father quickly remarried and fathered two more children. James was often at odds with his stepmother and unhappy at home, but nevertheless applied himself at the village's Free Church school, where his subjects included Latin and Greek. His habit of study and self-improvement remained with Taylor all his life and was key to his later success as a pioneer planter. Physically strong, he was also expected to 'muck in' with farmwork and he almost certainly inherited a practical streak from his father.

At fourteen, he became a pupil/teacher at Fordoun. It seems that his family had a bride and small-town respectability in mind for him, but Taylor had other plans. Peter Moir, a cousin of his mother's, was 'in coffee' in Ceylon. (A cousin of Peter's lies in the Garrison Cemetery.) On his first home-leave in six years, Peter Moir met and impressed the young Taylor with his stories of planting life. Moir was a key link in a pattern of chain migration that saw Scots assist their kinfolk in securing posts abroad. By 1875, half of Ceylon's plantation managers were from Aberdeenshire or Kincardineshire.[5] At one point, fourteen men out of Lawrencekirk's population of 2,000 were working in Ceylon, thanks to Moir.[6]

Peter Moir pulled the strings that allowed Taylor and another of his mother's cousins, Henry Stiven, to sign up for jobs on the Ceylon coffee plantations owned by George Pride.

Messrs G. & J. A. Hadden London October 1851

Gentlemen,

I hereby engage myself to Mr George Pride of Kandy, Ceylon, for the space of three years to act in the capacity of assistant superintendent and to make myself generally useful and obey the orders of those set over me – at a salary of £100 (a Hundred Pounds) per annum to commencing from the time of my arrival on the estate and to have deducted from my salary the amount of money advance by you for my passage and outfit.

I am, Gentlemen,

Your obedient servant,

JAMES TAYLOR

In short, Taylor was to start as a 'creeper', a tyro planter who learned the job 'creeping', or shadowing, a more experienced man. The cousins' voyage took 122 days and their ship dropped anchor off Colombo on 20 February 1852. At this time, Ceylon coffee was well on the way to becoming an international brand and it was by far the island's most valuable export.[7] Within two days of landing at the port of Colombo, Taylor was on his way inland to begin work on a George Pride coffee estate near Kandy.

Pride was a demanding employer with a foul temper, given to cursing and stamping his feet in rage. Taylor's correspondence tells of how Pride once threw a tumbler at him, and how he once thrashed a coolie for nearly half an hour 'till the fellow was nearly dead'. Taylor spent only six weeks on his first estate before being ordered to Loolecondera, eighteen miles southeast of Kandy, where he shared a primitive, rat-infested wooden hut with a Portuguese assistant planter. It was so draughty that the wind sometimes blew out their hurricane lamp and was cold during the rainy season. One night Taylor recorded that four-and-a-half inches of rain fell, followed by another four inches in just twenty minutes the following morning. Despite the inconvenience of monsoons, high Loolecondera enjoys a healthy, temperate climate, much more suited to the Scottish constitution than hot and humid Colombo, which in 1865 claimed the life of his cousin and travelling companion Henry Stiven, then later Henry's wife.

Loolecondera estate had been bought from the Crown in 1841 by Mr James Joseph Mackenzie, but little had been done over the past decade to cultivate it. Lying between 900 and 1,500 metres above sea level, it was covered in dense forest, except where the bare bones of the mountain thrust through the soil. Taylor thought one such peak looked like Ben Macdui. He and 200 labourers set to work. Forest had to be felled and burned, roads carved out on the flanks of hills and the ground prepared for planting. Taylor was a practical man with a work ethic and a gift for problem-solving, engineering and keeping costs down. Once he had got Loolecondera cleared and planted with coffee, Taylor built himself a bungalow that he boasted was the envy of all the white planters in the district. The cost of it might have put him in conflict with his employer, but George Pride died in London that year and – not for the last time – the estate changed hands and Taylor had new bosses.

While owners came and went, Taylor was to spend the rest of his days at his beloved Loolecondera. Although manicured, emerald-green tea plants, not forest, cloak the hillsides today, the wide glens and craggy peaks of the estate remind the traveller of Highland Scotland. 'You will think I write a lot about the scenery, but if you saw it you would not think I said too much', Taylor wrote home in 1858. Visiting the estate in the 1960s, the writer Denys Forrest too was struck by the similarity to Highland Scotland: 'It is, one feels, what tea growing in the Cairngorms would be if such a thing were possible.'[18]

Loolecondera, of course, was founded to grow coffee. For at least a century before the arrival of the British, coffee had been grown on small plots by native peasant farmers, having probably been introduced by Arab traders. Seeing the potential of the plant, the British developed 'coffee mania'. Between 1830 and 1845 they carved out vast estates from virgin forest and built factories, roads, bridges and irrigation schemes to maximise efficiency and profit. While the Sinhalese had a fondness for coffee, they had no taste for repetitive and poorly paid labour on British estates and were mostly content to cultivate their own smallholdings. Faced with a labour shortage, the white planters imported huge numbers of Tamil labourers from southern India. By 1907, 400,000 Tamils were employed on 1,600 tea plantations, with most of them living in the 'coolie lines' of the estates that employed them, living off little more than subsistence wages.

In common with other planters, Taylor was not impressed with his Tamil workforce, thinking them lazy and inefficient, calling them 'a set of the greatest cheaters that existed'. As in India, the relationship between the whites and the native peoples grew cooler in the wake of the Indian Mutiny of 1857. There were innumerable cases of white brutality towards indentured Tamil coolies, often by planters who had previously worked in the Caribbean and whose attitudes had not changed since the abolition of slavery in 1833. Despite these difficulties, the descendants of the Tamil migrants from India are still the backbone of Sri Lanka's estates, although Tamil/

Sinhalese relations have often caused bloody conflict in the country. Taylor could never understand the reluctance of the native Singhalese to give up their traditional plots to work for wages on white estates. It was, as Angela McCarthy and Tom Devine have written, 'a conflict between the ethic of capitalism and the traditionalism of a peasant society'.[9]

Although Loolecondera was first and foremost a coffee estate, there was a move to diversify and Taylor began to cultivate cinchona. Such work had been pioneered at the Peradeniya Botanical Gardens, which had first been established a few miles west of Kandy by the Scottish botanist Alexander Moon[10] in 1821 and then formally established in 1843 on a horseshoe bend on the Mahaweli River, five miles south of Kandy, by his countryman George Gardner. Gardner was the gifted son of a gardener who worked on the estates of landed gentry in Ardentinny and Ardrossan. Today more than 4,000 plant species flourish at the Peradeniya garden.

As in Calcutta, the Peradeniya garden first cultivated plants that were potentially profitable to the British Empire and in 1839 specimen plants of the Assam *jat* were first grown there, sent over by Dr Nathaniel Wallich from Calcutta. Individual enthusiasts also raised Assam and China *jats* in their gardens, including Sir Anthony Oliphant, the Forgendenny-born Chief Justice of Ceylon. Tea bushes, probably grown from seeds from Peradeniya, seem to have been planted by individuals as curiosities and James Taylor records attempting to make tea from 'some old tea bushes in the garden' and from hedgerows along the roadside. But in 1867 James Taylor got serious about tea. He cleared nineteen acres of hillside jungle at Loolecondera and planted the Assam seed in what became the estate's Field Number 7. Because tea bushes only begin to yield a crop at between three and five years, this investment in time and labour on such a new venture was a risk. Taylor learned on the job. Planters from India, a Mr Noble and a W.J. Jenkins, showed him how to pluck, wither and roll the leaves. It began as a very amateur affair. E.G. Harding, who went to Ceylon as an assistant coffee planter in 1869, would sometimes pay Sunday visits to Taylor at Loolecondera and recalled: 'The factory was in the bungalow. The leaf was rolled on the veranda by hand, i.e. from wrists to elbow, while the firing was done in chulas or clay stoves, over charcoal fires, with wire trays to hold the leaf. The result was a delicious tea which we bought up locally at Rs 1.50 per lb.' The primitive roller/drier that Taylor used in these early days is preserved at the Ceylon Tea Museum in the former Hanthana Tea Factory, just south of Kandy.

The year that Harding witnessed his neighbour's first ramshackle efforts to make tea goes down in history as a momentous one – a watershed in Ceylon's economy, and the year in which James Taylor's great achievements began. In 1869 the fungus *Hemileia vastatrix*, known as 'coffee rust', first appeared in Ceylon. Originating in East Africa, the fungus spores may have been carried by monsoon winds or arrived on contaminated material imported into the country. Even today there is no cure; in 2012, there was an epidemic of it across ten Latin American and Caribbean countries. In Ceylon, throughout the 1870s, yellow/orange blotches began to appear on the underside of coffee bush leaves. The leaves would then drop off and the plant would die. Midlothian planter Leybourne Davidson, who went on to become a major figure at James Finlay's, recalled that when he first arrived in Ceylon there were 300,000 acres under coffee, all doomed to perish. Nothing halted the spread of the plague which, month on month, leapt from estate to estate. All planters could do was to grub out the stumps of their precious bushes for firewood. In just twenty years the island's coffee crop – its main export – dropped from five million kilos a year to half a million.[11] 'No such calamity has befallen Scotch colonists since the Darien disaster,' observed Arthur Sinclair, an Aberdeenshire-born traveller and planter 'from old Jacobite stock'. 'At this stage not a few planters lost heart and retired to the Antipodes and elsewhere.'[12] Some among the planting community may well have recalled the Highland Potato Famine of the 1840s and 1850s. But the devastated coffee estates were to be the stage for what tea historian William Ukers described as 'one of the most dramatic stories in the history of the industry'.

James Taylor led the way. Year on year, as the diseases that killed coffee spread, Taylor demonstrated that tea could be the estates' salvation. In 1871 he sold his first tea in Kandy and the following year exported twenty-three pounds of it to London, doubtless through the recently opened Suez Canal, which had slashed the cost of shipping. That same year he erected a custom-built tea house at Loolecondera and had between fifty and a hundred acres under tea. Noting that the rolling of leaves cost as much as the picking of them, Taylor turned his practical mind to designing a machine to do the job. In 1872 Taylor had a water-driven rolling machine built in Kandy and had it installed and working at Loolecondera early the following year. Crushing the leaves mechanically improved both flavour and output. Following Loolecondera's lead, many coffee planters switched to tea. Bankrupt coffee estates were snapped up at bargain prices by tea planters. The enormous infrastructure that had been painstakingly built to produce coffee – roads, bridges, irrigation systems, factories, houses – was quickly adapted for the new crop. Lessons that had been hard-learned in Darjeeling and Assam were now freely available to any Ceylon planter who cared to read them. Ceylon's mountainous interior offered opportunities for producing low- and high-grown teas from both the Assam and the China *jats*.

While others followed his example, Taylor simply continued to do what he knew best – cultivate Loolecondera estate to the best of his abilities. If he knew that he was the saviour of the Ceylon economy, he never crowed about it and his commitment to Loolecondera remained total. In 1874 Taylor took his one and only holiday away from Ceylon – not to Scotland to visit family, but to Darjeeling to study tea.

Taylor realised that 'fine picking' – taking only two leaves and a bud from the tip of each stem – produced a much finer and more profitable tea than the coarser ripping of leaves by the fistful. By 1876 he was selling his tea in Ceylon 'for well over twice the price we could get for it in London'. Such was the rush into this new, profitable crop that an auction market was established in Colombo in 1883 and shortly after that a tea dealers' association. The soil and climate of Ceylon had proved to be ideal for tea. In 1875 there were just 1,000 acres of it. Twenty years later there were 350,000 acres, and by 1930 there were 467,000 acres. At Sri Lanka's independence in 1948, more than half a million acres were devoted to tea growing, more than had ever been given over to coffee.

Taylor was an outdoor man who couldn't bear to be indoors during the hours of daylight. When not engaged in the multifarious jobs of an estate manager, he tended his flower garden and had his father send him seeds from Scotland. A brook-fed, forest-shaded natural pool where Taylor bathed his sweaty, dusty, six-foot-plus frame at the end of his long working days is still to be found at Loolecondera. Unlike many planters, Taylor did not have a reputation as a heavy drinker but, although he was not a regular 'club' man, he could be convivial in company. His nearest club would have been the Scots Club in Nuwara Eliya, now subsumed into the plush St Andrews Hotel, where the modern bar still features the old fireplace around which well-lubricated planters would gather on their visits to civilisation. Taylor could only have made occasional visits, writing that in the early days at Loolecondera he scarcely ever saw a white person but took great pleasure in receiving letters from home.

James Taylor's lifelong drive for self-improvement and his evenings of study probably saved him from the tyranny of loneliness and the bottle. He learned the Sinhala and Tamil languages and studied whatever subject he thought would be useful to him as a planter. Unlike many whites, Taylor subsisted on local foods rather than trying to recreate the meat-and-tatties diet of the old country. This may have been simply due to availability rather than preference, but it is hard to feel sympathy for a man who breakfasted on rotis served with daal, or sweet potato curry spiced up with the zinging local coconut sambal.

Despite broad hints from his family in Scotland, James Taylor never married, instead describing himself as a 'confirmed bachelor'. But, like other planters, he was no monk. He too was susceptible to the charms of Tamil girls who worked on estates. Many such inter-racial relations between the powerful white master and the vulnerable native employee would have been coercive, but not all. In his correspondence with his family in Scotland, Taylor never revealed that he had a native partner, although a photograph album of his features images of the same Tamil girl dressed both in a sari and in a Western crinoline. Why would a Tamil tea-picker have such a garment, and why would a planter photograph her in it if it was nothing more than an employer/employee relationship? Taylor's biographers, Professors Angela McCarthy and Tom Devine, suggest that a Tamil girl called Paarvathy is likely to have been Taylor's partner and that 'Paarvathy's sister', whom Taylor mentions being born in 1865, may have actually been his daughter by her. They suggest that Taylor may have been keeping note of Paarvathy's menstrual cycle. Could it be that Taylor was practising a form of birth control? When Paarvathy 'ran off', he later may have had a relationship with his Sinhalese housekeeper. What is certain is that Taylor left in his will money to the mother of his children, and to the housekeeper.

When I visited the Ceylon Tea Museum near Kandy, I was told by an excited member of staff that 'a descendent of James Taylor's' had visited about two years previously.

'A Sri Lankan?' I enquired, my hopes rising that I might trace one of Paarvathy's descendants.

'No, a European,' I was told. Frustratingly, he hadn't signed the visitors' book and nobody remembered where he came from. As I was absolutely certain that no such European descendant existed, the story was perplexing – until we happened to pass the 1867-founded Glenloch Tea Factory, perched on the steep valley side on the beautiful winding road from Nuwara Eliya to Colombo. We took the tour and, among the trays of the withering floor, rich with the heady aroma of fresh leaf, I questioned Ramees, our helpful guide.

'Who founded this estate?'

'George Taylor,' he replied with enthusiasm. 'A Scotsman.' Could the enthusiastic 'descendant' who visited the museum in Kandy have got his Taylor ancestry confused? From what we know about James Taylor's life, it seems the probable answer. Whatever descendants Glenloch's George Taylor may have, his tea estate and factory is still a thriving concern and its Golden Tips tea is delicious.

Tea estate relationships between the races feature in Barbara Cartland's novel set in Ceylon, *Moon Over Eden*, in which the real-life James Taylor appears as the friend and mentor to fictitious English aristocrat Lord Hawkston. Although Cartland only gives Lord Hawkston 'a pleasant liaison with a very pretty Portuguese in Kandy' (i.e. a white person) as a past sex life, she does not shy from telling of the common habit of planters to take native mistresses and often father children by them. Cartland, who visited Ceylon in 1975, suggests that such arrangements were common and governed by certain rules. But in *Moon Over Eden* Lord Hawkston's whisky-soaked nephew Gerald has 'broken the rules with a native girl', unleashing an orgy of betrayal, suicide, revenge, madness, murder and passion. By page 152, good has prevailed and James Taylor is best man at the wedding of the handsome Lord Hawkston and Dominica, the daughter of an impoverished clergyman.*

By all accounts, Taylor was liked, although held in awe, by his coolies, who referred to him as *Sami Dori* – 'the Master who is God'. He would have towered over them and, it is said, would knock a man down with a single blow for incompetence.[13] Only once, as far as it is known, was Taylor ever threatened by his workforce. An attack on him in his home, which left him bleeding from the ear, was variously put down to an attempted burglary or the revenge of a servant and washerwoman whom he had dismissed.

In 1888 Taylor's homeland celebrated his achievement in founding Ceylon's tea industry. At the International Exhibition of Industry, Science and Arts, held in Glasgow's Kelvingrove Park, Queen Victoria sipped a cup of Ceylon tea – one of more than 6,000 cups downed each week of the six-month event. A craze for the Ceylon brand was developing. The soft, light flavours of the island's high-grown teas went well with the cucumber sandwiches and scones of that increasingly popular meal, afternoon tea. Aberdeen tea dealer William Westland offered customers a choice of 'single estate' teas, in the manner of today's 'single malt' whiskies. One buyer for the major Liverpool tea traders, Harrisons and Crosfield, said that he had 'never since tasted a more perfect tea' than the Loolecondera product. Tea from well-managed estates in Ceylon and India had now outstripped the small-farmer-produced leaves from faraway China in quality, freshness and

---

* Taylor is not the only Scottish tea man to be hijacked by romantic fiction. An even larger-than-real-life Robert Fortune appears in the Scottish novelist Sara Sheridan's 2009 romp *The Secret Mandarin*.

affordability. The once-mighty China drink was in freefall in the West.

In 1929 Ceylon exported an astonishing 551,500,000 pounds of tea, and today Sri Lanka exports more than China and India. The journey from the disease-devastated coffee fields of the 1870s to market dominance of tea is a remarkable and dramatic one. James Taylor's countryman Sir Arthur Conan Doyle wrote: 'Not often is it that men have the heart, when their great one industry is withered, to rear up in a few years another as rich to take its place, and the tea fields of Ceylon are as true a monument to courage as is the lion at Waterloo.'[14]

In 1891, in recognition of Taylor's pioneering work on tea and for saving the economy of Ceylon, the Planters' Association presented him with an ornate silver tea service. Their praise for him, inscribed on the silver salver, was fulsome: 'To James Taylor Lolle Condura, in grateful appreciation of his successful efforts which laid the foundation of the tea and Cinchona Industries of Ceylon 1891.'

But dark clouds had gathered above Loolecondera. The rapid success of Ceylon tea had seen capital being concentrated in the hands of large British-based corporations and a wave of mergers had forced out small planters.[15] Taylor had only ever managed his estate and ownership had changed over the years. By 1887 Loolecondera was in the hands of the liquidator of the Oriental Bank Corporation. In 1892 – just six months after Taylor's presentation by the Planters' Association – the new management ordered him to take six months leave away from the estate for health reasons. Taylor denied that there was anything wrong with him and refused to go. He was asked to resign. His friends recalled him being confused, dumfounded and in despair. Within days Taylor contracted dysentery and died on the estate. He had been a strong, fit, intelligent man who had lived and prospered for over forty years in Ceylon

– yet died as soon as he was sacked from his post on his beloved Loolecondera. Like the death of Tchaikovsky the following year (probably of cholera from drinking contaminated water, and possibly by suicide), suspicions were aroused. Many concluded that James Taylor died of a broken heart.

A writer to the *Overland Times of Ceylon* commented: 'It is certainly the universal opinion of those who knew him well that poor James Taylor died of a broken heart at the ordeal of having to leave the estate he loved so much and cared for so well and for so long.' A second wrote: 'Poor Taylor! He deserved a better end than to die a broken hearted man.' Another believed that there was 'more than mere coincidence' in the fact that the healthy Taylor died so soon after he got the sack. Taylor's most recent biographers do not dismiss the possibility that the stricken Taylor took his own life.[16]

In life, Taylor had been a big man. In death he was a deadweight. Early on the morning following his demise, two teams of twelve men, taking turns every four miles, carried his body the eighteen miles to Kandy. At 4 p.m. they reached the hillside cemetery at Mahaiyawa. After a memorial service at St Paul's Anglican Church's Chapel of Rest, James Taylor was laid to rest.[17]

Two helpful gardeners at Mahaiyawa led me to the grave, hurriedly clearing vegetation from around the high and ornately carved cross as I prepared to photograph it. The inscription is simple, but a testimony to Taylor's achievement.

In Pious Memory

Of James Taylor

Loolecondera Estate, Ceylon

The Pioneer of the

Tea and Cinchona Enterprises

In This Island

Who Died May 2Nd 1892

Aged 57 Years

I had come a long way to see this site, was in no hurry to leave, and stood for a while trying to imagine the procession of estate workers who carried their *Sami Dori*, 'the Master who is God', to his final resting place. I prowled around for a while, photographing Celtic crosses and gravestones with Scottish names, until the gardeners shouted to me that the recent drought had driven snakes down the hill to the overgrown area where I was treading. It was the sort of hazard that James Taylor faced every day of his forty-one years as a planter – he once stepped on a cobra – but the warning had me hurrying for the safety of the hard path.

Today, the 900-acre Loolecondera estate and tea factory are owned by Janatha Estate Development Board (i.e. the Sri Lankan government). Estate Superintendent Dhammika Kodituwallu manages forty staff and 525 plantation workers. They make up a little hill-country community complete with small shops and roadside Hindu temples. Most of the field workers are ethnic Tamils, not Buddhist Sinhalese, and descendants of those first brought over from South India by the British in the nineteenth century. With such a workforce, Dhammika is a busy man, and my interview with him is interrupted by an insistent phone and the need to issue a stream of orders, but he still finds time to greet James Taylor seekers cordially and to maintain the various signs and monuments around the estate that pay tribute to the father of Ceylon tea. Of the nineteen acres of Taylor's Field Number 7, five acres of his venerable bushes still remain. Many of the roads on the estate and some of the irrigation channels were created by the ever-busy Taylor. Loolecondera also boasts 'Taylor's

Seat', a prominent viewpoint where the Scot would sit on a rock to view his growing domain. Our guide Neel Perara's low-clearance car wouldn't have made it up the steep and rough track, so we hired a tuktuk and held on tightly. Arriving there, I was briefly disappointed that Loolecondera was cloaked in mist but consoled by the thought that, as a North-east man, Taylor would have sat on the very same spot on such a day recalling the *haar* of his homeland that he would never see again.

The fireplace and tall stone chimney of a building said to be Taylor's house still stand amid the estate, now protected by a corrugated roof from the monsoon rains. The walls would have been made of mud, according to Dhammika Kodituwallu, and have long dissolved and been washed away. What remains of the house doesn't seem to match his own description of the bungalow he built, but some visitors have noted that the fire-place, with its hearth raised well off the floor, is common in the Mearns where Taylor was born and raised. A (frankly bizarre) larger-than-life statue of Taylor also stands on the estate.

Tea is grown pretty well as it was done in Taylor's time. Seeds are planted on carefully prepared and terraced ground in October and November and take at least three years to mature enough to be picked. At Loolecondera picking can go on all year, with two or three picks per month during the dry season (January to March and July to September) and up to five picks a month during the rest of the year. In this way the estate produces an astonishing 200,000 kilos of black tea a year. 'James Taylor would be happy to see how tea has thrived,' says Dhammika Kodituwallu with a broad smile.

Taylor was just one of a huge colony of Scots in Ceylon, many of them in tea. He claimed that if an estate was doing well 'it is a Scotchman that is on it', and when the Planters' Association of Ceylon was founded in 1854, two Scots – Captain John Keith Jolly and Alexander 'Sandy' Brown – were its chairman and secretary. The very names of many of the estates betray the Scottish influence: Abbotsford, Barra, Caledonia, Cameron's Land, Craigie Lea, Culloden, Dalhousie, Dunedin, Dunsinnane, Eildon, Ettrick, Fassifern, Forres, Glasgow, Glen Alpin, Glencairn, Gleneagles, Glenloch, Glen Lyon, Holyrood, Kelburne,Kellie, Kelvin, Lochiel, Lochnagar, Logie, Lorne, MacKenzie's Land, Moray, St Andrews, Seaforth, Stair, Stirling, Strathspey, Tulibody and Ury.

Not all the Scots who made their mark on Ceylon were planters. John Walker had been an apprentice engineer at the Deanston Cotton Mill of James Finlay & Company near Glasgow before moving to Ceylon. He joined Wilson Ritchie & Co. of Colombo in 1842, but along with his brother William (another Deanston man) founded engineering and manufacturing businesses Walker Sons & Co., and Walker & Greig. They developed machines that became the industry standard in Ceylon and beyond – the Walker Economic Tea Roller and the Colombo Drier. A Walker water-wheel can still be seen at Glenloch Tea Factory. Walkers were associated with Walter Lamont and David Kinloch Michie, two Scots who built tea-drying and tea-sifting machines in Ceylon, including the 1930s one I discovered still rattling away on the Kolukkumalai Tea Estate in Kerala. John Brown, born near Aberdeen in 1826, went to India when he was twenty-two to work on the railways. Moving to Ceylon, he specialised in important irrigation projects, and later became the managing director of the company that owned Glen Appin and Spring Valley estates.

In 1893 James Finlay & Company of Glasgow opened a Colombo branch under manager Alexander Fairlie. The intrusion of such a major company disturbed the established planting community, creating a sudden new demand for labour and an exodus of skilled hands to the newcomer's estates. Labour was a constant headache for planters, as the company's official history recalls:

There were many troubles other than those which nature so plentifully supplied. Labour was difficult to obtain, and afterwards there was the problem of keeping the workers settled and contented. Unused to the routine of large scale commercial management they were restless and hard to handle. Once, more than a thousand marched to Colombo and sat down opposite the Queen's House, the official residence of the Governor. This embarrassingly passive form of protest presented Mr Fairlie with a sore problem. However, he arranged for the feeding and the housing of them all until they decided to return to work.

Today, Finlay's owns eighteen Sri Lankan tea estates, five combined tea and rubber estates, and two rubber estates and a coconut estate. Like other companies in Sri Lanka, Finlay's is now involved in tea tourism, offering factory tours and accommodation in former estate bungalows.

Scots tamed Ceylon jungle, carved out plantations, built infrastructure and founded companies that still thrive in modern Sri Lanka, but – inevitably – they also left a genetic inheritance. One such man was George Thain Davidson. Born in 1871, Davidson was the son of a Broughty Ferry minister who had taken charge of the 'Scotch' Presbyterian church in London's Islington and who himself was the son of a 'Disruption' minister from Dundee. The young Davidson – with no intention of following family tradition and donning a dog collar – tried his hand at cattle ranching in California before sailing for Ceylon on the Clyde-built Royal Mail Ship *Dunottar Castle* in 1893 to become a 'creeper' at Invery estate, owned by the Scottish Ceylon Tea Company.

George was soon befriended by Alfred William Leslie, the Ceylon-born son of a Scottish planter. Through a Sinhalese man who supervised the native labour on their estates, the two young Scots were introduced to the well-respected Kasthuri Arachchi family at their sprawling home in the hill-country village of Naranwita. The family, which was of Sinhalese nobility, had three daughters in their teens or early twenties – Dingirimenike, Muthumenike and Punchimenike. Muthumenike was already spoken for, but George was smitten by Dingirimenike, and his friend Alfred by Punchimenike. The two young Scots moved in with their girls at their family home but they were clearly more than just 'bidie-ins' (as non-married, live-in sexual partners are referred to in Scotland). With a respected family like the Kasthuri Arachchis – and especially in this era – co-habiting would only have been possible if formal engagements had taken place according to Ceylonese custom. Even today, an 'engagement' in Sri Lanka is a witnessed and registered commitment to marriage that may or may not require a further public ceremony, so the domestic arrangements of the young Scots were perfectly respectable – at least in Sinhalese eyes, if not Victorian, racist, British ones.

George gave his Ceylon family the surname Robinson, and his first child, Lorna Janet Robinson, was born in 1904. Did he feel the need to distance his Ceylonese family from his ultra-respectable Davidson relations? And why Robinson? It was Captain J.C. Robinson of the RMS *Dunottar Castle* who had brought Davidson to Ceylon, so it may be that George chose 'Robinson' as being symbolic of a new life with a new family in a new country where Victorian values could be flouted. George Davidson's planter friend Alfred Leslie also raised a family with his Sinhalese wife and later settled with them at Bangalore in India, where he continued as a tea planter.

George worked on a number of plantations, clearly making a reputation for himself as an able man. His grandson,

Norman Martinesz, suspects that George may previously have met Thomas Lipton in America, but we know for certain that in 1907 George was appointed Lipton's tea estates manager and visiting agent, and spent most of his career at Lipton's Dambatenne Tea Estate and factory. Davidson had become a key man in Lipton's Ceylon empire. In 1905 George's first son, Henry, was born, followed by Mary (1906), Kate (1907), Albert (1909) and Marguerite (1910).

George Davidson was now living in the house known as Lipton's Bungalow, a building with breathtaking views and a cool climate that his grandson, Norman, believes must have reminded him of Scotland. The house still stands, occupied by whichever manager is in charge of the Dambatenne estate. George continued to live there after his retirement in 1922. That year he treated himself to a visit to the UK and a world tour – while at the same time arranging for the purchase of an extensive coconut and rubber estate near Kandy and the construction of 'Woodlands', a large house designed by his son Henry. The sprawling, high-roofed, coconut-palm-thatched building was home to George's extended family for many years.

In 1926 his daughter Lorna married Terence Wilfred Martinesz at St Paul's Church, Kandy. With the nuptials over, George set off for a cruise to America, but suffered from some sort of fit while at sea. Returning home, he quickly recovered and planned further travels. Early on the morning of 11 February 1927 George's chauffeur came to pick him up at the Grand Hotel, Anuradhapura, in northern Ceylon. When his boss didn't respond to the car's horn, the chauffeur went to his room, where he found George lying helpless on the floor. George Davidson passed away the following morning.

George Thain Davidson's legacy to Ceylon was more than the efficient stewardship of Thomas Lipton's plantations. The family he raised – officially 'Ceylonese Eurasian' – benefited from a comfortable and loving home life and the best of educations. The Robinsons and their children went on to make their mark on Ceylonese life as engineers, military personnel, clergy and planters.

One can only speculate about the attitude of George Davidson's reverend father to his son having a Ceylonese, Buddhist 'wife' – through an arrangement not recognised by the Church of Scotland – and six mixed-race children with her. If there was a difficulty in accepting this Robinson 'sept' of the Davidson clan, it was not felt by the Robinsons or their descendants. Norman Martinesz, the youngest son of George's first child, Lorna Robinson, is entirely comfortable with his Scots/Sinhalese heritage: 'I cannot recall any difference been shown to who or what we were, nor who our ancestors were. It did not matter to anyone, it was never an issue. There are many families who have descended from mixed marriages and liaisons that go back to Portuguese, Dutch, British rule, and the Arabian occupation, or traders with the island. In recent times the need to migrate for whatever reason has led people to look for Western or Australian connections to lend a positive bias to their applications for travel visas.'[18]

Throughout the British Empire the authority of the white planter often led to the sexual exploitation of native women, but the story of George Davidson and his friend Albert Leslie show that some Scots broke with the conventions and narrow views of the Victorian era and entered into relationships that were loving and respectful, and would be quite normal and unremarkable today.

In the first half of the twentieth century, young Scots continued to arrive in Ceylon to begin careers that would last through two world wars and up to Sri Lankan independence in 1948. Alexander 'Mac' McLaren is a late example of that

Celtic connection that flooded the empire with Scots. As the youngest of 13 children growing up on a farm at Tannadice, near Forfar, albeit quite a prosperous one, he had to seek a living furth of Scotland. The McLarens had been ships chandlers before they were farmers, and through that, according to Mac's grandson Richard Ross, 'appear to have had plenty of connections with the wider world of empire'. Barbados and Ceylon were the options being considered by the lad, but his mother knew a Geordie Thomson who was 'in tea' in Ceylon.

Another link in Scotland's chain-of-migration was forged and Mac became a 'creeper' to Geordie Thomson, working at the Spring Valley estate just before the start of the First World War. Mac remained in Ceylon during the war years, signing up as a Royal Flying Corps reservist and making the tea that we encountered in Chapter 1 that was keeping Iain Hay's *The First Hundred Thousand* alert at their posts. By the 1920s Mac had risen to manage a group of estates. During the Second World War, Japanese bombing raids caused widespread panic in Ceylon and Mac's wife and daughter were evacuated to South Africa. As tea was deemed essential to British morale, Mac stayed on at the plantations. The McLarens returned to Scotland in 1946, a few years before Sri Lanka's independence, but not before Mac had begun the building of a new tea factory at Darty estate, Gampola.[19]

The year that followed the Great Exhibition in Kelvingrove, where Queen Victoria sipped the Ceylon brew, a highly successful Glasgow grocer took ship for Ceylon with a pile of money.

Thomas Lipton was a Gorbals boy – the son of Ulster-Scots smallholders who had been driven from their home by the potato famine and had settled in Glasgow in 1847. Thomas was probably born the following year and was the only one of the Liptons' four children to survive infancy. His parents took over a shop in Crown Street, selling basic provisions, and Tommy left school at 13, eventually going to sea as a cabin boy. He spent five years odd-jobbing his way around America before returning to Glasgow in 1870 to start 'Lipton's Market', a provisions shop in the Anderson district. Lipton was a born salesman and in an early stunt paraded pigs through Glasgow with signs saying 'Home fed and bound for Liptons'. He later had an elephant pull a giant wheel of cheese through Leicester, and another time hired skinny men to march to one of his shops with placards saying, 'Going to Lipton's' – and then sent out fat men with signs reading 'Coming from Lipton's'.[20] Raised in poverty, he knew that cost was king for most customers and that low prices would be made up for by high turnover. By the time of the 1888 exhibition he had 300 shops throughout Britain.

Lipton arrived in Ceylon just in time to snap up some bargain-basement coffee plantations. He spent £75,000 on this shopping spree, acquiring twelve estates and becoming the island's biggest tea proprietor.[21] There were grumblings that Ceylon was no longer a British colony but a Lipton colony.[22] A great salesman is almost certainly a great exaggerator, and Lipton's claim to have cut out the middleman to bring customers their favourite drink 'from tea garden to tea pot' was certainly an exaggeration because he did buy tea from other estates. But his gift for publicity firmly established Ceylon tea in the public mind as a quality product, and his vast chain of shops sold tea that a growing public could afford. While Lipton never really had his own colony in Ceylon, tea-drinking settlers in Saskatchewan, Canada, named their small village after him.[23]

For countless working-class Scots 'tea' became Lipton's Ceylon tea – and Ceylon's tea was James Taylor's tea. But while

Taylor's pioneering work and example had re-booted Ceylon's plantation economy, not all planters benefited. Some of the failed coffee men no doubt found other employment in Ceylon or went home in despair. Others dusted themselves down and started all over again in pastures new. Such a man was Henry Brown.

CHAPTER 7

A Handful of Seeds

In 1891 a Scottish coffee planter from Ceylon – a botanical refugee from the devastating *Hemileia vastatrix* fungus – wandered into the garden of the Church of Scotland mission at Blantyre, in what was then British Central Africa. The town, now the commercial centre of Malawi, was busily growing up around the mission station built in honour of the doctor, missionary and explorer David Livingstone, and named after his birthplace. Livingstone had first ventured into the area in 1859, and Free Church of Scotland and Church of Scotland missionaries had followed in 1875 and 1876.

Forty-one-year-old Henry Brown arrived in time to witness the completion of the brick-built St Michael and All Angels Church that had risen over the past three years on the site of the original mission. Whatever spiritual solace the uprooted coffee planter found in the church, its garden was a revelation. Blantyre's missionaries liked to introduce plants to Africa that they thought might be nutritionally and economically useful to the local people, and Jonathan Duncan, the mission gardener, had first imported a Wardian case of tea and coffee plants from the Edinburgh Botanical Gardens to Blantyre in 1878. Low rainfall may have killed his first plants, but a decade later Scots missionary Dr Walter Elmslie arrived from Edinburgh with another batch, from which Duncan successfully raised two healthy tea bushes. They were of robust stock and it is said that one of Duncan's plants survived into the 1970s.

Jonathan Duncan hadn't been the only plantsman to dream of African tea. In 1850 it was grown as an experimental crop at the Durban Botanical Gardens, but it wasn't until 1877, when the local coffee crop failed, that tea was taken seriously in the Natal region of what is now South Africa. Like the tea seeds, Natal's plantation workers were imported from India – and when immigration rules stemmed the supply of skilled Indians, Natal's tea industry began to wither.[1] By 1911 Natal tea was in terminal decline, however Jonathan Duncan's plants had quietly flourished in the Blantyre Mission garden, where they had caught the eye of the enterprising Henry Brown.

According to Glasgow-born missionary the Rev. John Archibald Smith, Henry was walking one day in the mission garden when he spotted Duncan's tea bushes. Gathering around twenty seeds, Brown went on to plant about half of them on an estate which he had recently bought from the African Lakes Company.[2] The remaining seeds he gave to his neighbour, John Moir, who planted them on his nearby Lauderdale estate. Moir was one of two Edinburgh-born brothers who managed the African Lakes Company, which had been set up by Scots businessmen in 1877 as a commercial operation that would support Free Church missions. The company developed lake and river transport, leased land and established trading posts, and at one point even waged a small, but unsuccessful, war against Swahili slave traders.

The Lakes Company had an early interest in tea as a crop. Five years before Henry Brown arrived in Africa, John Moir had written to Kew Gardens for tea plants and seeds to be sent to him. These were duly dispatched on the *Garth Castle*, the Govan-built UK-to-Cape mail ship, in the care of Aberdeen-born missionary Dr Robert Laws, who was on his way back to Africa. 'Nothing is known of the fate of these consignments,' recalled the chairman of the Nyasaland Tea Growers' Association, 'and it is only reasonable to assume that they perished.' The tea that would finally take root in Africa was Jonathan Duncan's, carefully cultivated by Henry Brown on his Thornwood estate, seventy-five miles west of Blantyre, close to the majestic Mulanje Massif and the Mozambique border. The Mulanje peaks are magnets for cloud and rain, and the estate beneath them, lying between 2,000 and 3,000 feet, enjoys cool winters and hot, wet summers. Brown's pocketful of seeds thrived in the rich, red soil and would make him the father of African tea. But Henry Brown's story begins nearly 8,000 miles away in the Aberdeenshire town of Banff.

Henry Brown was born in 1850 in a town that seems to have forgotten him, for there is no reference to him in the town's museum or the local Heritage Society's *Book of Banff*. And while Wikipedia lists a premier of Tasmania, a bodybuilding strongman and singer-songwriter Sandi Thom amongst Banff's notable sons and daughters, Henry Brown is shamefully forgotten.

Henry was the first son of John Brown and his English-born wife Bridget Devine. The couple lived at the 'top of Gallowhill', presumably close to where the tinker outlaw James Macpherson played a 'rant' on his fiddle prior to being hanged and immortalised by Robert Burns.

Sae rantingly, sae wantonly,
Sae dauntingly gaed he;
He play'd a tune, and danc'd it roon'
Below the gallows-tree.

The 1851 census describes John Brown as a sailor, a not unusual job in this community, where fishing for herring, and the export of them, was nearing its height. But within a decade John Brown had moved on. While Bridget and her two sons, Henry and James, are recorded in the 1861 census as still living in Banff, John Brown is absent; Bridget is described as 'a coffee planter's wife'.

At some stage, probably around 1873, young Henry moved to Ceylon, where *Hemileia vastatrix* was already wreaking havoc among coffee plantations. The coffee might have been dying, but North-east Scots flourished there. Brown's Doric-tinged accent would hardly have stood out. Henry was related to a well-established and influential Ceylon planter. An African newspaper[3] described Henry as 'a relative of Alexander Brown of Ceylon'. As well as being 'a picturesque pioneer type' who controlled a large number of estates, Alexander 'Sandy' Brown (1820–76) was the first secretary and treasurer of the Planters' Association of Ceylon and was the author of the snappily titled book *The Coffee Planter's Manual, to Which is Added a Variety of Information Useful to Planters, Including a Summary of Practical Opinions on the Manuring of Coffee Estates Etc.*[4]

Henry found love and, in 1878, at the age of twenty-eight, married the eighteen-year-old Mary Ann Imlah, the daughter of a Scots coffee planter from an estate near Matale, north of Kandy. Mary Ann's upbringing on an estate seems to have prepared her for the role of pioneering wife. Henry and Mary Ann had two children, Henry James Brown, born in 1880, and Helen Devine Brown, born in 1884.

With a family to support, and coffee rust destroying crops and livelihoods, Brown upped sticks and headed for the rough-and-ready territory of British Central Africa. It was untamed country where the mortality rate among Europeans was high, so Mary Ann and the children were packed off to Glasgow, where they appear in the 1891 census, before joining Henry in Africa four years later.

In the late 1800s the Protectorate of British Central Africa, which became Nyasaland, and then became Malawi, was a turbulent region, beset with slave trading and war. For whites, the chaos presented the perfect opportunity for a land grab. Europeans with guns and influence quickly snapped up land 'rights' from tribal chiefs who were seeking protection from enemies and slavers. White settlers bamboozled black chiefs with contracts they couldn't read, acquiring huge tracts of land in exchange for a few guns and gewgaws. The chiefs were almost always cheated. Sometimes they didn't have the authority to sell tribal territory in the first place, and often the lands 'sold' were found to be overlapping, leaving more than one buyer claiming it. Even when land was deemed to have been legally sold, the price was derisory. For landless Africans the white estates only provided low-wage jobs, but for hard-working Europeans, prepared to put up with isolation, privation and danger, there were opportunities.

An experienced planter, Henry soon found work establishing the Lauderdale estate, belonging to the Lakes Company, growing coffee and tobacco. Much of the land was virgin, requiring the application of sharp-bladed panga, hoe and sweat to tame it. A talented agriculturalist, with a gift for working with local labour, Brown swiftly made his mark and soon took over the nearby Thornwood estate for himself. It was from the rich, red soil of Lauderdale and Thornwood that the shoots of Africa's gigantic tea industry first sprouted. The ambitious Henry Brown entered into the scrabble for African land with gusto. Within a decade of arriving, he became the proprietor of more than 2,000 acres of Mulanje, including Thornwood, Dunraven and Swazi estates.[5]

Brown was physically and psychologically robust. But his response, in 1894, to a survey about the effect of climate on

Europeans reveals something of the danger and hardship that pioneer planters faced.

> There is doubtless a great mortality among Europeans which is caused by want of knowledge of diseases, which are common in all tropical climates, and how to treat them. Poor fellows often live far away from medical advice without even a white face to look at them, console or comfort them during illness. Such has always been the case in opening up new countries, with pioneers isolated far from the centre of civilisation; often hundreds of miles from the sea coast without an expedient means of conveyance, without even a horse, donkey, coach, bullock, rickshaw or road to travel by. The great secret is knowing how to live and doctor oneself which is only taught by experience ... The stamp of men wanted here are those which might be recruited from the middle of gentleman class, with a little capital which many a father is often ready to give his son to start him in life and glad to get rid of him instead of having him loafing at home, idling away his years doing no good to himself or those connected with him.

The worldly wise Scot was suited to this style of life, but his enormous drive and capacity for hard work came with some predictable personality traits. He was impatient, hot-tempered and stubborn, and frequently in conflict with the colonial administration, often bringing down the wrath of the Forestry Department for illegally grazing his cattle on the Mulanje plateau.

In 1891 Brown purchased – or thought he had purchased – a huge tract of land from Chief Mwambula. But in the colonial scramble for territory, this land ended up on the wrong side of the border between British Central Africa and the

Portuguese territory that is now Mozambique. Despite being told that he had no legal right to the land, Brown continued to plant coffee on it – bringing down threats of prosecution. The following year Chief Mwambula denied selling the land to Brown, saying that he had only given him permission to plant coffee and build a small house on it, and that, as a gift, Brown had given him 'two kegs of powder, one piece of red cloth, one piece of handkerchiefs, three packets of pink beads – this is all, together with seven night caps'.

Brown lost his case but was incorrigible. In September 1882 after he began developing land he claimed to have bought at Kukumba on the Ruo River, he received a sharp rebuke from colonial official W.M. Farrell: 'Your claim to that country is recognised by nobody but yourself. Under the circumstance I insist on your stopping this work immediately or I shall send or take a police force to stop it for you.'

The man ultimately responsible for reining in Brown – stopping him from snaffling parcels of land that didn't belong to him and rebuking him for his rudeness to government officials – was British Commissioner Harry Johnston, a highly experienced explorer-turned-colonial administrator. A letter from Johnston sent in September 1892 to Brown ends: 'Please understand that, after this letter, if you continue clearing or in any way interfering with land to which you have no right, you will incur a very serious responsibility as I shall consider your conduct wholly inexcusable.'

Although the correspondence between Johnston and the recalcitrant Scot was sometimes acrimonious, Johnston had a regard for Brown and took time to write sympathetically to him when he fell ill.

I was sorry to learn that you had a touch of fever today. We have all been out of sorts here ... This country is so beautiful that it argues a certain spite on the part of providence to have made it unhealthy. Poor martyr man! The thought of us having to toil & suffer incessantly to remedy the want of finish in our surroundings often gives my view on Africa an irreligious bias. Dwelling in paved streets, with hot & cold water laid on, with the electric light, & the butcher and baker calling for orders daily, it is easy enough to believe in all-wise providence: but here ...!

Although cantankerous, Brown was capable of firm friendship. He was stingy when it came to using writing paper – he wrote his letters on torn scraps – but was hospitable and generous. Befriending Edward Laidlaw Thomson, who was John Moir's assistant at Lauderdale and the Lakes Company, Brown would lend the young Scot his rifle and shotgun, and once gave him a pair of Ceylon water sapphires to send to his mother. When Brown fell out with John Moir, Thomson wrote home in July 1893:

> Brown, the man who opened up this whole estate and knows the country round better than any other man, has quarrelled with Moir, and at present intends on leaving him. I must say, I side entirely with Brown, or nearly so ... I am awfully sorry about Brown leaving. He has been very kind to me in many ways.

A month later, Thomson wrote: 'Brown left on Monday.'

One of the things that impressed Thomson about Brown, apart from his generosity, was the relationship he had with the estate workers, who called him *Mlanghi* (advisor or mentor). He wrote: 'Brown is, in their eyes, the best example of a *Mzungu** they have seen.' Brown's role at the Lakes Company's

---

* A Bantu word for white person.

Lauderdale estate was taken over by fellow Scot George Garden.

The energetic Brown now gave his full attention to building up his own estate at Thornwood. The Mulanje District is 200 square miles of tableland from which great granite peaks rise to over 9,800 feet. Brown's estate was at just over 6,000 feet, where the climate is north-temperate, the water pure and plentiful, and the pasture rich. It was a place where a hard-working man could prosper. The arrival from Glasgow of Henry's strong-minded wife in 1895 only made him even more formidable. 'If Henry was the actual pioneer of tea planting, there is little doubt that the drive behind the enterprise was that of his wife's, for "Ma" was the dominant partner,' wrote planter Henry Westrop in *Green Gold*, his memoir of tea planting in Nyasaland.

It wasn't the arrival of Ma that stirred Edward Laidlaw Thomson, who wrote home:

> Mrs Brown's awfully nice, but when you remember that for two and a half years I have not seen an unattached woman under ten stone in weight, you can make allowance for any hyperbolic allusions to what Cox calls 'a blooming angel'. Just fancy a girl with hair down her back in this black, benighted B.C.A.!

This 'blooming angel' of a girl with hair down her back must have been eleven- or twelve-year-old Miss Nellie Brown, not her formidable thirty-five-year-old mother. Clearly young Thomson had been out in the sticks for some time.

Henry Brown now had tea plants mature enough to harvest. Even if he had been paying close attention to the pioneering work of James Taylor in Ceylon, he had none of the technology that had been developed by estates in India and Ceylon. But, by hand-rolling the leaves and firing them in a pan over a charcoal burner, Henry made tea. No doubt it was initially for his own use, but in September 1896 he entered his tea in the Mulanje Horticultural & Agricultural Show, winning first prize. This couldn't have been much of an accolade, as the tea was widely thought to be 'awful'.

Brown persevered, winning first prize again two years later, beating his former colleague, John Moir, who came in second. His 1900 tea at the same show drew the comment: 'It was awful; in fact, so awful that it merited the well-known word beginning with "b" which prefixed the awful.' Local tea seems to have been pretty well hit or miss. The Rev. John Archibald Smith recalled drinking the Blantyre Mission's tea: 'We did not pronounce favourably upon it. Oh, the horror of it!'[6]

But African tea was improving – or at least showing potential. Mr J. McClounie, the Protectorate's scientific officer based at its capital in Zomba, reported from the Lauderdale and Thornwood estates:

> Tea seems to do well here ... the bushes shew good growth, and a very palatable tea made entirely by natives who were, I understand, instructed by Mrs Moir. Tea has been largely planted throughout the upper part of the estate and were more attention given to the preparation of the leaves no doubt a tea of good class would be the result ... Mr Brown's interesting estate at Thornwood was next visited. The soil at Thornwood is deep, of rich reddish chocolate colour, apparently suited to the cultivation of tea which is also grown here. There is about 6 acres under cultivation and doing well; the older bushes are vigorous and very promising in appearance.

Three years earlier Henry Brown had been quoted in the *Central African Times* as claiming, 'I am trying to get up an acreage of tea and now have 12 acres planted with a very good jat.'

Whatever acreage of tea Brown actually had, he was harvesting favourable press coverage. In April 1903 the *Government Gazette*'s editorial said:

> We are glad to note the progress which is being made in the cultivation of tea at Mlanje, at both Thornwood and Lauderdale Estates. Indeed, tea has reached what might be termed the commercial stage, and the product is on the local market, with a quality which is certainly gratifying to the growers. Like all pure teas, it has a distinctive flavour of its own, but the flavour is one which grows upon one with use ... we believe Mlanje tea has come to stay.

Not all planters who tangled with tea succeeded. John Buchanan, a Scot who had come to Central Africa as a lay-member of Blantyre Mission, had established extensive estates with his brothers in the Zomba region but failed to grow tea successfully. Reporting the failure, Mr McClounie noted that the rainfall in the Zomba region was about a half to a third of the estates beneath the Mulanje Mountains.

Africa could not only destroy dreams and profits, it extracted a heavy toll on people too, especially Europeans with no immunity to tropical diseases. In 1900 Henry wrote of his worry about his son, Henry (Harry) James Brown, 'at the front' in the Boer War, where he saw considerable service, but it was blackwater fever, a severe form of malaria, that killed the twenty-three year old in 1903.

That year Sir Alfred Sharpe, who had taken over from Harry Johnston as commissioner, sent tea samples to the Imperial Institute in London, a showcase for the produce of Empire. Hopes of getting an Imperial thumbs-up were dashed, as Henry Brown's tea had been packed together with other produce and 'the true aroma of the tea was masked by that of tobacco'. But although the flavour was ruined, the teas were sent to a commercial broker for evaluation. The brokers 'read the leaves', even if they didn't taste the tea, and reported: 'The infused leaves were moderately bright, and in the two broken mixed and two Orange Pekoes the leaf appeared to have been fairly well manipulated and contained a small quantity of tips. The value given were from 4¼d. to 7½d. per lb.'[7]

Tea may have been a passion for Brown, but it alone did not provide him with a living. He raised cattle, felled timber, built roads and was one of the region's leading tobacco farmers, producing cigars and pipe tobacco. His Thornwood estate had its own blacksmith's forge, a carpenter's shop, and raised poultry and maize to feed his workers. Year on year, more tea was planted at Mulanje. In 1904 there were over 200 acres of tea at Thornwood and 50 at Lauderdale, and for the first time tea figured among British Central Africa's exports – with around four tons of tea being exported at a value of £40.

Two years later, the country's agricultural report noted that while 395 acres of tea at Mulanje was expected to produce 1,500 pounds of tea, a 'large area' was also planted with young, immature bushes. Tea, however, was well down the table of the region's produce, coming after coffee, cotton, tobacco, chillies and rubber.

By 1911 the annual report was taking tea more seriously: 'For some years tea was looked upon as a hobby of Mr H. Brown of Mlanje, but everything points that he is a pioneer of what will intimately become an important minor cultivation of Nyasaland.' The report also stated: 'Even with a smaller yield than Ceylon, tea would be a most profitable crop in Nyasaland as labour is at least 50 per cent cheaper.'[8]

Where Brown led, others followed, but Henry – right from

the start – was acclaimed as the founder of the tea industry in the region. In 1912 the Rev. Smith, who spent much of his career as a missionary and teacher in Nyasaland, reported: 'While tea seed has been imported by others, the real pioneer of tea in Nyasaland is undoubtedly Mr Henry Brown who has for many years persevered through sunshine and storm to make the industry a success.'[9] By this time Brown was ramping up his commitment and investment, and was using tea dryers, a tea cutter and a gas engine. His product had moved on from being simply a home brew to inspiring an entire community of planters. In 1914 the annual report of the Tea Brokers' Association in London contains numerous references to the sale of 'Nyasaland' tea. Blenders just couldn't get enough of the inexpensive leaf that was conveniently available during Assam's winter months.

Henry Brown's tastes and interests were well suited to the colonial life. He enjoyed outdoor pursuits, camping and spending weekends in the simple clapboard Pioneer Cottage which he had built on Mulanje Mountain. Like many of the planter breed, he hunted and filled his home with trophies. But like the botanically minded Scottish doctors of India, Brown had a serious interest in the natural history of the country he had found himself in. For at least sixteen years the planter sent zoological and other specimens to museum curators in Glasgow – often to order – at a time when the new Kelvingrove Museum and Art Gallery was being built and was hungry for exotica from around the world. The creation of the baroque red-sandstone Kelvingrove Museum was partly due to the efforts of that emerging Glasgow tea magnate John Muir of James Finlay Ltd. Today, among more than a million artefacts stored in Glasgow Museums' resource centre are about 2,000 supplied by Henry Brown, including at least 500 bird skins, along with hundreds of insects, plants and mammal pelts, tribal bowls, pipes, snuff boxes and knives.

Glasgow Museums also has revealing letters from Brown to the museum superintendent, James Paton, and his colleague, Mr Campbell. Written thriftily, on both sides of extremely flimsy paper, through which the ink has bled, they have been painstakingly decoded and transcribed. Even a handful of extracts reveal Henry Brown to be a serious and dedicated collector, and one with an intense interest in the new museum that was being constructed in Glasgow.

Dunraven Estate, Mlanji, B.C.A.

11 February 1897

Dear Mr Paton,

I have been going to write to you for some time, but have always put off intending to send some more big game specimens, but the season has passed without my being able to procure any more. In Aug last I went out some 60 miles to get big game & only managed to get a zebra, buffalo & water-buck, the two latter had good heads. I left the skins to be sent by the African Lakes Co steamer to the coast ... I trust reached you in good order. I gave instructions to have the specimens sprinkled with turpentine before dispatch which may have saved them & they were fairly well preserved when I left them ...

The great difficulty in sending things from this country is the transport. We are 280 odd miles from the coast ...

I enclose a bill for expenses in connection with the specimens sent home, the amount £15 might be paid out to my son Harry c/o Mrs Burnett, 21 Kent Road,

Glasgow & the receipt sent out to me for signature if necessary.

When is the new museum to be ready?

Yours sincerely

Henry Brown

                                        Mlanjj, B.C. Africa
                                        10th March '99

Dear Mr Campbell,

I send by today's post a skin of a young Bush Buck. Sorry the head was eaten by my dog, also the skull of our Baboon monkey, shot in my potato garden.

I hope the Zebra & other skins reached you all right. I would be much obliged if you would send me out some preservation powder, arsenical soap etc. & I would make a collection during the dry season. (Is) your new museum open yet?

With kind regards to Mr Paton & yourself,

Yours very truly

Henry Brown

                                        Thornwood Estate
                                        M'lanje
                                        18th Feby 1908

Dear Mr Paton,

I sent by Mr Austin, a Mlanje planter who went home 2 months ago, the skeleton of a leopard that was a determined man eater but was killed in the end by a man, whom he attacked, with a big cane knife. The cuts on the skull are quite sizeable & the man recovered altho [sic] badly torn on face, neck & arms. Would you kindly ask your museum manager to send me by post some napthalin [sic] & camphor.

With kind regards. Yours truly,

H. B.

Once in Glasgow, many of Brown's specimens were sent to the Sauchiehall Street premises of Charles Kirk, Scotland's leading taxidermist. Kirk, along with being the taxidermist for the Bombay Natural History Society, was also responsible for stuffing Sir Roger, Kelvingrove's popular pachyderm.

Henry Brown shot photographs, as well as animals, and recorded the development of his estate and gatherings of friends, although he seldom put himself in the frame. His photos, and many papers relating to his life and work, are held at Mandala House, the oldest building in Blantyre and the home of the invaluable library and archives of the Malawi Society. Built in 1882, in the colonial style, with an all-around veranda, it was a residence for African Lakes Company managers. As a one-time Lakes Company employee, Henry Brown may well have visited and socialised in this very building.

In common with most other tea planters, Henry was not exactly teetotal, although his wife Mary Ann most certainly was and banned alcohol from their house. The resourceful Henry got around this by 'planking' bottles around his estate, and 'inspecting' them on his daily rounds. Visiting male friends would be invited to join him on such lubricated excursions. While staying at Pioneer Cottage, Henry would send notes to friends to send him a bottle of whisky from the planters' club, and sometimes several bottles would arrive in response to a flurry of begging letters.

Hospitality among planters in lonely stations was common where hotels were scarce and Henry was no exception. 'We shall be glad to see you with any of your friends at any time,' he wrote to an acquaintance.[10] Annually the planters gathered for a Sports Week, which was popular and highly convivial, although when the teetotal John Moir attempted to form a golf club, it failed – because it lacked a 19th hole. Any social events that the Browns attended would have had a strong Scottish accent, as the 1911 census shows that almost half of the Nyasaland settlers were Scots-born, making it 'more or less a Scottish colony'.[11]

In the 1920s, imported seeds from India and Ceylon superseded the original Blantyre Mission stock, and in 1924 Nyasaland's tea exports hit the £1 million mark. Henry Brown lived to see this milestone, but the following year died at Mulanje on 17 August at the age of seventy-five, having seen his pocketful of seeds grow into a major industry. He was buried on Thornwood estate – the land he had carved out of the wild African landscape. His grave was surrounded by a brick wall in a tea field and in the shade of a venerable mahogany tree. The following year the Lyons Tea company acquired 6,000 acres of tea plantation in Nyasaland. It seemed the days of the true pioneer planter had passed . . . but not quite.

Mary Ann, 'Ma' Brown, survived her husband by twenty-one years, dying at the age of eighty-five in Blantyre Hospital after a short illness and was buried alongside Henry at Thornwood. The writer and self-styled guru Laurens Van Der Post, in *Venture into the Interior*, dismisses Ma Brown as 'an eccentric old lady who kept some cows up there' on Mount Mulanje. But the old fraud underestimated Ma. Although she lived a quiet, pious and frugal life, she was an able farmer and had remained a formidable force in the Mulanje planters' circle.

Major Vincent John Keyte, a former Protectorate official, who was in his eighties when recorded in 1984, remembered: 'I knew her well and I was frightened of her. She very seldom came to the Club, where my spiritual home was. She was a formidable old lady. She would shout you down if you argued with her, but she was a very knowledgeable person on tea.' Keyte went on to say that Ma was 'a dear old thing' and that 'everyone loved her'.

Another insight into Ma's personality was revealed to me – over lunch, suitably, in Glasgow's old-worldy Butterfly & Pig Tea Room – by Max Docherty, whose mother, Isabella, spent more than six years living with Ma and her daughter Nellie at Thornwood. Through a complicated family entanglement, Ma was Isabella's step-great-grandmother.

'At nineteen,' said Max, 'my mother seems to have been something of a "wild child" and was shipped off from Milngavie to Nyasaland. I gather she worked round the estate. Ma Brown insisted that the estate workers should be spoken to in their own language and my mother spent six years there and learned Swahili. She enjoyed the social life of the Europeans in Nyasaland and attended balls at the governor's residence in Blantyre. She seems to have enjoyed life there and I think she was quite close to Nellie.'

Max believed that Isabella may have left Thornwood because Presbyterian Ma 'disapproved quite strongly of my mother's intention to become a Catholic – she had been very impressed by the White Father Missionaries'. The breach, however, was healed, and Nellie once wrote to Isabella offering her husband a job on the estate, although he never took it. 'My mother wasn't a blood relation of Ma's,' Max told me, 'but she was seen as "family" all the same.'

Ma's obituary in the *Nyasaland Times* reveals that she and Nellie continued running the family estates after Henry's death. Major Keyte recalled: 'Nellie was very knowledgeable about tea, although she was henpecked. I'm sure she would never have married because she was Ma's factotum.' Nellie never did marry. Local tradition had it that Ma saw off suitors with a shotgun. In her will, Ma left everything to Nellie, including 2,000 acres of land, 900 under tea cultivation. Nellie would not enjoy the fruit of her parents' struggle. Only three months after her mother's death, Nellie died at the age of sixty-two and was buried beside her parents at Thornwood. Legend has it that on hearing of Nellie's death a local planter said, 'I thought that might happen. When Ma got up aloft, she must have found that there was no one to fetch and carry for her. No "Nellie do this, Nellie do that." So she just shouted down, "Nellie, come here." And she came!'[12]

Nellie left her fortune – valued at £88,000 – to the Nyasaland government on the understanding that it be used to build a road up to Lichenya, close to Pioneer Cottage, and a European school there. The government baulked at this and declared the will invalid, claiming that there was no case for a European school, as Europeans had their children educated in the 'old country' and, in any case, the legacy was insufficient to build both the road and the school. But when the Browns' property was auctioned off at the Town Hall in Blantyre the Thornwood estate, and its more than 700 acres of tea, sold for £155,000. The sale of the smaller estates and the cottages brought the total amount to £250,000. But even this enormous sum (worth over £10 million today) was thought insufficient to realise Nellie's dream of a school and in 1952 the money went to the newly formed Henry Brown Trust, which devoted itself to the care of Nyasaland's lepers.

In a fascinating essay on Henry Brown, written for *The Society of Malawi Journal* in 1992, Barbara Lamport-Stokes, lamented: 'Today there are no individually owned tea estates and the Brown properties have been sold to various tea companies, many of whose employees will never have heard of Henry Brown, who started it all.'

In 1891 Henry Brown had left a strongly Scottish planting community on Ceylon and helped to create an equally Scottish one on Africa. The role of Scots in Nyasaland didn't escape the attention of the generously initialled chairman of the Nyasaland Tea Association, G.G.S.J. Hadlow.

> As an Englishman I feel I should end my talk with a tribute to all the Scotsmen who played a major part in the beginnings of tea in Nyasaland. Practically every name I have mentioned has a Doric sound (if not the intonation), the Moirs, the Buchanans, Dr Elmslie, Dr Laws, Henry Brown (although he could have been an Englishman, but wasn't) and George Garden, together with all the Scottish Missionaries who played their part in those early days.[13]

Most of us have drunk Malawian tea, even though we don't know it. In its pure form it is difficult to buy, even from specialised shops, but its anonymous presence imparts to many quality British blends a deep red colour that looks and tastes great with a splash of milk. In 2016 Malawi's exports were worth $932 million, of which $74.1 million was tea, the country's fourth-biggest export after raw tobacco, gold and sugar. The country produces more than 45 million kilos of tea annually – providing jobs for thousands of workers and valuable foreign currency for this relatively poor country. It is an extraordinary journey for an industry, the seeds of which were pocketed by a Scotsman in the Blantyre Mission garden.

Henry Brown's Thornwood estate, where Africa's tea industry began, is still flourishing. Today it is owned by Eastern Produce Malawi Ltd, whose parent company is Camellia Plc. Based in the UK, Camellia operates across twelve countries, has a staff of nearly 80,000 and is the second-largest private producer of tea in the world. But even under the management of this global giant, an echo of Scotland can be detected. Camellia's website proudly traces the company's origins to 1859, when a young Scot, Walter Duncan, first arrived in Calcutta in search of his fortune. With his brother William, he eventually set up a successful tea enterprise which – through mergers, takeovers and rebranding – eventually evolved into the global Camellia Plc.

The Scottish-founded tea company James Finlay & Co. today has a presence in Malawi, but it was also a leading pioneer of the massive tea industry in Kenya. Among the first settlers to plant tea in Kenya were the Orchardson brothers, sons of the famous Scottish painter Sir William Quiller Orchardson. Engravings of Sir William's *Napoleon on Board the Bellerophon* hung on the walls of many a Victorian schoolroom. The Orchardsons were certainly growing tea in the Kericho District for their own consumption from 1916. Brooke Bond began to develop an estate at Limuru in 1924, and two years later James Finlay's chairman announced to the annual meeting of shareholders that the company had 'for a year or two, been keeping an eye on East Africa' and had now acquired a 'compact block of land in Kenya' (about 23,000 acres!) where, with partners, it had formed a company to develop it as a tea estate.

A book, privately printed by Finlay's[14], reveals a fascinating history of the Kenyan investment. Shortly after the First World War, the British East African Disabled Officers' Colony (BEADOC) was launched in Kenya to support ex-servicemen. More than seventy ex-officers shared an estate of fine rolling land in the Kericho District, with the idea that each would have his own plot but that they would work collectively, sharing machinery and expertise. 'It was,' the book states, 'an admirable idea in theory, but one which unfortunately failed to work out in practice, largely due to inadequate capital, insufficient experience and, it is feared, unsound advice which probably proved to be a good example of the old saying about "too many cooks".'

The plan had been for the old soldiers to grow flax, but when the bottom fell out of the flax market in 1922 BEADOC was surrendered to the liquidator. Two years later, tea estate manager R.D. Armstrong decided to take a break from Finlay's Kanan Devan Hills Produce Company in what is now Kerala in south-west India and visit relations in Kenya. Hearing of the demise of BEADOC, he visited the abandoned land, was impressed, and on New Year's Day 1925 wrote a report that whetted the appetites of the James Finlay directors in Glasgow's West Nile Street. Armstrong also reported that Lipton's was showing an interest in the property. After further investigation, Finlay's snapped up most of the BEADOC land – 20,000 acres of it – in partnership with four other companies. The remaining land was bought by Brooke Bond. It was a good buy. Tea growing this close to the equator makes an all-year production possible, while the altitude (just over 7,000 feet) brings ample rain and moderates the heat of the sun. Like Sri Lanka, it has two rainy seasons and allows picking almost all year round.

But despite the generosity of the geography, Finlay's new offshoot, the African Highlands Produce Company, was a very bold investment, and it was seen by colonists in Kenya as more than a reckless one. Old Africa hands doubted if suitable labour could be found to work the proposed plantations, and when the first manager of the new estate, William Lee, revealed to Kenya's chief native commissioner that his long-term plan was to recruit 20,000 workers, the commissioner waited until Lee had left his office, tapped his forehead and murmured, 'Mad, quite mad!' Lee began work with no experience of local conditions, no knowledge of the language and no labour force. But by sharing the cost of the investment with partners and drawing on their own staff, with their in-depth experience of tea growing in India, the canny Scots prevailed. Soon a hundred labourers, recruited from those who had worked for BEADOC, were busy hacking out a thirty-acre tea nursery from the virgin bush and 25,600 pounds of seed was on its way from India. In 1928 the first Kenyan tea reached the London salerooms. By 1930, the Glasgow-incorporated African Highlands Produce Company had 1,213 acres of tea planted. Today, James Finlay's still grows tea on the former BEADOC land – a testimony to the astute recommendation of R.D. Armstrong. Some of the bushes being picked today are the same ones planted by the first pioneers.[15]

Little more than a century ago a handful of planters like the Orchardson brothers were producing just about enough tea for their own consumption. Now, Kenya is a major exporter producing more tea than the rest of Africa put together. While 'speciality' or 'artisan' Kenya tea is hard (though not impossible) to find, all of us who make our first morning quencher with a teabag will have unknowingly enjoyed its brightness and zest. Where Malawi had led, Kenya had followed. It is remarkable that the seeds of the giant African tea industry once rattled around in Henry Brown's pocket.

CHAPTER 8

Home for Tea

The foothills of the Himalayas, the craggy Western Ghats of South India and the hill-country of Sri Lanka are all likely to remind a Scottish traveller of their own Highlands. I am not the first tea pilgrim to comment on this, and writer Denys Forrest took the idea further when he gazed out from James Taylor's Loolecondera estate: 'It is, one feels, what tea growing in the Cairngorms would be if such a thing were possible.'[1]

And why not? A temperate climate, acidic soil, lots of rain and well-drained hillsides are exactly what tea needs to flourish and what Scotland has aplenty. We Scots also have a drouth that only tea will satisfy and, consequently, a potentially healthy home market. On the negative side are the high costs of native labour and the withering winds that dictate that the Cairngorms, or anywhere else in Scotland, are never going to provide the mass-produced leaf needed to fill supermarket teabags. But, nevertheless, Scotland has joined the ranks of the tea-producing nations. Its tradition of plantsmanship, which fed its people and nurtured its botanically minded doctors, who were so influential in world tea, today inspires many artisan pioneers who are producing world-class food and drink. In sheltered spots throughout the land, some of these inspired souls are growing and processing quality teas in a variety of *jats.* I reckon, at the time of writing, there are about forty fairly serious tea growers in Scotland, although many more people may have a few specimen plants.*

Although Sri Lanka is alluring to Scots as a land of 'bens and glens', it was to take a break from her successful business career that Beverly-Claire Wainwright first moved there. Her new challenge was as a VSO volunteer, working with a Sri Lankan rural chamber of commerce to help develop agri-businesses. A meeting with one of the owners of Amba Tea Estate led to her being offered the job of business development manager once her post as a volunteer ended. The job was wide-ranging, but essentially it was to figure out a way of reviving the ailing estate and creating sustainable livelihoods for local people.

Only twenty acres of the Amba's 110 were planted with tea, and most of the bushes were more than seventy years old and producing very little leaf. The estate didn't have its own factory but simply packed its leaf off to be processed for the massmarket. Beverly-Claire launched herself onto a steep learning curve – visiting factories and the country's Tea Research Institute, and avidly reading all the research she could lay her hands on.

Most of Sri Lanka's tea is factory-produced, but Beverly-Claire spotted a gap in the market: a growing international interest in handmade specialty tea. After a visit to the estate by international tea consultant Nigel Melican, she started to make small batches of hand-rolled tea. For the best part of a year, in addition to running the estate, she continued to experiment and finally created a tea that she was happy with. It turned out that others were happy with it, too – Fortnum & Mason and

---

* Here I should admit to having had such a plant, which I shamefully killed through either neglect or over-watering.

Harney & Sons, which both placed orders. Beverly-Claire's dedication and success led to the building of a small-scale tea factory at Amba estate, the creation of many new jobs, a share scheme for the workers and a turnaround in the fortunes of the estate.

After seven years in Sri Lanka, Beverly-Claire returned to Scotland and a job as associate tea consultant working with Nigel Melican at Teacraft Ltd. Her first job was for the Great Mississippi Tea Company, where she created their first teas to win awards in the TOTUS (Tea of the United States) competition. Beverly-Claire has since helped set up another two micro-factories and developed several new teas in Sri Lanka and Myanmar. In Scotland she has become the 'go-to' consultant for the tea-growing culture that has been steadily taking root in Scottish soil. Her first client was Susie Walker-Munro at Kinnettles in Angus, whom she helped develop her first batches of Kinnettles Gold Tea. Susie is now an established producer of quality, high-value tea, albeit one with a tiny output.

In 2018 Beverly-Claire was able to open Scotland's first small-scale tea factory, at Comrie Croft near Crieff in the southern Highlands. The project was partly funded by a grant she had won from the Perth and Kinross LEADER Fund, which supports rural development. The factory and its demonstration tea garden support Scottish growers by offering tea-processing services, tea-making courses and expert consultancy. A licensed trainer for the UK Tea Academy, Beverly-Claire teaches professional-level tea courses for people in the food and drink industry. She sees tea education as the first step in raising the bar in Scotland from the teabag towards high-quality specialty teas.

Whilst her early tea education was won in Sri Lanka, Beverly-Claire isn't attempting to reproduce the same style of tea. Tea plants grow slowly in Scotland, taking six years to mature in conditions that are marginal. She says that 'the

Scottish soil and weather lead us to cultivating certain tea bushes, and these three elements conspire to make Scottish tea unique.' She also says that 'developing a new tea is a slow process; it takes many experiments and test batches to work out the best processing methods. You need to work with the leaf to bring out the best flavours in order to create a tea that can truly reflect our natural environment and identify as Scottish'.

Even if history doesn't actually repeat itself, I am pretty certain that it does echo down the corridor of time. The thought of James Taylor hand-rolling his leaves on his veranda at Loolecondera in the 1860s, then Beverly-Claire Wainwright conducting her first tea experiments at the Ambra estate a century and a half later pleases me immensely.

We sip China tea – first green, then black – served with simple ceremony in tiny cups as we sit in a little wooden shack while a light wind torments wind-chimes that hang outside, close to thriving young tea bushes. I'm nearer to Perth than Peking, for my host is Monica Griesbaum, who grows organic tea at Windy Hollow Tea Estate at Trinity Gask, near Auchterarder, just north of the Ochil Hills.

Monica's off-grid eco-home, which she shares with her family, lies at the end of a bumpy track. When we arrive, she's waiting for us, playing with her spaniel, Cookie, and raring to go and guide us enthusiastically around her plantation. In her mid-forties, Monica exudes the youthful enthusiasm of someone much younger, talking softly but rapidly as we walk, but stopping frequently to smile in appreciation of what she sees. She delights in the wildflowers and wildlife that thrive all over her pesticide-free farm, and she is dedicated to growing her tea organically, biodynamically and in harmony with the nature that surrounds her. 'I want to encourage natural predators like toads and ladybirds,' she says, as we carefully step around a well-fed specimen of the former.

While Monica made an early decision to raise her first young plants from seeds in polytunnels, more mature plants now survive Perthshire's sometimes keening wind and occasional sub-zero temperatures in small enclosures protected only by windbreaks of cut broom, woven between upright stobs hammered into the ground. Monica hates plastic and eventually wants to do away with her three polytunnels. The wind that screeches over her the aptly named farm is helping her do that, having flayed the skin from one of them already. The plants growing beneath the naked metal ribs of the wreck seemed healthy enough. Soon, she says, she'll demolish the other two, leaving the healthy young bushes unprotected in the soil.

After tramping round the farm, examining and comparing bushes, even nibbling the raw leaves, my wife Jenni and I take tea in Monica's tasting hut. Leaves ... hot water ... a little time to whet the appetite during which we sniff leaves, rubbing them between our fingers ... and then we drink, in appreciative sips. The tea is delicious but, sadly, not Monica's own, which was all sold almost as soon as she had processed it and, she hopes, drunk very shortly afterwards, as she firmly believes that fresh is best when it comes to tea. I make a mental note to get my order in early next year.

Today we first drink a fine and expensive green brew. We sip, sometimes in silence, appreciating the taste, the company and the situation, and sometimes chatting about tea, China, India and travel. The infusion loosens our tongues and lubricates the interaction between people who were strangers an hour before. Then Monica brews a black China tea, once again a premium-quality leaf. It's completely different from the previous drink, refreshing but 'nuttier' and with a mysterious undertone of chocolate! We keep sipping, swapping thoughts and impressions of it as it works its magic on our palettes. I'm reminded of evenings doing the same with malt whiskies in the company of my late friend Carl Reavey. And here's the magic. Like music, art, fine food and good books, tea can not only stimulate and challenge your perceptions but, shared with others, be life-affirming, bringing people together in harmony, strengthening old friendships and forging new ones. In essence, I think drinking tea together is about taking the time out of busy lives to enjoy something made with skill and passion in comfortable companionship with others. There – that's as mystical about tea as I'm going to get.

Although tea is now Monica's passion, it wasn't her top priority when she took over Windy Hollow. 'Tea really wasn't the first thing for me; the farm was first; being a natural organic farmer came first for me and us a family,' she admits. With only twenty-four acres to farm, she realised that she would need to concentrate on high-value specialised crops. But this hard economic fact corresponded with her deeply held values. Growing up in Germany, Monica had been deeply influenced by the rise of the Green Party, concern over the environment and by the resurgence of interest in organic farming. 'I had a strong passion for natural growing and I see the farm as a whole ecosystem and that's really, really important. Tea is now one of the core plants within this system.'

As soon as she acquired her first nut-like tea seeds, Monica began to feel a responsibility for them. Because tea bushes can live a century or more, she thought seriously about where exactly to plant them. Where she could, she put them in sheltered spots. Where she couldn't, she built windbreaks woven from broom.

She tells us: 'You don't know what's going to happen, you don't know if they like our soil. You invite these plants and seeds in, but if they don't like it where you are, it's not meant to be. They don't like the minus-10 degrees here, but they really like the soil, they like our spring water and I do actually believe that it's different to giving plants tap water. So, yes, it was very special when they first came out. You see them grow, you look after them, you do get used to them and they have a presence.'

'Like part of the family?' I ask.

'Yeah, they are. They very much are.'

The more Monica learned about tea, the more intrigued she became. 'That's the beauty of the tea. It's so rich in history and flavour and excitement, and possibly health as well. Many people say they feel much healthier since they've started to drink very fine teas.' For Monica, tea now engages her in three ways. 'One is enjoying tea and training my palate for really fine teas, and that continues all through your life. The second is growing and loving your plants and understanding what they need, and the third is processing tea.'

Monica travelled to Taiwan to stay and study with an organic tea maker. While there, she tasted fine machine-made oolong teas, but it was hand-rolled leaf that really inspired her. 'Machines have their place, but for me the beauty of hand-rolling is making tea in a very, very ancient way. When they first started to make tea, they didn't have machines. They tried leaving it in the sun, not leaving it in the sun; leaving it in the shade at various temperatures; rolling it, breaking it, shaking it. I am interested in what nuances you can tease out of the beautiful plant with all these different techniques. That's what I'm drawn to.'

When it comes to physical, psychological and spiritual balance sheets, tea has been a sound investment for Monica and her family, but how do the finances stack up? Can Scottish tea producers make a living, or will it only ever be a lifestyle choice? With bushes taking several years to mature, there is a hefty investment upfront. Organic tea grows slowly and Monica's plants are still small, her crop meagre, although her BlackGold tea fetches high prices and is in demand. While blending home-grown tea with other leaf – or combining tea growing with dealing in imported quality teas – is an option for Scottish producers, Monica refuses to go down these routes. 'I understand financial pressure to say, "I could have some income this year while they are still growing so I'm going to buy some tea and mix it." That's a decision you may have to take for the survival of your farm, but my decision is to be a single estate and only to sell my own produce, and I will never blend.'

I visited Monica early in my research for this book and caught up with her again just days before I finished it. She had good news for me. Windy Hollow has become the only certi-fied organic tea plantation in the UK (and possibly in Europe) and is now certified as a tea producer by the Biodynamic Association UK. And, more importantly, she now produces two delicious Scottish teas, GreenWander and BlackGold.

The organisation Tea Scotland represents sixteen independ-ent tea growers across the country, from Orkney to Galloway and from the Isle of Arran to the coast of Fife. They joined up to collaborate and share experience, to promote awareness of Scottish tea as a product wholly grown, and processed, in Scotland, and to uphold the quality of the product and ethics of the business. Tea Scotland is also in touch with, and tries to encourage, seventeen other growers across Scotland, and it has close ties with the tea factory recently established near Comrie by Beverly-Claire Wainwright. Tea Scotland's chairman, Richard Ross, gave me an overview of the group's activities.

'Growing tea in Scotland is a new adventure for all of us. So far, there are no textbooks on the subject! We aim to share as much information as we can, and help each other to work out solutions to problems and offer general moral support. We come together to console each other when our plants look miserable. As with any new tea region, it takes a while to

understand how climate, soils, weather conditions and growing methods affect the plants, and ultimately affect the finished
tea, so it's a slow path to success.'

The Scottish tea growers whom I have met and corresponded with are deeply committed to what they do. But
of all the tea plantations that I have visited in the East, only
the Okamoto family's tea garden in Japan was run without
employing a large squad of low-paid labour. Harvesting costs
are high, and only by producing tea of the very highest quality
can Scottish growers charge the price they need in order not
to splatter red ink over their annual accounts. Richard Ross
is confident, however, that the quality of the local product
and the 'story' of tea grown and crafted in Scotland will find
a ready market. 'There's now a growing market for premium,
high-quality tea from different parts of the world, especially
when the teas have a good backstory too. Even ten years ago it
would have been a very hard sell to convince consumers to pay
a premium for Scottish-grown tea, at a price level necessary
for the work and time involved to create it. We are confident
there's a good potential market for genuine high-quality tea
grown and made in Scotland.'

To this end, Tea Scotland has adopted a robust constitution and a thorough reporting regime that tracks the number
of bushes each producer has and their garden's output. It is
often said that four times as much Darjeeling is sold than is
actually grown* – Tea Scotland's measures aim to ensure that
'Scottish tea' is tea that is guaranteed to be both grown and
processed in Scotland.

Bad winters, with their Darwinian thinning-out of young
bushes, are a challenge to the viability of growers as well as
tea bushes, but Richard believes that the plants that survive

---

* Not all such teas are fraudulent, as some are clearly sold as
  Darjeeling blends.

and thrive can produce exceptionally good tea. 'The flavour compounds produced in plants which have to struggle a bit to survive are often more complex than those in softer climes. In China, mountain teas are generally regarded as the highest quality, partly for this reason. So tough conditions can pay dividends in the finished tea.'

Richard, who is a wine journalist, cultivates 700 bushes on family-owned land near Dunkeld – from where we hear a north-east accent whisper to us down the corridor of time. One hundred years (to the day) before Richard planted his first bush, his grandfather set out from Tannadice, near Forfar – just forty miles from Richard's garden – to become a tea planter in Ceylon. That ancestor was Alexander 'Mac' McLaren, whom we met in Chapter 5, growing tea through two world wars.

At the time of writing, nobody has begun cultivating tea on Islay, my own home and the birthplace of Archibald Campbell of Ardmore and Darjeeling, but I feel that it is only a matter of time, for other Hebridean islands have their tea gardens. The high-value/low-weight ratio works in favour of small-scale artisan production in the clean environment of Scotland's islands.

Lismore lies in Loch Linnhe, at the western end of the Great Glen Fault. In Gaelic it is called *Lios Mòr*, which may mean 'garden' or 'great enclosure', and the fertility of the soil rather supports that interpretation. The traveller John Knox, writing in 1787, found the people 'indigent and frequently obliged to import meal for their subsistence', but thought the limestone-rich landscape could be the 'granary of that coast'. Farming, along with fishing, is the main occupation of the islanders. Low-lying, with furrows that run along the length of the island, Lismore has sheltered spots where creative gardening can flourish.

Such a place is Baleveolan Croft, where Clare Haworth and Mike Hyatt run a smallholding where they grow tea. The couple fetched up on Lismore after a quarter of a century of holidaying – and dreaming of settling – in Argyll. Their first job on taking over Baleveolan in 2011 was to plant the first of 12,000 trees – partly as windbreaks for the smallholding they planned – and to repair their cottage. An income-earning bunkhouse followed, and crops were planted.

'We are experimenting with a wide range of fruit and edible plants with the idea that in the future we can produce food of high value but low weight to overcome the disadvantage of island transport costs,' Mike told me. 'Other crops might be sea buckthorn, mulberries, lingonberry – even truffles. All experiments just now, but we do have sixty heritage fruit trees that are doing well.'

Mike, a professional landscape architect, operating from Glasgow and Lismore, has strong views on the importance of small-scale rural enterprise. 'Smallholdings and crofts have a huge potential to feed Scotland in a healthy and sustainable way without the need to import massive amounts of food from distant places with the associated carbon footprint. There are many young families we have come across who want a small area of land in rural Scotland to grow food and live. If the Scottish government can put more effort into encouraging landowners to release land for new crofts, then it would be a boost to rural communities, which are still declining in Argyll.'

Into Mike and Clare's mix of fruit and vegetables went small cuttings of tea plants that have now been established for three years and are doing well. Mike describes the origin of their bushes as 'a bit of a mystery' but believes they may come from Turkish stock. Their 450 bushes are planted in what look like traditional Hebridean lazy beds and survive the wind, occasional sub-zero temperatures, variable pH levels and uprooting by voles to produce just two or three hundred grams a year. It's a tiny amount, but they adhere to the 'two leaves and a bud' regime in order to keep the quality high.

Thirsty for knowledge and skills, the couple have found the pioneering work of Beverly-Claire Wainwright inspirational. 'Beverly-Claire is the epicentre of all the skills and information in Scotland,' says Mike. The couple attended one of Beverly-Claire's tea-making courses at her Comrie tea factory, and on that course processed their first home-grown tea. While they plan to process some of their tea on the croft to develop their own knowledge and skill (and because 'it is enjoyable and interesting'), they will probably send future crops to Beverly-Claire for processing once they grow more volume. Mike believes that a fully commercial and profitable Scottish tea garden would have to use polytunnels to extend the season by two picks a year. And while he and Clare have no plans to do this, they still have ambitions to produce a high-value speciality tea.

'We hope to be commercial tea growers by making small quantities of a high-quality tea,' says Mike. 'There are more complex flavours and variations on what you can produce using the basic ingredient of fresh tea leaf than any other type of drink I can think of, and there is a growing interest in specialty teas around the world. We are doing experiments in crop growing with the James Hutton Institute and the Soil Association, and tea is part of the mix. A cup of our own produced tea and a bowl of porridge from our oats would be a great breakfast to achieve.'

Mike believes that Scotland's forty or so growers are still at the stage of 'all learning together'. In the future he predicts that the industry may shake itself out, with some growers falling by the wayside as certain areas and conditions are recognised to be more or less favourable to tea growing. 'I think if current growers have success in their area, it may encourage other growers in the same area to start growing tea. Other places, where it is less successful, will decline. There may ultimately be parts of Scotland that become known for their tea production in the same way that good whisky and wine can be regional. Certainly the tea will be different from different parts of Scotland!'

It is a two-ferry odyssey – but a short hop for a seagull – from Lismore to Mull, where Liz and Martyn Gibson cultivate about 250 bushes on their ten-acre croft near Craignure. Their original plan was to grow soft fruit organically for the local market, but reports of other tea growers in Scotland caught their eye and in 2014 an area of hillside that had been laboriously cleared of bracken was planted with fifty tea plants. Corrugated-iron windbreaks were erected to shelter the young bushes, but they were flattened by Atlantic gales, leaving Liz and Martyn's investment at the mercy of the blast.'We thought we'd made an expensive mistake and were about to admit defeat,' Liz admitted.

Advice was sought, given and implemented. A different site on the croft was selected and new bushes planted while the old ones were turned into stem tea. Windbreaks were woven from natural material, with some of the labour being provided by volunteers, including WWOOFers.* About a hundred of their bushes are now six years old and doing fine, although smaller than they would be under less challenging conditions. Until recently, another hundred three-year-old bushes were struggling but are now benefiting from improved screening and growing healthier. In the early days, knowing when and how much to pick, and processing the leaves themselves without

---

* Volunteers from Worldwide Opportunities on Organic Farms (WWOOFers) swap their labour for experience and training from the farmers and growers who host them.

equipment or supervision, were skills that were hard-learned. 'But,' says Liz, 'we're getting the hang of it now.'

There are strong environmental, psychological and spiritual impulses to Liz and Martyn's endeavours, which is not surprising, given that Liz is a Church of Scotland minister, although currently one without a parish so that she can experiment with 'other ways of doing ministry'. The couple had their first taste of tea-growing on a Fairtrade trip to Peru. The journey was mostly to do with handicrafts but included a visit to a small coffee and tea producer. What they saw happening in that estate chimed with their own views on justice, small-scale production, low-carbon miles and the importance of a direct connection between the grower and the land. The Gibsons have put these ideas into practice on their Mull croft, which at the time of writing was about to be certified organic by the Soil Association.

In the early days, the Gibsons sent their leaves away to be processed, but recently have experimented with processing their tea themselves. Output of their tea has been tiny, but they have also produced a bonus crop from stem cuttings. Stem tea, or twig tea, is a popular Japanese specialty, often chosen for its low-caffeine content. 'I intend to take a lot more cuttings this year,' Liz told me, revealing a new market. 'We are currently selling what we produce to Tobermory Distillery which uses it as one of the botanicals in its new gin. This hasn't yet been launched. The plan is to up our tea-growing significantly and also to grow other botanicals for them.'

The Gibsons are still pondering the best way to process their tea crop in the future. In the meantime, Liz has founded Grow Grow Grow CIC, a community interest company. It has been set up to raise healthy staple crops for local consumption. As well as growing produce on the Gibsons' croft, the volunteers utilise unused and underused ground elsewhere – around public buildings, including churches and sheltered housing, and private gardens that owners can't look after themselves. WWOOFers are, and will remain, a key part of Grow Grow Grow, but the social enterprise company also aims to employ local people.

In the Gibsons' busy life, tea has to take its place alongside much else, but the ambition to increase production still burns. 'Growing tea has been fun and mostly a good experience,' says Liz. 'We're delighted to be actually growing tea on Mull and in Scotland. So we know it's possible and can increase.'

Liz and Martyn's main tea so far has been matcha, a green tea that is ground into a fine powder and is traditionally at the centre of the Japanese tea ceremony. However, it was their Scottish Antler stem tea that won limelight on the international stage when it was included in a pack presented by Scotland's First Minister Nicola Sturgeon to President Barack Obama during her visit to the United States in 2015. Such success must be cheering to Liz and Martyn during long, cold Scottish winter nights on their croft, especially in the knowledge that each year the roots of their precious tea bushes are imbedding themselves more deeply into the soil of Mull.

At her family farm near Forfar, Susie Walker-Munro grows her cold-hardy tea bushes from Georgian and Nepalese stock in a venerable walled garden, in polytunnels and increasingly outside on a loamy, south-facing hillside of the Strathmore Valley. It's a business she started from scratch, and her first tea bushes had taken root before she realised that tea ran in her blood.

Susie's decision to grow tea at Mains of Kinnettles (where she and her husband Euan run an arable farm) prompted a rummage around the collective family memory bank – which revealed that, on her mother's side, Susie is the great-great-great-granddaughter of Charles Alexander Bruce, one of the

Assam brother-adventurers we encountered in Chapter 3. Robert and Charles Bruce turned the world's tea industry on its head with the discovery that indigenous tea grew in the jungles of the Brahmaputra River. The echoing corridor of time is now becoming a noisy place!

Charles Bruce was made superintendent of the government-led project to develop tea in Assam, and in 1871 he was awarded the Royal Society of Arts Gold Medal for his pioneering work. Enthused by her discovery of her ancestor's achievements, Susie and her mother, Jean Walker, made a pilgrimage in 2015 to Assam and visited Charles's grave at Tezpur on the banks of the Brahmaputra.

So, if it was not her illustrious ancestor who inspired her to grow tea, what was it? Mundane as it sounds, the epiphany came as Susie read a magazine article about tea-growing in Cornwall, while sitting in a dentist's waiting room. Although with a balmier clime than Angus, Cornwall also has cool, wet weather, and the article triggered a momentous 'why not?' in her imagination. In 2007 she bought her first twenty tea-bush cuttings. Twelve years later, her Kinnettles Gold orange pekoe tea sells for £2,500 a kilo!

So, is Mrs Walker-Munro on her way to Thomas Lipton levels of wealth? Alas, no. Her top-quality, delicately apple-flavoured product, launched in 2015, is produced in such tiny quantities – about two-and-a-half kilos a year – that she herself can only sample it for quality control, as daily use would consume all her crop and profit. But, as well as growing tea, Susie also offers educational tours, classes and tastings as part of her business. For the tea enthusiast, a tea garden tour is akin to the distillery tours proffered to the whisky buff, and an equally enjoyable (although more weather-dependent) experience. Susie has hosted knowledgeable Japanese devotees at Kinnettles, and it seems that the wealthy of this discerning tea-drinking nation have added the discovery of boutique, hand-rolled teas from out-of-the-way places to their reasons for visiting Scotland.

We began our tour in the first polytunnel, home to a high-mountain variety of tea bushes with small leathery leaves that concentrate the caffeine and are consequently resilient against insect attack. The roof of the polytunnel was shaded with green netting to simulate the cloudy skies of the Himalayas, and along its sides are sheets of sticky blue plastic – traps for parasitic insects. The result is a tea reminiscent of Darjeeling.

While current output is small, the Kinnettles ambition is big. The walled garden shelters 4,000 bushes and the polytunnels 300 more, while 2,000 are exposed to the elements on the hillside. Twelve years previously, in 2007, Susie bought her first twenty cuttings from the Tregothnan Tea Estate in Cornwall and slowly built up her stock in the face of lack of experience, bad winters and vine weevil. 'It was really very difficult for these little bushes to cope with the cold climate,' she told me. 'They didn't have a root system that anchored them properly against the high winds because cuttings are very, very shallow-rooted.' Setbacks only increased Susie's fascination and determination, and the plants that had endured were moved into polytunnels where enough survived and thrived to convince Susie that she really could make lovely tea. In 2015 Beverly-Claire Wainwright leant her shoulder to the wheel as Kinnettles' consultant, and the following year Susie was granted permission to import tea seed from north-east Nepal. Kinnettles now has home-grown bushes from both Nepalese and Georgian* seeds.

---

* Scottish soldier Jacob McNamara played a major role in the development of tea in Georgia after the ship he was on was wrecked in the Black Sea during the Crimean War. Although taken prisoner, McNamara met, courted and married a local aristocrat. Missing his tea, he prompted the growing of it in several Georgian estates.

In 2016 Susie was a founder of the Tea Gardens of Scotland, initially a vehicle to 'bulk buy' expensive tea seed, but also a forum where knowledge is exchanged, and a body that has attracted European funding to help pay for consultation and research. All nine members are based in Angus, Fife and Perthshire, and share the goal of diversifying farms or utilising the micro-climates of old walled gardens. They have plans to market together in the future and perhaps even create a tea-tourist-trail, although Susie emphasises that the members go at their own paces and make their own decisions. 'The Tea Gardens of Scotland group is really about nine women feeling their way through this together and working out the best way to do this. We're still experimenting with our teas. While we're not trying to reinvent the wheel, we have to discover the best practice for our own conditions.'

Some of the earliest practical advice on growing tea came from Susie's own ancestor. In a letter of 1837 to Nathaniel Wallich in Calcutta, a government official recommended Charles Bruce's paper, *An Account of the Manufacture of Black Tea as Now Practiced at Sudeya in Upper Assam by the Chinamen sent hither for that purpose:* 'Mr Bruce has here given all the information on the manufacture of black tea that is obtainable by him, and it may probably not be without use to those who are attempting to manufacture tea elsewhere.' How extraordinary that Bruce's advice might benefit his own great-great-great-granddaughter nearly two centuries later, 5,000 miles away in his native land. Here is Charles Bruce's first note on best practice:

> In the first place the youngest and most tender leaves are gathered; but when there are many hands and a great quantity of leaves to be collected, the people employed nip off with the forefinger and thumb the

fine end of the branch with about four leaves on, and sometimes even more if they look tender.

To give tea a chance in Scotland is demanding work, right from the start. Susie's early experiments of growing from cuttings were disappointing, but raising bushes from seeds proved successful. Seed-grown plants have longer tap roots and are more frost- and wind-resistant. For the first two years, the plants have to be thoroughly weeded until the bushes push out, covering the soil around them. Susie generally prepares the ground for tea bushes by planting clover, the roots of which attract nodules of nitrogen that are then released into the soil when the clover is cut and its roots die off. After planting, the tea bushes are carefully fed and watered, using only organic material as the tea reaches the stage where it can be picked. Beyond the walled garden is the stinking heart of Susie's feeding regime. With all the relish of a weird sister adding a toe of newt to her bubbling cauldron, she stirs reeking tubs of rotting nettles, comfrey and dock leaf that are her staple fertilisers. She delights in the awfulness of the stench, knowing what magic the foul, but fair, liquid will work on her bushes.

I visited Susie at Kinnettles just in the aftermath of rumours of malpractice in the Scottish artisan tea industry, a subject she has written about.[2] While tea was certainly not adulterated in the old Chinese manner (with Prussian blue, hedgerow plants and even gunpowder), there were claims that imported tea may have been mixed with the expensive home-grown variety to hoodwink the public and increase profits. Such deception has been revealed in recent years in the whisky industry, the 'hand-dived' scallop market, and the meat trade. You have to be sharp to discern the important difference between 'Scottish smoked salmon' and 'smoked Scottish salmon'. However, in the case of tea, fraud can now be detected. The elemental profile of the soil from each Scottish tea garden can be recognised using ionomic analysis by the School of Biological Studies at Aberdeen University. As well as giving authority to the concept of *terrior*, or the character bestowed on a product by its unique habitat, it means that the chemical fingerprint of Scottish teas can be recognised. Scottish science has taken us from 'buyer beware' to 'fraudster beware'.

We end our visit to Susie's with a treat – a dish of potential Kinnettles Gold that was rolled only a few hours earlier that we sip from porcelain spoons. The tea is delicious, but it doesn't make the grade, as far as its creator is concerned. 'Not as fragrant and complex as I would like. It's a little too dry in the mouth feel. I'd like it softer. It's black tea, so you want a little astringency, but you don't want the dryness in the mouth . . . I probably should have left it to oxidise for longer. I wouldn't be selling this to Jon at Pekoe Tea – it's fine for us lot at home.'

With the slurping over, Susie declares, 'When you're pushing that really high end, you have to be critical. It's usually in the oxidation that you get it wrong, so I'll know what to do next time. There is no quick fix. You need patience. By tweaking the process of making the tea, we managed to turn it from something worth £250 a kilogram to £2,500.'

The Scots who put the tea in Britain – and much of the rest of the world – have been great company during the writing of this book. What adventures I have shared with them! Robert Fortune risking his life and liberty to smuggle tea bushes from China; Robert and Charles Bruce discovering indigenous tea in the Brahmaputra jungle; the ever-inquisitive doctor-botanists of Kew, Calcutta and Saharanpur botanical gardens; the pioneers Archibald Campbell of Darjeeling, James Taylor of Ceylon, and Henry Brown of Central Africa; the young planters who faced death by disease, tigers, elephants and snakes to grow tea; the entrepreneurs who gave the names Finlay, Melrose and Lipton to famous brands; and the estimable Miss Catherine Cranston and her artist protégés.

I began this journey drinking tea in Darjeeling, where my curiosity about Archibald Campbell and his fellow country-men's role in making *Camellia sinensis* the world's favourite drink was first whetted, and I ended it slurping Scottish-grown tea from a bowl with a porcelain spoon with a descendant of Charles Alexander Bruce of Assam in rural Angus. As some-one who loves to travel, but who yearns to come home to Scotland, it was a fitting end to a fascinating journey.

A Note for the Botanically Curious

For millennia, people all over the world have brewed plant infusions, tisanes and teas to warm, comfort, refresh and delight themselves. In South America today, they have mate; in South Africa, rooibos; in the West, a plethora of commercial herbal and fruit choices – all of which I dismiss collectively as 'sage & onion'. My own interest is confined strictly to the brew made from the leaves of *Camellia sinensis* – what we recognise as the 'tea' plant. Rather than interrupt my narrative of Scotland's extraordinary role in the development of tea with an explanation of what tea is and how it is made, I have prepared this note for the botanically curious.

Camellia sinensis is a lush, evergreen perennial, deep in colour and with slightly serrated leaves. The species evolved in Southeast Asia, almost certainly in the Highlands where India, Burma, China and Tibet huddle together, but it has proved to be highly adaptable and, with human help, has travelled the world. It is a jungle plant and, left to its own devices, will sprout thirty or forty feet to seek light above the forest canopy. This vigorous growth long confused Westerners, who perceived the tea plant not as a tree but as a bush, the top of which could be plucked simply by bending over it.

The 'jungle' tea that was discovered and recognised by the

Bruce brothers in the Brahmaputra Valley of Assam in the 1820s is a variety of the tea the Chinese had long cultivated, and it is described scientifically as *Camellia sinensis var. assamica*. Much money, heartache and research went into discovering which of the two varieties of plant suited which region, but today most tea bushes claim both parents and many are cultivars that have been developed by humankind for quality of taste or hardiness in the face of excessive heat, cold, drought or insect attack.

Newly planted bushes take about three years to mature before they can be harvested. Bushes are usually rooted-out and replaced after about fifty years, but they can live for centuries. At Loolecondera estate in Sri Lanka several acres of the tea bushes James Taylor planted in 1867 are still being harvested. It is commonly held that older plants give less yield but a deeper, richer flavour.

Spells of leaf growth are known as 'flushes', and successive flushes are recognised as producing different qualities of tea. Two harvests of these flushes a year is common, but some climates and terrains can allow more. Traditionally tea is gathered by 'plucking' – picking by hand or, more precisely in the case of the finest tea, by forefinger and thumb. Nowadays shears and machines do most of the work to keep labour costs down. For the finest teas, known as orange pekoe teas, only the bud and two lower leaves are plucked. In eye-wateringly expensive teas, only the bud is picked.

The picked tea is then withered – laid out on mesh to be air-dried, either in the sun or in a well-ventilated room – during which the leaves can lose a quarter of their weight. When you consider that leaves may enter the tea factory during very dry or very rainy spells, judging the drying time is ever-challenging and it will, to a significant extent, determine the value of the final product. The withered leaves are then distressed, to break down their structure and allow the enzymes in the leaves to react with oxygen in the air. Vigorously tossing and shaking the leaves in a bamboo basket was the ancient way of doing this, but 'leaf maceration' is now done by mechanical rollers. Much mass-produced tea is made by the ferocious CTC – or Crush, Tear and Curl – process, which produces cost effective and easily brewed tea to the detriment of subtle complexity.

The newly rolled, now coppery-coloured leaves are called *dhool*. Rolling allows what is confusingly called 'fermentation' in the tea trade, but it is actually enzymatic oxidation. Exposed to the air, the leaves darken as the chlorophyll they contain breaks down and 'tannins' are released. Like 'fermentation', tannin is a tea-trade misnomer. What is actually released are astringent polyphenols unrelated to tannic acid.

Here green and black teas part company. Such was the success of Imperial China's jealous protection of its tea plants and know-how that generations of Western tea drinkers believed that green and black tea were made from different plants. It was Scotland's Robert Fortune who – much to his own astonishment – discovered that it was process not plant that made the difference. Apart from initial withering, green teas undergo very little or no oxidation. Black teas, however, are well 'fermented', increasing their polyphenols and deepening their flavour. Brighter, lighter-flavoured teas require less fermentation, while the stronger ones that benefit from adding milk will take longer. The creativity of tea makers has also produced a flavour-led spectrum of oxidation between the lightest green and the black tea bruisers, and oolong and Darjeeling teas occupy a place midway on this scale. Great skill is required to know when the *dhool* is sufficiently oxidized, and on this skill depends the brightness, strength and flavour of the cup that it will produce.

The fermenting process is halted by heating the leaves to 35°C and drying them out to the consistency that a buyer of loose tea would recognise. Experimenting with his first crop of tea in Ceylon, James Taylor used a traditional wok over an open fire to 'fix' his leaves. Today the process is done by baking the *dhool* in rolling drums. Either way, great skill and experience are needed to make sure that the leaves are sufficiently dried to stop further oxidation but not scorched – or, in tea parlance, 'bakey'.

At this stage, tea is a mixture of everything from twigs to dust. Traditionally, the tea was passed through a series of sieves to remove the stalks and sort the leaves into batches of different sizes or grades. Today, electrostatic rollers do much of the sorting. At the low end of tea quality are the 'fannings' or 'dust'. This is the tea of India's ubiquitous tea stalls and much of the content of British tea bags, but even the fannings from top quality pekoes can produce a very fine brew.

Sturdy foil-lined plywood chests – much recycled by skiffle groups and the removal men of Aberdeen's Shore Porters Society that I remember from my parents' house moves – are little used today. Tea is mostly packed for shipping in brown paper sacks. About 90 per cent of the tea that reaches Britain is then blended to produce the popular everyday teas we buy in supermarkets. Teas of different types from different continents are tasted and blended by experts to ensure that consumers experience exactly the same quality and flavour every time they buy that blend, despite any differences in the teas that the blender is importing. In Britain, teas have often been blended to suit the hardness or softness of water in certain areas. Although 'single estate' leaves are increasingly popular among connoisseurs, blending tea is the final of the many great skills needed to bring tea from bush to cup.

Notes

Introduction

1   Tom Devine, *Scotland's Empire 1600–1815*, Allen Lane, 2003.
2   Michael Fry, *The Scottish Empire*, Tuckwell Press & Birlinn Ltd, 2001.
3   Benjamin Wilkie, *History Scotland*, Vol. 17, No. 4, 2017.
4   David Hamilton, *The Healers: A History of Medicine in Scotland*, Canongate, 1981.
5   Agnes Repplier, *To Think of Tea*, 1932.
6   The Daily Mash, 13 August 2018.

1: To Drink a Dish of Tea, Sir?

1   William H. Ukers, *All About Tea*, Tea & Coffee Trade Journal Company, 1935.
2   F. Marian McNeill, *The Scots Kitchen*, 1929.
3   F. Marian McNeill, *The Scots Kitchen*, 1929.
4   William Anderson Smith, *Lewsiana*, 1875.
5   *Dictionary of National Biography, 1885–1900*, vol. 19.
6   Agnes Repplier, *To Think of Tea*, 1932.
7   Robert Chambers, *Domestic Annals of Scotland*, 1885.
8   T.C. Smout & Sydney Wood, *Scottish Voices*, William Collins and Sons, 1990.

9   Lord Kames (Henry Home), *Sketches of the History of Man*, vol. 1, 1778.

10 John Knox, *A Tour Through the Hebrides*, 1787.

11 John Griffiths, *Tea: A History of the Drink That Changed the World*, André Deutsch, 2007.

12 T.C. Smout & Sydney Wood, *Scottish Voices*, William Collins and Sons, 1990.

13 Tom Devine, *Scotland's Empire 1606–1815*, Allan Lane, 2003.

14 Michael Lynch, *Scotland: A New History*, Pimlico, 1991

15 Thomas Trotter MD, *A View of the Nervous Temperament*, 1807.

16 T.C. Smout & Sydney Wood, *Scottish Voices*, William Collins and Sons, 1990.

17 Carol Foreman, *Lost Glasgow*, Birlinn, 2013.

18 Perilla Kinchin, *Miss Cranston: Patron of Charles Rennie Mackintosh*, National Museums of Scotland, 2018.

19 Perilla Kinchin, *Miss Cranston: Patron of Charles Rennie Mackintosh*, National Museums of Scotland, 2018.

20 Hugh MacDiarmid and Lewis Grassic Gibbon, *Scottish Scene, Or, The Intelligent Man's Guide to Albyn*, 1910.

21 H.V. Morton, *In Search of Scotland*, Methuen, 1929.

22 Robbie & Nora Kydd, *Growing Up in Scotland: An Anthology*, Polygon, 1998.

23 Diary of Captain Ronald Rose of the 1st Cameronians (Scottish Rifles), Historylinks website (http://www.history links.org.uk).

2: Without Milk, Sugar – or Tax!

1   Alex M. Cain, *The Cornchest for Scotland: Scots in India*, National Library of Scotland, 1986.

2   Andrew Mackillop, 'A Union for Empire? Scotland, the East India Company and the British Union', *The Scottish Historical Review*, 2008.

3   Rudyard Kipling, 'In an Opium Factory', *Pioneer* newspapers, 1888.

4   John Griffiths, *Tea: A History of the Drink that Changed the World*, André Deutsch, 2007.

5   Simon Schama, *A History of Britain, The Fate of Empire 1776–2000*, The Bodley Head, 2009.

6   Michael Fry, *The Scottish Empire*, Tuckwell Press & Birlinn Ltd, 2001.

7   Robert Fortune, *Three Years' Wanderings in the Northern Provinces of China*, 1847.

8   Professor Peter Ward Fay, 'The Opening of China', an essay in *The Thistle and the Jade: A Celebration of 150 Years of Jardine, Matheson & Co.*, edited by Maggie Keswick, Octopus Books, 1982.

9   Arthur Herman, *How the Scots Invented the Modern World*, 2001, versus John Griffiths, *Tea: A History of the Drink that Changed the World*, André Deutsch, 2007.

10 Hoh-cheung Mui & Lorna H. Mui, *The Management of Monopoly*, 1984.

11 Hoh-cheung Mui & Lorna H. Mui, *The Management of Monopoly*, 1984.

12 Denys Forrest, *Tea for the British*, Chatto & Windus, 1973.

13 Derek Janes, *The Smuggler's Coast*, Upfront Publishing, 2016.

14 Derek Janes, *The Smuggler's Coast*, Upfront Publishing, 2016.

15 Essay by Derek Janes in *The New Coastal History: Cultural and Environmental Perspectives from Scotland and Beyond*, ed. David Worthington. Palgrave MacMillan, 2017.

16 Henry Home, Lord Kames, *Sketches of the History of Man*, vol. 2, 1778.

17 Sir Walter Scott, *Guy Mannering*, 1815.

18 Letter to Kirkman Finlay from Sir Thomas Munro, Bt., K.C.B., Governor of Madras, 15 August 1825. Quoted in *James Finlay & Company Limited*, privately printed for James Finlay & Company, 1951.

19 Duncan Gilmour, 'Out of China into India', Finlay's house magazine, June 2018.

20 *Memoirs and Portraits of 100 Glasgow Men*, James Maclehose and Sons, 1886.

21 Kirkman Finlay, letter to his son, Alexander Finlay, in Bombay, 20 September 1837, from company history, *James Finlay & Company Limited, 1750–1950*.

22 *Memoirs and Portraits of 100 Glasgow Men*, James Maclehose and Sons, 1886.

23 Hoh-cheung Mui & Lorna H. Mui, *The Management of Monopoly*, 1984.

3: Take Things Coolly and Never Lose Your Temper

1   P.J. Banyard, *A History of the Tea Trade*, Thompson, Lloyd & Ewart, 1981.

2   Dunse History Society website.

3   *Entering China's Service: Robert Hart's Journals, 1854–1863*, Volume 1, Harvard Univ. Asia Center, 1986.

4   Robert Fortune, *Three Years' Wanderings in the Northern Provinces of China*, 1847.

5   Denys Forrest, *Tea for the British*, Chatto & Windus, 1973.

6   The Chelsea Physic Garden, signage, 2017.

7   Shashi Tharoor, *Inglorious Empire: What the British Did to India*, Hurst & Company, 2017.

8   Fa-ti Fan, *British Naturalists in Quing China: Science, Empire and Cultural Encounter*, Harvard University Press, 2003.

9   Jeff Koehler, *Darjeeling: A History of the World's Greatest Tea*, Bloomsbury, 2016.

10 Sarah Rose, *For All the Tea in China*, Arrow, 2010.

11 Sam Jefferson, *Clipper Ships and the Golden Age of Sail*, Bloomsbury, 2014.

12 Hoh-cheung Mui and Lorna H. Mui, *William Melrose in China 1845–1855*, The Scottish History Society, 1984.

13 Raymond Dawson, *The Chinese Chameleon: An Analysis of European Conceptions of Chinese Civilization*, Oxford University Press, 1967.

14 Robert Hart's Journals, *Entering China's Service: 1854–1863*, vol. 1, Harvard Univ. Asia Center, 1986.

15 Stuart Heaver, *South China Post Magazine*, 9 Nov. 2013.

16 Robert Fortune, *A Journey to the Tea Countries of China*, 1852.

17 *Memoirs of the Rev. Walter M. Lowrie, Missionary*, edited by his father. Philadelphia: Presbyterian Board of Publication, 1854.

18 *The Nautical Magazine and Naval Chronicle for 1852*, Cambridge University Press, 2013.

4: The Days for Gathering Rupees

1 Professor H. Montgomery Hyde, *Dr George Govan and the Saharunpore Botanical Gardens*, Journal of the Royal Central Asia Society, Volume 49, 1962.

2 C.W. Dilke, *Greater Britain: A Record of Travel in English-Speaking Countries During 1866 and 1867*, J.B. Lippincott & Co. Philadelphia, 1868.

3 Joseph Dalton Hooker, *Himalayan Journals*, vol. 1, 1854.

4 T.M. Devine, *Scotland's Empire 1600–1815*, Allen Lane, 2003.

5 M. Kelway Bamber, *A Text Book on the Chemistry and Agriculture of Tea*, Calcutta, 1893.

6 Kyd to Governor-General, 1 June 1786, Dawson Turner collection, Natural History Museum, London.

7 William H. Ukers, *All About Tea*, The Tea and Coffee Trade Journal Company, New York, 1935.

8 B.C. Kundu, K.C. Basak, and P.B. Sarcar, *Jute in India*, Indian Central Jute Committee, Calcutta, 1959.

9 John D. Comrie, *History of Scottish Medicine*, Wellcome Historical Medical Museum, 1932.

10 Alan Macfarlane and Iris Macfarlane, *Green Gold: The Empire of Tea*, Edbury Press, 2003.

11 Samuel Ball, *An Account of the Cultivation and Manufacture of Tea in China*, 1848.

12 David Crole, *Tea: A Textbook of Tea Planting and Manufacture*, London, 1897.

13 David Burton, *The Raj at Table*, Faber & Faber, 1993.

14 *Australia & New Zealand Trade Journal*, January 1884.

15 Will Battle, *The World Tea Encyclopaedia*, Matador, 2017.

16 H.A. Antrobus, *History of the Assam Company*, T. & A Constable Ltd, 1957.

17 *Encyclopaedia Britannica*, 1911.

18 F.W.F. Staveacre, *Tea and Tea Dealing,*1929.

19 Samuel Baildon, *Tea in Assam, a Pamphlet on the Origin, Culture and Manufacture of Tea in Assam*, W. Newman & Co., Calcutta, 1877.

20 Stephanie Jones, *Merchants of the Raj: British Managing Agency Houses in Calcutta Yesterday and Today*, MacMillan Press, 1992.

21 John Carnegie letters, India Office Library, British Library.

22 Jayeeta Sharma, *'Lazy' Natives, Coolie Labour, and the Assam Tea Industry*. Modern Asian Studies, 2009.

23 Website of the Scots Cemetery in Bengal.

24 T.M. Devine, *Scotland's Empire 1600–1815*, Allen Lane, 2003.

25 Yvonne Singh, 'The Forgotten World, How Scotland Erased Guyana from Its Past', *The Guardian*, 16 April 2019.

26 *The Hindu*, 24 September 2013.

27 Interview with the author.

28 Neal Ascherson, *Stone Voices, The Search for Scotland*, Granta Books, 2002.

29 Michael Fry, *The Scottish Empire*, Tuckwell Press & Birlinn Ltd, 2001.

30 William H. Ukers, *All About Tea*, The Tea and Coffee Trade Journal Company, New York, 1935.

31 William H. Ukers, *All About Tea*, The Tea and Coffee Trade Journal Company, New York, 1935.

5: The Place of Thunderbolts

1 Cecil Sinclair, *Jock Tamson's Bairns: A History of the General Register Office for Scotland*, 2000.

2 *Old Statistical Account of Scotland*, vol. XI, 1794.

3 Obituary of Dr Archibald Campbell, *The Journal of the*

Anthropological Institute of Great Britain and Ireland, vol. VII, 1878.

4   Obituary of Dr Archibald Campbell, *The Journal of the Anthropological Institute of Great Britain and Ireland*, vol. VII, 1878.

5   Carolyn Fry, *The Plant Hunters*, André Deutsch, 2009.

6   Joseph Hooker, *Himalayan Journals*, Vol. 2, 1854.

7   Thomas Pakenham, *The Company of Trees*, Weidenfeld & Nicolson, 2015.

8   Basant B. Lama, *The Story of Darjeeling*, 2009.

9   Joseph Hooker, *Himalayan Journals*, Vol. 2, 1854.

10 Joseph Hooker, *Himalayan Journals*, Vol. 2, 1854.

11 *Encyclopaedia Britannica*. 1911.

12 L.S.S. O'Malley, *Indian Civil Service, Bengal District Gazetteers*, Darjeeling, 1907.

13 Alex McKay, International Institute of Asian Studies. *A Difficult Country, A Hostile Chief, and a Still More Hostile Minister: The Anglo-Sikkim War of 1861*, Bulletin of Tibetology, 2010.

14 Darwin Correspondence Project, Cambridge University, http://www.darwinproject.ac.uk./DCP-LETT-4996

15 Obituary, *The Journal of the Anthropological Institute of Great Britain and Ireland*, vol. VII, 1878.

16 James R. Minto, *Graham of Kalimpong*, Blackwood, 1974

17 William Dalrymple, *White Mughals*, HarperCollins, 2003.

18 John Griffiths, *Tea: A History of the Drink that Changed the World*, André Deutsch, 2007.

19 George Orwell, *Burmese Days*, Victor Gollancz, 1934.

20 Iris Macfarlane, 'Memoirs of a Memsahib', from *Green Gold: The Empire of Tea* by Alan Macfarlane and Iris Macfarlane, Ebury Press, 2004.

21 Jeff Koehler, *Darjeeling*, Bloomsbury, 2016.

22 T. F. Bourdillon, Conservator of Forests, Travancore, *Report on the Forests of Travancore*, Government of Travancore Press, 1892.

23 *The History of Parliament: The House of Commons 1820–1831*,

Members Biographies, ed. D.R. Fisher, Cambridge University Press, 2009.

24 The Rev. Samuel Mateer, London Missionary Society, *The Land of Charity, A descriptive Account of Travancore and its People, with Especial Reference to Missionary Labour,* John Snow & Co., 1871.

25 T.F. Bourdillon, Conservator of Forests, Travancore, *Report on the Forests of Travancore,* Government of Travancore Press, 1892.

26 Administrative/Biographical History, Scottish Indian Coffee Company Limited, Lloyds Banking Group Archives (Edinburgh).

27 General William Cullen, report of 1859, quoted in William H. Uker's *All About Tea,* Tea & Coffee Trade Journal Company, 1935.

28 John Daniel Munro, *The High Ranges of Travancore,* 1880.

29 Samuel Mateer, *Native Life in Travancore,* W.H. Allen & Co., 1883.

30 *Gulf Times,* 19 February 2015.

31 http://www.nishkamariarajesh.com/HISTORY.htm.

32 Dick Tewson, *Char Walla,* privately printed memoir, 1990, James Finlay & Co. archive, Glasgow University.

33 *Ferguson's Ceylon Directory,* 1912.

34 Shashi Tharoor, *Inglorious Empire: What the British Did to India,* Hurst & Company, 2017.

6: The Master Who Is God

1 E. Jaiwant Paul, *The Story of Tea,* Roli Books, 2001.

2 John Ferguson, *Ceylon in 1903,* 1903.

3 J. Penry Lewis, *Tombstones and Monuments of Ceylon,* 1913.

4 John Still, *The Jungle Tide,* William Blackwood & Sons Ltd, 1930.

5 Michael Fry, *The Scottish Empire,* Tuckwell Press & Birlinn Ltd, 2001.

6 Angela McCarthy & T.M. Devine, *Tea and Empire: James Taylor in Victorian Ceylon,* Manchester University Press, 2017.

7   D.M. Forrest, *A Hundred Years of Ceylon Tea, 1867–1967*, Chatto & Windus, 1967.

8   Denys Forrest, *Tea for the British*, Chatto & Windus, 1973.

9   Angela McCarthy & T.M. Devine, *Tea and Empire: James Taylor in Victorian Ceylon*, Manchester University Press, 2017.

10 Umberto Quattrocchi, *CRC World Dictionary of Plant Names*, CRC Press, 1999.

11 John Griffiths, *Tea: A History of the Drink that Changed the World*, André Deutsch, 2007.

12 Arthur Sinclair, *In tropical lands: recent travels to the sources of the Amazon, the West Indian Islands, and Ceylon*, Aberdeen, 1895.

13 John Griffiths, *Tea: A History of the Drink that Changed the World*, André Deutsch, 2007.

14 Sir Arthur Conan Doyle, 'De Profundis', from *The Last Galley*, 1911.

15 Stanley Paliwoda & Michael Thomas, *International Marketing*, Routledge, 2013.

16 Angela McCarthy & T.M. Devine, *Tea and Empire: James Taylor in Victorian Ceylon*, Manchester University Press, 2017.

17 Website of St Paul's Church, Kandy, https://www.stpaulschurchkandy.lk/Mahaiyawa.html.

18 Correspondence with the author, March 2019.

19 Correspondence between Richard Ross, Alexander 'Mac' McLaren's grandson, and the author.

20 Richard Shotton, 'What the Victorians Can Teach Us', *Campaign Magazine*, 11 June 2015.

21 Michael Fry, *The Scottish Empire*, Tuckwell Press & Birlinn Ltd, 2001.

22 E. Jaiwant Paul, *The Story of Tea*, Roli Books, 2001.

23 www.villageoflipton.com/.

7: A Handful of Seeds

1   William H. Ukers, *All About Tea*, Tea & Coffee Trade Journal Company, 1935.

2   Brian Morris, *An Environmental History of Southern Malawi: Land and People of the Shire Highlands*, Palgrave MacMillan, 2016.

3   *Central African Planter*, September 1895.

4   William H. Ukers, *All About Tea*, Tea & Coffee Trade Journal Company, 1935

5   Brian Morris, *An Environmental History of Southern Malawi: Land and People of the Shire Highlands*, Palgrave MacMillan, 2016.

6   G.G.S.J. Hadlow, Chairman of the Nyasaland Tea Association, Speech given to Nyasaland Society,3 June 1959.

7   G.G.S.J. Hadlow, Chairman of the Nyasaland Tea Association, Speech given to Nyasaland Society, 3 June 1959.

8   F.G.H. Lupton, 'History of Ruo Estate', *The Society of Malawi Journal*, Vol. 49, No. 2, 1996.

9   Barbara Lamport-Stokes, 'Henry Brown: Planter', *The Society of Malawi Journal*, Vol. 45, No. 2, 1992.

10 Barbara Lamport-Stokes, 'Henry Brown: Planter', *The Society of Malawi Journal*, Vol. 45, No. 2, 1992.

11 Michael Fry, *The Scottish Empire*, Tuckwell Press & Birlinn Ltd, 2001.

12 Arthur Westrop, *Green Gold*, privately published, 1956.

13 G.G.S.J. Hadlow, Chairman of the Nyasaland Tea Association, Speech given to Nyasaland Society, 3 June 1959.

14 Hugh O. Douglas, *African Highlands: A Brief History of the African Highlands Produce Company Limited*, James Finlay & Company, 1959.

15 Will Battle, *The World Tea Encyclopaedia*, Matador, 2017.

8: Home for Tea

1   Denys Forrest, *Tea for the British*, Chatto & Windus, 1973

2   Susie Walker-Munro, 'Fighting Food Fraud', *Scottish Field*, June 2019

Bibliography

Bamber, M. Kelway, *A Text Book on the Chemistry and Agriculture of Tea*, Calcutta, 1893

Battle, Will, *The World Tea Encyclopaedia*, Matador, 2017

Cain, Alex M., *The Cornchest for Scotland: Scots in India*, National Library of Scotland, 1986

Cartland, Barbara, *Moon Over Eden*, Pan Books, 1976

Chambers, Robert, *Domestic Annals of Scotland*, 1885

Crole, David, *A Text Book of Tea Planting and Manufacture*, London, 1897

Dalrymple, William, *White Mughals*, HarperCollins, 2003

Devine, T.M., *Scotland's Empire 1600–1815*, Allen Lane, 2003

Dictionary of National Biography, 1885–1900, Volume 19 (on Duncan Forbes)

Douglas, Hugh O., *African Highlands: A Brief History of the African Highlands Produce Company Limited*, privately published for James Finlay & Co. Ltd, 1959

Fan, Fa-ti, *British Naturalists in Qing China: Science, Empire and Cultural Encounter*, Harvard University Press, 2003

Fay, Professor Peter Ward, 'The Opening of China', an essay in *The Thistle and the Jade: A Celebration of 150 Years of Jardine, Matheson & Co.*, edited by Maggie Keswick, Octopus Books, 1982

James Finlay & Company Limited, *James Finlay & Company Limited, 1750–1950*, privately published, 1951

Foreman, Carol, *Lost Glasgow*, Birlinn, 2013

Forrest, Denys M., *A Hundred Years of Ceylon Tea 1867–1967*, Chatto & Windus, 1967

Forrest, Denys M., *Tea for the British: The Social and Economic History of a Famous Trade*, Chatto & Windus, 1973

Fortune, Robert, *Three Years' Wanderings in the Northern Provinces of China*, John Murray, 1847

Fortune, Robert, *A Journey to the Tea Countries of China*, John Murray, 1852

Fry, Michael, *The Scottish Empire*, Tuckwell Press & Birlinn Ltd, 2001

Gilmour, Duncan, 'Out of China into India', Finlay's in-house magazine, June 2018

Grassic Gibbon, Lewis (with Hugh MacDiarmid), *Scottish Scene, Or, the Intelligent Man's Guide to Albyn*, 1910

Griffiths, John, *Tea: A History of the Drink that Changed the World*, André Deutsch, 2007

Hadlow, G.G.S.J., speech given to Nyasaland Society, 3 June 1959

Hart, Sir Robert, *Entering China's Service: Robert Hart's Journals, 1854–1863*, Volume 1, Harvard University Asia Centre, 1986

Hay, Ian, *The First Hundred Thousand*, William Blackwood & Sons,1915

Heaver, Stuart, 'Affairs of our Hart' in *South China Post Magazine*, 9 November 2013

Herman, Arthur, *How the Scots Invented the Modern World*, Crown Publishers, 2001

Home, Henry, Lord Kames, *Sketches of the History of Man*, Volume 1 & 2, 1778

Hooker, Joseph, *Himalayan Journals, or Notes of a Naturalist in Bengal, The Sikkim and Nepal Himalayas*, 1854

Janes, Derek, *The Smugglers' Coast: The Story of Smuggling around Eyemouth*, Upfront Publishing, 2016

Janes, Derek, essay in *The New Coastal History: Cultural and Environmental Perspectives from Scotland and Beyond*, ed. David Worthington, Palgrave MacMillan, 2017

Jefferson, Sam, *Clipper Ships and the Golden Age of Sail*, Bloomsbury, 2014

Journal of the Anthropological Institute of Great Britain and Ireland, Volume VII, obituary of Archibald Campbell

Kinchin, Perilla, *Miss Cranston: Patron of Charles Rennie Macintosh*, National Museums of Scotland, 2018

Kipling, Rudyard, 'In an Opium Factory', *Pioneer* newspaper, 1888

Knox, John, *A Tour Through the Hebrides*, 1787

Koehler, Jeff, *Darjeeling: A History of the World's Greatest Tea*, Bloomsbury, 2016

Kundu, B.C., Basak, K.C. and Sarcar, P.B., *Jute in India*, Indian Central Jute Committee, Calcutta, 1959

Kydd, Robbie and Kydd, Nora (eds), *Growing Up In Scotland: An Anthology*, Polygon, 1998

Lamport-Stokes, Barbara, 'Henry Brown, Planter', *The Society of Malawi Journal*, Volume 45, No. 2, 1992

Lewis, J. Penry, *Tombstones and Monuments of Ceylon*, 1913

——*Memoirs and Portraits of 100 Glasgow Men*, James Maclehose and Sons, 1886

Lowrie, Walter, *Memoirs of the Rev. Walter M. Lowrie, Missionary*, edited by his father. Philadelphia: Presbyterian Board of Publication, 1854

McCarthy, Angela and Devine, T.M., *Tea & Empire: James Taylor in Victorian Ceylon*, Manchester University Press, 2017

Macfarlane, Alan & Macfarlane, Iris, *Green Gold: The Empire of Tea*, Ebury Press, 2003

McKay, Alex, 'A Difficult Country, A Hostile Chief, and a Still More Hostile Minister: The Anglo-Sikkim War of 1861', *Bulletin of Tibetology*, 2010

Mackillop, Andrew, 'A Union for Empire? Scotland the East India Company and the British Union', *The Scottish Historical Review*, 2008

McNeill, F. Marian, *The Scots Kitchen*, 1929

Melrose, William, *William Melrose in China 1845–1855, The Letters of a Scottish Tea Merchant*, Hoh-cheung Mui and Lorna H. Mui (eds), Scottish History Society publications, 1973

Minto, James R., *Graham of Kalimpong*, William Blackwood, 1974

Morris, Jan, *Heaven's Command*, Faber & Faber, 1973

Morton, H.V., *In Search of Scotland*, Methuen, 1929

Mui, Hoh-cheung and Mui, Lorna H., *The Management of Monopoly: A Study of the East India Company's Conduct of Its Tea Trade, 1784–1833*, University of British Columbia Press, 1984

The Nautical Magazine and Naval Chronicle for 1852, Cambridge University Press, 2013

Quattrocchi, Umberto, *CRC World Dictionary of Plant Names*, CRC Press, 1999

Repplier, Agnes, *To Think of Tea*, Houghton Mifflin, 1932

Rose, Capt. R., *War Diary of Captain Ronald Rose of the 1st Cameronians* (Scottish Rifles), Historylinks website (http://www.historylinks.org.uk)

Rose, Sarah, *For All the Tea in China*, Arrow, 2010

Scott, Sir Walter, *Guy Mannering*, 1815

Short, Thomas, *A Dissertation upon Tea, Explaining its Nature and Properties by Many New experiments . . . to Which is Added the Natural History of Tea and a Detection of the Several Frauds Used in Preparing it*, 1730.

Smith, Rev. J.A., 'Life and Work', in the magazine of the Church of Scotland, Nov/Dec 1912

Smith, William Anderson, *Lewsiana*, Daldy Isbister, London, 1875

Smout, T.C. *A Century of the Scottish People 1830–1950*, William Collins, 1986

Smout, T.C. and Wood, Sydney, *Scottish Voices*, William Collins, 1990

Still, John, *The Jungle Tide*, William Blackwood & Sons Ltd, 1930

Tharoor, Shashi, *Inglorious Empire: What the British Did to India*, Hurst & Company, 2017

Trotter MD, Thomas, *A View of the Nervous Temperament*, 1807

Ukers, William H., *All About Tea*, The Tea and Coffee Trade Journal Company, New York, 1935

Westrop, Arthur, *Green Gold*, privately published, 1956

Index

Acknowledgements

First and foremost, I am indebted to my wife Jenni Minto, who has been my constant travelling companion in my pursuit of the Scots who put the tea in Britain, and my long-suffering, but supportive, writing-widow, as I laboured at my desk to shape the material I found. It was her family's connection to Dr Graham's Homes in Kalimpong that first took us to Darjeeling and set me on the tea trail. A special thanks, then, to my very own tea-Jenni.

Many other people and institutions have been invaluable guides and deserve my sincere gratitude:

The Argyll & Bute archives, Lochgilphead.

Barbara Armstrong, for tracing the origins of Henry Brown. I swear that I'll never refer to my genealogy-obsessed wee sister as 'the ancestor worshipper' ever again.

Neil Bartlett for pointing me in the direction of Lewis's 'field of tea'.

Margaret Bennett for sharing her Nova Scotian lore.

The staff of the British Library.

The staff of the Ceylon Tea Museum, Kandy.

Charles Carmichael, my guide to the Garrison Cemetery, the last resting place of many Ceylon planters.

Ian Davidson and John Davison, Assam planters who generously shared their memories with me.

Max Docherty, who related stories of his mother's time on the Nyasaland Tea Estate of 'Ma', the widow of Henry Brown.

Duncan Gilmour, my generous and enthusiastic expert in all things connected to James Finlay Ltd, and my guide through the company's extensive archives.

Marilyn Gahm in Wisconsin, USA, who (once again) has saved me from my comma-scattering, sloppy-typing self.

The staff of Glasgow University Archives.

Nick Hide, Clan Davidson historian and the man who pointed me to the Ceylon of George Thain Davidson.

Dhammika Kodituwallu, Superintendent of Loolecondera Tea Estate, Sri Lanka, where James Taylor changed Ceylon's history.

Alan Donald James Macfarlane, for permission to quote his mother Iris's account of 'the club' from their joint book, *Green Gold: The Empire of Tea.*

Norman Martinesz, the grandson of George Thain Davidson, and my trusted advisor on all things Sri Lankan. *Ayubowan*, Norman.

The staff of the Mitchell Library, Glasgow.

Ronald Morrison, secretary, Dunse History Society, for his information about the early life of Robert Fortune.

The staff of the National Library of Scotland.

Neel Pereira, our driver and knowledgeable guide in Sri Lanka.

The Society of Malawi, especially its former and current honorary secretaries, Mike Bamford and Kathy Paul.

Subair MS, our guide and unflappable driver from Chennai to Cochin (via numerous tea plantations).

Richard Sutcliffe, Glasgow Museums' Natural Sciences research manager, and my enthusiastic guide to Henry Brown's zoological specimens and correspondence at the museums.

And finally, to the inspired growers who have brought tea home to Scottish soil – Liz and Martyn Gibson on Mull; Monica Griesbaum at Windy Hollow near Auchterarder; Clare Haworth and Mike Hyatt on Lismore; Richard Ross, chairman of Tea Scotland and grower near Dunkeld; Susie Walker-Munro of Mains of Kinnettles in Strathmore; and the guru of Scottish tea, Beverly-Claire Wainwright of Comrie. Thank you all for your precious time, support and slurps.